AMERICAN
FORTS
YESTERDAY
AND TODAY

AMERICAN
FORTS
YESTERDAY
AND TODAY

By BRUCE GRANT

Illustrated by LORENCE F. BJORKLUND

E. P. DUTTON & CO., INC.
NEW YORK

To Brooke and Grant

Acknowledgments

To name all the persons who have so kindly and sympathetically helped me in this project would require many, many pages. I have had correspondence with directors and heads of all the fifty state historical societies, and many of the county and city historical groups. With few exceptions all have been most cooperative. I extend my sincere thanks to them for their informative letters and printed material.

Mr. Herbert E. Kahler, chief of the Division of History and Archeology of the National Park Service, called my attention to several important source books. From General Services Information, National Archives, Washington, D.C., I was able to obtain microfilm records of more than six hundred military forts and army posts. Marion Dittman, editor, the American Library Association, opened up new areas of research. Wright Howes, dean of Americana book dealers and author of *U.S.-iana, 1650–1950*, guided me in the selection of bibliographical material. Earl Schenck Miers, author of many historical books, followed my work with interest and offered encouragement. Jane Taylor uncomplainingly typed and retyped the manuscript. To all these, and scores of others, I am most grateful.

My chief source of information, of course, was several hundred reference books. Biographies and autobiographies of famous explorers, military leaders, and pioneers were among those books I consulted. Encyclopedias, pamphlets and other publications were extremely valuable. And for those who wish more detailed information concerning forts, I have provided a short bibliography at the end of the book.

B.G.

Contents

Introduction

The story of American forts is woven into almost every phase of the history of this country for the past four centuries. No matter how small a fort, it had some historical significance.

Built for the most part on strategic sites—at the mouth or confluence of rivers, at canoe portages, on commanding eminences, along important trails, in harbors, and at points marking the progress of civilization along the frontiers—hundreds of forts formed the nuclei of settlements that grew into towns and cities and even metropolises, retaining their original names intact or dropping the designation "fort" and using the proper name alone. Today, listed in atlases, are more than one hundred towns and cities carrying the name "Fort."

The term "fort" had a broad meaning in this country. There were stockades, palisades, blockhouses, redoubts, military garrisons, army posts or camps, and even fortresses; but in the United States a fortified place, whether a log cabin, with loopholes for rifles, or a huge pile of stone with a hundred or more great guns mounted on its walls, went by the name "fort."

Whereas in Europe or the Old Country a fort usually was the product of scientific engineering skills and built on basic principles laid down by such geniuses as the Seigneur de Vauban or the Baron Menno van Coehoorn, in America hastily constructed trading posts and even some churches and missions were often designated as forts. The word took on a new and romantic meaning in the New World, and in connection with each fort, big or little, there occurred one or more colorful or highly significant events that contributed to the history of the United States.

One point is of special interest. Forts were sometimes named for individuals of some importance during their time. The identities of many such persons have been lost to history, remaining only in the names of forts even though the fort itself has long disappeared. Investigation into the history of forts often brings to light many a so-called "forgotten hero."

Many forts were named for America's familiar heroes. There are, for instance, scores of Fort Washingtons throughout the nation. The fascinating history of forts often reveals the stories not only of military men and engineers who helped to found America but also of the presidents and generals, the politicians and visionaries, the *voyageurs* and the mountain men, the cattlemen and tillers of the soil, and, too, the Indians and bad men, rascals and promoters, gamblers and claim-jumpers. The story of forts embraces all types of men, as well as many nationalities. For there were French, Dutch, English, Spanish, Russian, and Swedish forts, as well as those built by men from other foreign lands.

As wave after wave of foreigners arrived in this country, they built their forts. The English were not great fort builders. But French forts extended in a well-organized line from the mouth of the St. Lawrence River west and south through the Greak Lakes region down the Mississippi River to the Gulf of Mexico. The French built one of the first strongholds in this country in 1564—Fort Caroline at the mouth of the St. Johns River in Florida. Spain erected great bastions to enable her to maintain title to newly discovered land, and the old forts at St. Augustine and at Pensacola, both in Florida, remain as relics of her former power.

Of the fortifications of the Dutch on the Hudson River and the Swedes on the Delaware River, nothing remains today.

Forts were established by colonists during the early Indian wars, such as the Pequot War and King Philip's War. The Indians, too, had their own forts. During the French and Indian War George Washington planned 125 forts in Virginia.

By 1783, at the close of the Revolution, the United States extended from the Atlantic to the Mississippi River, and forts had a key role in holding and protecting the land. Then, when the Louisiana Purchase in 1803 added a vast territory from the Gulf of Mexico to the Canadian Border west of the Mississippi River, more forts were necessary.

By 1808, some of the forts that were built during the Revolutionary War were considered inadequate for the defense of harbors. In that year Congress, because of the arrogant maritime pretensions of England over our neutral commerce, voted to place the country in an attitude of defense by increasing the Army and making large appropriations for fortifications and ordnance. When a species of so-called "Washington Stars" were ordered for the Eastern Department, there were protests from the young engineers out of West Point that such forts were the result of the study of outmoded treatises on fortifications in the Middle Ages.

Henry Adams, in his *History of the United States*, declared:

Another significant result of the War [of 1812] was the sudden development of scientific engineering in the United States. This branch of the military service owed its efficiency and almost its existence to the military school at West Point, established in 1802. The school was at first much neglected by the government. The number of graduates before the year 1812 was very small; but at the outbreak of the war the corps of engineers was already efficient. Its chief was Colonel Joseph Gardner Swift, of Massachusetts, the first graduate of the academy; Colonel Swift planned the defenses of New York Harbor. The lieutenant-colonel in 1812 was Walker Keith Armistead, of Virginia—the third graduate, who planned the defenses of Norfolk. Major William McRee of North Carolina became chief engineer to General [Jacob] Brown and constructed the fortifications at Fort Erie, which cost the British general Drummond the loss of half his army, besides the mortification of defeat. Captain Eleazer Derby Wood, of New York, constructed Fort Meigs, which enabled Harrison to defeat the attack of Proctor in May, 1813. Captain Joseph Gilbert Totten, of New York, was chief engineer to General Izard at Plattsburg, where he directed fortifications which stopped the advance of Prevost's great army. None of the works constructed by a graduate of

West Point was captured by the enemy, and had an engineer been employed by Armstrong and Winder at Washington, the city would have been saved.

But the British had landed and burned Washington. After the war was over, a great era of fort building began. Despite all the efficient engineers out of West Point, President Monroe invited Simon Bernard, former chief engineer of Napoleon, to the United States in 1816 and made him senior member of the Board of Engineers for Seacoast Fortifications. General Bernard had grandiose ideas, and drew up plans for such great forts as Fort Monroe and Fort Pulaski. As America's own engineers watched with a jaundiced eye, they came to the conclusion that such gigantic piles were unnecessary, as they were "separated by a deep wet moat of 3,000 miles from any European besieger." Nevertheless, millions were spent.

Though many of these forts had their day in the Civil War, for the most part the forts that sprang up during the War Between the States were makeshift affairs, and sometimes were nothing but a series of trenches on a hill. The great fort-building period was over.

Earlier, military forts began to dot the western country. In 1834 John Dougherty, Indian agent at Fort Leavenworth, Kansas, wrote a letter to the War Department recommending a chain of military posts to protect the Indians "as untutored children." The next year the territory was explored and sites were recommended. A so-called "permanent Indian frontier" had been established, marked by Fort Snelling, Minnesota, to the north; Fort Leavenworth, Kansas, in the center, and Fort Jesup, Louisiana, in the south. Most of the western forts had no fortifications and were merely stations for troops. Some did have stockades and blockhouses, but a typical example was Fort Kearny, Nebraska, with its five unpainted wooden houses, two dozen long, low mud (sod or adobe) buildings, and cleared parade ground.

When California came into the possession of the United States, along with other territory ceded by the Mexican Government in 1848, this country acquired a remarkable chain of forts, or presidios, along the Pacific Coast. Some of these garrisoned posts, usually attached to Spanish missions, were utilized by the United States Government. But forts were becoming things of the past. There was a flurry to recondition some during the Spanish-American War, but no attack was made on our coasts. In later years the remaining forts either became relics or cantonments and training centers. In 1922, by an Act of Congress, sites of forts could be purchased by states, as the buildings and lands were no longer needed for military purposes. Thus many today are state-owned.

America in recent years has become highly fort-conscious. Many important forts are National Historic Monuments such as: Castle Pinckney, South Carolina; Fort Frederica, Georgia; Fort Jefferson, Florida; Fort Laramie, Wyoming; Fort McHenry, Maryland; Fort Marion (Castillo de San Marcos), Florida; Fort Matanzas, Florida; Fort Pulaski, Georgia; Fort Union, New Mexico, and Fort Vancouver, Washington. Fort Necessity, Pennsylvania, is a National Battlefield Site, and Fort Raleigh, North Carolina, is a National Historic Site. The National Park Service is considering many more forts for like distinction.

Scores of fort sites are state parks and state historic sites, and many picturesque forts have been reconstructed, among them Fort Osage, Missouri; Fort Nashborough, Tennessee, and Fort Ticonderoga, New York. The Boy Scouts of America have a special program wherein sites of old forts throughout the nation are located and tabulated. Someone has called forts "outdoor archives."

As forts were abandoned and crumbled away, settlers salvaged building materials with which to erect their homes, and thus many an old private building standing today contains all that is left of some romantic and historic fortification.

BRUCE GRANT

January 24, 1965
Winnetka, Illinois

The Northeast States

MAINE

NEW HAMPSHIRE

VERMONT

MASSACHUSETTS

CONNECTICUT

RHODE ISLAND

NEW YORK

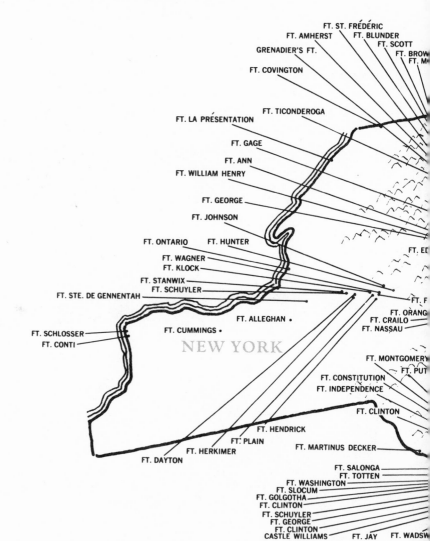

SCALE OF MILES

| 0 | 50 | 100 | 150 | 200 |

FT. ST. FRÉDÉRIC
FT. AMHERST   FT. BLUNDER
GRENADIER'S FT.   FT. SCOTT
FT. BROW
FT. COVINGTON   FT. M

FT. TICONDEROGA
FT. LA PRÉSENTATION

FT. GAGE

FT. ANN
FT. WILLIAM HENRY

FT. GEORGE
FT. JOHNSON

FT. ONTARIO   FT. HUNTER
FT. WAGNER
FT. KLOCK
FT. STANWIX
FT. STE. DE GENNENTAH   FT. SCHUYLER   FT. EI

FT. F
FT. ALLEGHAN •   FT. ORANG
FT. CRAILO
FT. CUMMINGS •   FT. NASSAU
FT. SCHLOSSER
FT. CONTI
NEW YORK   FT. MONTGOMERY
FT. PUT

FT. CONSTITUTION
FT. INDEPENDENCE

FT. CLINTON

FT. HENDRICK
FT. PLAIN   FT. MARTINUS DECKER
FT. HERKIMER
FT. DAYTON

FT. SALONGA
FT. TOTTEN
FT. WASHINGTON
FT. SLOCUM
FT. GOLGOTHA
FT. CLINTON
FT. SCHUYLER
FT. GEORGE
FT. CLINTON
CASTLE WILLIAMS   FT. JAY   FT. WADSW
FT. HA
FT.

18

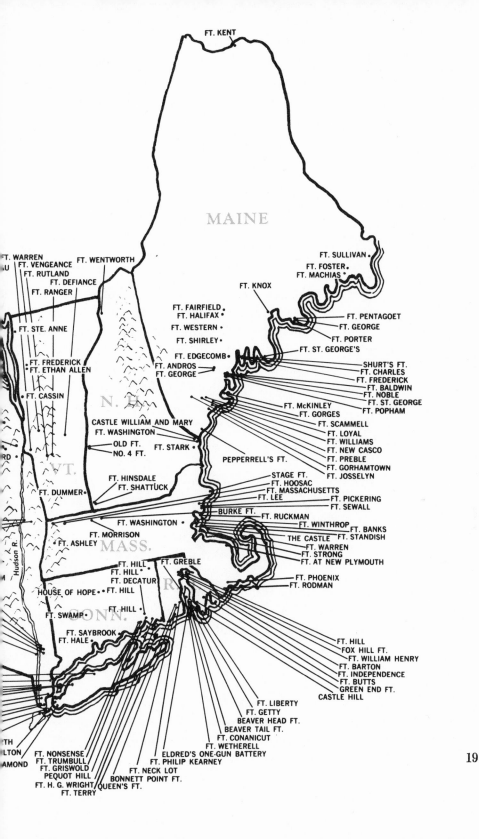

FT. KENT

MAINE

FT. WARREN
FT. VENGEANCE   FT. WENTWORTH
FT. RUTLAND
FT. DEFIANCE
FT. RANGER

FT. STE. ANNE

FT. FREDERICK
FT. ETHAN ALLEN

FT. CASSIN

N. H.

CASTLE WILLIAM AND MARY
FT. WASHINGTON
OLD FT.
NO. 4 FT.   FT. STARK •

VT.

FT. DUMMER •

FT. HINSDALE
FT. SHATTUCK

FT. WASHINGTON •
FT. MORRISON
FT. ASHLEY   MASS.

FT. HILL
FT. HILL •
FT. DECATUR
HOUSE OF HOPE • • FT. HILL
FT. HILL •

FT. SWAMP •

CONN.

FT. SAYBROOK
FT. HALE

FT. GREBLE

R.

FT. SULLIVAN •
FT. FOSTER •
FT. MACHIAS •

FT. KNOX

FT. FAIRFIELD •
FT. HALIFAX •
FT. WESTERN •
FT. SHIRLEY •

FT. EDGECOMB •
FT. ANDROS
FT. GEORGE

PEPPERRELL'S FT.

STAGE FT.
FT. HOOSAC
FT. MASSACHUSETTS
FT. LEE

BURKE FT.   FT. RUCKMAN

FT. PENTAGOET
FT. GEORGE
FT. PORTER
FT. ST. GEORGE'S

SHURT'S FT.
FT. CHARLES
FT. FREDERICK
FT. BALDWIN
FT. NOBLE
FT. ST. GEORGE
FT. McKINLEY   FT. POPHAM
FT. GORGES
FT. SCAMMELL
FT. LOYAL
FT. WILLIAMS
FT. NEW CASCO
FT. PREBLE
FT. GORHAMTOWN
FT. JOSSELYN

FT. PICKERING
FT. SEWALL

FT. WINTHROP   FT. BANKS
THE CASTLE   FT. STANDISH
FT. WARREN
FT. STRONG
FT. AT NEW PLYMOUTH

FT. PHOENIX
FT. RODMAN

FT. HILL
FOX HILL FT.
FT. WILLIAM HENRY
FT. BARTON
FT. INDEPENDENCE
FT. BUTTS
GREEN END FT.
CASTLE HILL

FT. LIBERTY
FT. GETTY
BEAVER HEAD FT.
BEAVER TAIL FT.
FT. CONANICUT
FT. WETHERELL
ELDRED'S ONE-GUN BATTERY
FT. PHILIP KEARNEY
FT. NECK LOT
BONNETT POINT FT.
QUEEN'S FT.

FT. NONSENSE
FT. TRUMBULL
FT. GRISWOLD
PEQUOT HILL
FT. H. G. WRIGHT
FT. TERRY

Hudson R.

19

MAINE

*Formerly a part of Massachusetts. Admitted to
the Union as the twenty-third state in 1820.*

The good ships *Gift of God,* commanded by Captain George Popham, and *Mary and John,* under Captain Raleigh Gilbert, dropped
anchor off the shore of a promising site for a colony in the mouth
of the Kennebec River on August 19, 1607.

The 120 persons who had sailed from Plymouth, England, to
settle in what was then known as North Virginia, went ashore.
They took possession of the ground in the name of King James I of
England, and the Reverend Richard Seymour read the service of
the Church of England and preached a sermon.

The next day the colonists set to work in earnest. "All went to
shore again, and there began to entrench and make a fort and to
build a storehouse," reads the account of their historian. They called
the fort **FORT ST. GEORGE,** and it was on the site of the present
town of Phippsburg. But the colony was short-lived. The winter was
severe, and word came in the spring that Sir John Popham, who
with Sir Ferdinando Gorges had been awarded the region by a
charter of their Plymouth Company, had died. The fort was abandoned, and the colonists returned to England.

But afterward, because of the need to defend a long border and
a long coastline, many fortifications of various types were built
in Maine.

SHURT'S FORT marked the beginnings of an English settlement
on the Pemaquid Peninsula in 1630. Though it was hardly more
than a stockade, it was the site of several more important forts at a
later date. Shurt's Fort, at the place then known as Jamestown (now
Pemaquid), had a short life. Dixey Bull, a notorious pirate, thor-
oughly pillaged the town and fort in 1633.

Next, **FORT CHARLES** was erected at Pemaquid under orders
of Edmund Andros, governor of the Province of New York, following the Indian uprising known as King Philip's War, when the

20

government of New York, under royal letters patent, assumed control of that area. The strong timber redoubt with a bastioned outwork, or projection, built in 1677, became the refuge of settlers fleeing from the Indians and the French, and was garrisoned by soldiers from New York. But the French, who settled on the Castine Peninsula, claimed the territory, and in August, 1689, Baron Vincent de Castine led a war party of whites and Indians against Fort Charles, wiping out the fort and village.

FORT WILLIAM HENRY, built in 1692 at Pemaquid, was a symbol of British determination to occupy this place. Again, four years later, Castine attacked and destroyed the fort. In 1729 the English erected here **FORT FREDERICK,** named for the Prince of Wales. Colonel David Dunbar built it under royal commission, but local residents destroyed it during the Revolution to prevent it from falling into British hands. Today a reproduction of the tower of Fort William Henry faces the beach, and inside is to be found the great rocky foundation of Fort Frederick. The house Colonel Dunbar constructed for himself is now a private residence.

FORT PENTAGOET, on the site of present-day Castine, was the stronghold of the French in Maine. Named for the Pentagoet (or Penobscot) Indians of that region, it was built in 1635 on a spot where a trading post had stood in 1613. It was captured by the English in 1674. It was returned to the French some years later by the Treaty of Brenda, but in 1688 Sir Edmund Andros, now governor general of the New England colonies, in a dispute over the territory, descended on the fort and settlement and plundered them. Baron de Castine retaliated by wiping out Fort William Henry at Pemaquid. The French retained Castine, but in 1722 the English again razed the fort and seized the territory. The grass-covered ruins still are to be seen on Perkins Street in Castine.

FORT SCAMMELL, on House Island in Portland Harbor, had its origin in a blockhouse erected on the site in 1661. The fort was built and named for Colonel Alexander Scammell, of the Revolutionary War, in 1808, under the direction of H. A. S. Dearborn, son of the Secretary of War. It was an octagonal blockhouse, with a porthole and gun on each side and a battery on the upper story. The structure was topped by a carved wooden eagle with extended wings. During the Civil War it was enlarged until it housed seventeen guns. It still stands.

FORT LOYAL was built under authorization of the Massachusetts Government in 1690 where Portland now stands. Ten years later it was enlarged into a stronger fortification with four blockhouses and eight cannon. But in May of that year French and Indians destroyed all the houses of the new community (Falmouth), and three days after all the refugees had gone into the fort, it surrendered. The old fort stood on a bluff about thirty feet higher than the Grand Trunk Railroad Station. Eight years after Fort Loyal fell, **FORT NEW CASCO** was erected nearby. It withstood an attack from French and Indians in 1703, but was demolished thirteen years later by order of the Massachusetts Government to avoid the expense of maintaining a garrison.

FORT ANDROS, built at Brunswick (then Pejepscot) by Governor General Edmund Andros in 1688, had a short existence, as it was destroyed by French and Indians two years later. In 1699 a treaty with the Indians was ratified, and after a group of eight men known as the Pejepscot Proprietors had purchased and laid out most of what is now Brunswick, **FORT GEORGE** was erected near the site of old Fort Andros in 1715. The town was once more attacked and razed by Indians seven years later, and in 1737 the fort was dismantled by the Massachusetts Government.

Iroquois

FORT McCLARY, on Gerrish Island, Kittery, was erected in 1680 by the English and was first known by the name of **PEPPER-RELL'S FORT,** from Sir William Pepperrell, and later as **FORT WILLIAM,** also in honor of Sir William. The present name was given during the Revolutionary War as a tribute to Major Andrew McClary, who fell at Bunker Hill. The fort was repaired, added to, and garrisoned during the Civil War. An interesting feature is the old blockhouse with overhang that was built in 1812. This old fort, partly in ruins, is on the Fort McClary Military Reservation.

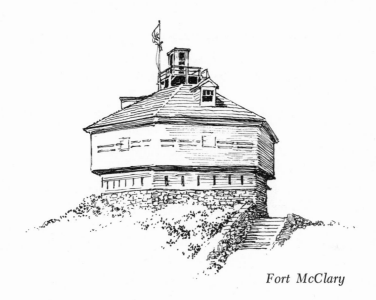

Fort McClary

FORT WESTERN, on the site of Augusta, was one of three forts erected by Governor William Shirley along the Kennebec River during the French and Indian War in 1754. The fort was named for Thomas Western, of Sussex, England, a friend of the governor's. The defeat of Montcalm at Quebec made the Kennebec safe, and the fort was dismantled except for the Garrison House, which has been restored. It was here that Benedict Arnold's expedition on Quebec gathered for a week in September, 1775. **FORT SHIRLEY,** named for the governor, was another of these forts, and was on the site of the present town of Dresden. The third was **FORT HALI-**

FAX, erected on the site of the present town of Winslow. The fort was abandoned after the Treaty of Paris in 1762, but the blockhouse still stands.

FORT MACHIAS, on the west bank of the Machias River, was erected on orders of General George Washington in 1775. It also was called FORT O'BRIEN, as it was built through the activities of the O'Briens. Jeremiah O'Brien, his brother, and others from Machias, captured the British schooner *Margaretta* on June 12, 1775, in what has been termed "the first naval battle of the Revolution." Fearing reprisals, Washington ordered a regiment of men to protect the settlement, and therefore this fort and FORT FOSTER on the other bank were built. Fort Foster was named for Benjamin Foster, a church deacon and one of the leaders in the capture of the British schooner. In 1781 Fort Machias was made a part of the national defense. In 1814 the British captured the fort and burned the barracks. It was again fortified in the Civil War.

FORT GEORGE, at Castine, was built by the British in 1779. In the same year colonists tried to take the town but failed, and it was this failure that blasted the hopes of Paul Revere for a military career. He was forced to return to his task of casting cannon for the Army. In the War of 1812, the British once more occupied the fort in 1814–1815 and added nearby batteries at the same time they built the canal that crosses the Peninsula at its narrowest part.

FORT ST. GEORGE'S, on the bank of the St. George's River and on the site of the town by that name, was built in 1809 and garrisoned during the War of 1812. Earthworks 6 feet high and 50 feet long are all that remains of the crescent-shaped rampart upon which 15-pounder guns once were mounted. In 1814 the British ship *Bulwark* sailed up the river, captured the fort, and spiked its guns.

FORT MADISON, built in 1811 by the Americans, as the largest of the batteries at Castine, was captured by the British in the War of 1812 and renamed FORT CASTINE. It had originally been named for President James Madison, of course, but when it was returned to the United States after the Treaty of Ghent it was called FORT PORTER, for Major Moses Porter, Army engineer. When rebuilt during the Civil War it was called **UNITED STATES FORT.** The fort still stands.

FORT EDGECOMB, at Edgecomb, built in 1808–1809 on Davis Island, as an octagonal blockhouse, was named for Lord Edgecomb, a friend of the American Colonies. On March 4, 1809, the 18-pounder and one 50-pounder were fired in honor of the inauguration of President James Madison. Gun emplacements and earthworks still are to be seen.

FORT PREBLE, on Cape Elizabeth, with a view of Portland Harbor, was built in 1808–1811 and named in honor of Commodore Edward Preble, early naval officer. Its whitewashed brick and heavy timber ramparts are well preserved.

FORT KNOX, a massive structure of Mount Waldo granite, was built at Prospect on the west side of the Penobscot River in 1846. It was named for General Henry Knox, first Secretary of War under President Washington. The fort was never finished, but troops trained there during the Civil War.

FORT GORGES, on Hog Island in Portland Harbor, was begun in 1858 but was not completed until 1865. A huge stone structure, it was designed to receive 195 guns, but modern artillery made its period of usefulness brief. It was named in honor of Sir Ferdinando Gorges. Other Portland defenses were **FORT WILLIAMS** at Cape Cottage and **FORT McKINLEY** on Great Diamond Island.

Earlier forts for defense against the French and Indians included **FORT JOSSELYN,** at Scarboro, built in 1703 and named for Henry and John Josselyn. Eight men here fought off 500 French and Indians. Others were **FORT GORHAMTOWN** at Gorham, built in 1728, and **FORT NOBLE** at Phippsburg on the southern end of Fiddlers Reach, built in 1734.

The boundary dispute between Great Britain and the United States sometimes termed the Aroostook War, involving the county and river of that name, created such a stir that 50,000 men were authorized by Congress to aid Maine, and caused the building of two forts: **FORT FAIRFIELD,** at Fairfield, and **FORT KENT** at Kent. Both were erected in 1839 and named for governors of the state.

General John Sullivan, heroic figure of the Revolutionary War, had been captured once by the British and then exchanged. **FORT SULLIVAN,** at Eastport, built in 1808 and named for the general, had a similar experience. It surrendered to the British in 1814, but reverted to the United States at the end of the War of 1812.

FORT POPHAM, at Phippsburg, an impressive granite and brick structure begun in 1861, was never completed. It became a State Reservation in 1924. **FORT BALDWIN,** also at Phippsburg, named for Colonel Jeduthan Baldwin of the Revolutionary Army, and built in 1905–1912, also is now a forty-five-acre State Park.

NEW HAMPSHIRE

One of the Thirteen Original Colonies.

Four months before the stirring events at Concord and Lexington, Paul Revere rode from Boston to Portsmouth to inform the Committee of Safety of a British order that no gunpowder or military stores would be exported to America. There were immediate cries from the angry colonists: "On to the fort!" Thus came the first organized fight of the Revolution. On December 14, 1774, the Sons of Liberty with the patriots of New Castle, one of the dependencies of Portsmouth, under Major General John Sullivan of the Continental Army and Captain John Langdon stormed **CASTLE** (or **FORT**) **WILLIAM AND MARY** and forced the British Captain John Cochran to surrender. The 400 patriots then carried away 100 barrels of powder and hid them under the meetinghouse pulpit at Durham. The powder was used at Bunker Hill. At the time of attack, the patriots also took sixteen cannon and about sixty muskets.

Castle William and Mary, which later become known as **FORT CONSTITUTION,** is one of the most historic forts in New England.

It stands on a rocky projection in the Piscataqua River at the entrance to the harbor of the City of Portsmouth. Its history dates back to the early beginnings of a settlement on the New England Coast. In 1665 commissioners of Charles II began to erect a fortification there but were halted by the Massachusetts fathers. But history records that by 1700 a fort was in existence on "Great Island," which later was to be known as Castle William and Mary. While there is no record of fighting, the fort undoubtedly did its part in frightening off French invasions during the French and Indian War, and in guarding the flourishing little city of Portsmouth.

French private,
French and Indian War

Government troops occupied it in 1806. It was strengthened during the War of 1812 by the addition of a martello tower on a rocky eminence overlooking the fort. At the time two British cruisers were lying nearby off the Isle of Shoals. Old Fort Constitution, with its rough stone walls topped by brick, presents an imposing appearance today.

FORT STARK, at Jaffrey's Point, Rye, the site of which is now a part of the United States Military Reservation, was one of New Hampshire's earliest coastal defense works. Next to the spot where the fort stood is Jaffrey Cottage, the meeting place of the Provincial Assembly in 1682–1683, after New Hampshire had become a separate royal province. Previously it had been a dependent of the Massachusetts Colony. The fort was named for John Stark, later a Revolutionary War general.

OLD FORT, the site of Charlestown on the Connecticut River, was built by settlers from Massachusetts in 1744. It was 180 feet long, with log flankers at the corners to allow a raking fire along the sides. In 1747, while under the command of Captain Phineas Stevens, it was besieged in vain by French and Indian forces, who finally gave up and withdrew.

FORT WENTWORTH was built in 1755 at the mouth of the Ammonoosuc River by Major Robert Rogers, the famous commander of Rogers' Rangers in the French and Indian War. He named it in honor of the then New Hampshire Governor Benning Wentworth. Settlers used the fort as a refuge from Indians, and it was the meeting place of Rogers' Rangers on their return from destroying the village of the St. Francis Indians on the edge of Canada. The St. Francis had long been a terror to the frontier settlers of New England. Fort Wentworth was occupied during the Revolutionary War by Colonel Timothy Bedel of the Continental Army in 1778. A boulder between Potter House and the cemetery in Northumberland marks the site.

While there is some question as to the actual location of this fort, it is plainly marked on a map inscribed on a foot-long powder horn

owned by a New Hampshire resident. The relic carries the inscription, "John Wells his horn A.D. 1757." Besides eight other forts shown on the horn in Vermont and New York, it also marks **NO. 4 FORT**, several miles down the Connecticut River, which a contemporary writer also mentions, saying that in the retreat of Rogers' men from St. Francis "some found their way to Number-four, after having suffered much hunger and fatigue."

In 1741 when the Massachusetts–New Hampshire boundary was established, a tract of land four miles long and 197 rods wide was cut off from Northfield, Massachusetts, given to New Hampshire, and called the town of Fort Dummer. The actual Fort Dummer was in Vermont across the Connecticut River. Later, Colonel Ebenezer Hinsdale, who had been chaplain of Fort Dummer, built **FORT HINSDALE,** petitioned for a division of the town, and after it was granted named his section Hinsdale. Daniel Shattuck then built **FORT SHATTUCK.** Both forts were refuges from Indian attacks. Soon the name Fort Dummer disappeared as that of one section of the town, and both were incorporated under the name Hinsdale.

FORT WASHINGTON, an extensive earthwork built in 1775 between Peirce's and Seavey's Islands, is now in ruins. It is the site of the present United States Navy Yard.

VERMONT

First state to be admitted to the Union, in 1791, after the adoption of the Constitution by the Thirteen Original Colonies.

The first white men to settle in Vermont, although they did not remain long, were the French. In 1665 they built **FORT STE. ANNE,** together with Ste. Anne's Shrine, on the western part of

Isle La Motte at the northern end of Lake Champlain. The fort was erected under the direction of Captain Sieur de la Motte as a protion against the Mohawk Indians. The site of the old fort was used in 1814 when the British anchored their fleet off the island and placed a battery of three long 18-pounders there to support the landing of supplies on the New York shore at Chazy. Several days later, Commodore Thomas Macdonough, of the United States Navy, defeated the British fleet on the lake.

Long 18-pounder

FORT DUMMER, near the present town of Brattleboro, marks the site of the first permanent white settlement on Vermont soil. The fort was built in 1724 and named for William Dummer, then lieutenant governor of Massachusetts. It was 180 feet square, of yellow pine timber, with a garrison of 55 men. Captain Timothy Dwight, whose son later was president of Yale College, was in command the first two years. The spot where the fort, dismantled in 1763, stood, is now covered by the backed-up waters of the Vernon Dam. A granite marker more than 2,000 feet away records the story of the fort. The Fort Dummer Historical Association, with headquarters in Brattleboro, is seeking to bring about a reconstruction of this important colonial stronghold. The association has on display a complete model of the fort.

FORT FREDERICK, built on the Winooski River by Ira Allen, younger brother of the famous Ethan Allen of the Green Mountain Boys, was one of the earliest military structures in Vermont. Near the fort, Ira Allen also established a shipyard and built the first vessel on the river, the schooner *Liberty*, in 1772. The site of the fort is on Main Street in Winooski at the bridge over the Winooski River. The fort was named to honor the Prince of Wales, father of George III.

FORT RANGER was built on a high bluff at Mead's Falls (now Gookin's Falls) in 1778 "to prevent the incursion of the enemy on the northern frontiers and to annoy them should they come within your reach," according to orders received by Captain Thomas Sawyer. Until 1781 Fort Ranger was headquarters for state troops, when the presence of a large British army on Lake Champlain caused the removal of the garrison to Fort Warren already established at Castleton at the foot of Lake Bomoseen. The old fort, oval in shape and accommodating from two hundred to three hundred persons, was used as a gathering place for people of the settlement after the troops left. **FORT RUTLAND,** another Revolutionary fort, had been established in Rutland in 1775.

British light infantryman, 1775

FORT WARREN, at Castleton, or a section of that township now known as Hydeville, was the westernmost of a group of four Revolutionary forts constituting the western and northern lines of defense of the state. A farmhouse now occupies a portion of the elevation upon which the fort stood, while other parts were demolished to make way for a highway and railway.

FORT VENGEANCE was built at Brandon in 1780 as a protection against invasion from Canada. The fort had no name when it was first occupied, but shortly afterward a soldier stationed there was killed by Indians. His comrades swore vengeance, and so named their fort.

FORT CASSIN, at what is now Basin Harbor, a popular Lake Champlain summer resort, was named in honor of Lieutenant Stephen Cassin, commander of the schooner *Ticonderoga* in the War of 1812. Lieutenant Cassin led the defense of this fortress on May 14, 1814, when the British attacked it in an attempt to sail up Otter Creek and destroy Commodore Thomas Macdonough's fleet, then under construction at Vergennes. The enemy was repulsed after a half hour's fighting, and Macdonough's fleet was saved to gain a notable victory later against the British on Lake Champlain. Cassin was awarded a gold medal by Congress.

FORT ETHAN ALLEN, named for the famous Vermont hero who at the head of his Green Mountain Boys captured Fort Ticonderoga in the Revolution, was built in 1892 and was one of the largest United States Cavalry posts in the country—and the last. It occupies 761 acres near Burlington.

FORT DEFIANCE, a garrisoned stronghold, was erected at Barnard in Windsor County, in the early part of the town's history as a protection against French and Indians. A bronze marker has been placed near the town to commemorate the site of this fort.

MASSACHUSETTS

One of the Thirteen Original Colonies.

FORT INDEPENDENCE, on Castle Island in Boston Harbor, is one of the oldest forts in America. In the early winter of 1630, members of the Massachusetts Bay Colony settled at what they called Boston after the name of their home in England. Governor John Winthrop and a party of Puritans set out to explore the island. They were detained there because of ice for a day and night. Despite their suffering without shelter, they became enthusiastic about the island as a possible location of a fort. Each man subscribed five pounds sterling, and subsequently a small fort was erected. Governor Winthrop named the place Castle Island because he thought its natural contours resembled a castle, and the fort was called **THE CASTLE.** Later, in 1689, the Crown donated a large sum of money, and a stronger structure, named **CASTLE WILLIAM,** was erected. In 1740 the fort was repaired, and new guns—twenty 42-pounders—were installed. In 1776 the Americans captured the fort and promptly renamed it Fort Independence. Lieutenant Colonel Paul Revere served there from 1777 to 1779. In 1801 a new fort was built, of which the greater part survives today. Edgar Allan Poe, under the name of E. A. Perry, was a soldier at this fort in 1827. In 1880 the fort was abandoned and eventually became a part of Marine Park. A notable thing about this fort is that, while it stood defiantly through all of America's wars, no shot was ever fired in anger from its guns.

Seven years before the Puritans settled Boston, **STAGE FORT,** overlooking Gloucester Harbor, was built along with the first fishing stage, or platform, for drying fish. On its site today is Stage Fort Park.

FORT AT NEW PLYMOUTH was built by the Pilgrims after they landed in December, 1620. Miles Standish, military commander in chief, and sometimes called "The Hero of New England," erected an 8-foot-high palisade around the log cabins of the settlers. This was strengthened the following year with thick, rough-hewn planks, and in 1622 a blockhouse was built upon a hill overlooking the harbor. It had an overhanging second story with embrasures for four cannon and with loopholes for rifles below. The palisade was lengthened from the settlement to enclose the blockhouse, making a wall some 2,700 feet long. In the center of the enclosure was a small stockade where four swivel guns were mounted, commanding the three gates to the palisade. As the fortification served no other purpose than to awe the Indians, it gradually was torn down and the timbers used for building houses. The site of this fort is in the center of present-day Plymouth. Just outside the city Plimoth (*sic*) Plantation, Inc., has reconstructed the original village and its fortifications.

BURKE FORT, near Bernardston, was one of the defenses erected during the bloody French and Indian wars. All that remains is a marker on the site where fifty persons took shelter during a raid in 1738. Another of this period was **FORT SEWALL,** built in 1742 at what is now the end of Front Street in Marblehead. It was named for Chief Justice Stephen Sewall, who at one time taught school in Marblehead. Fort Sewall saw action in the Revolution, keeping British ships at bay off Marblehead. It was rebuilt during the War of 1812, but has long since been abandoned and is now a small seaside park. **FORT MASSACHUSETTS** was erected by the Massachusetts Bay Colony in 1745 at North Adams. Although built to guard against attacks by the French and Indians, it also served to stop Dutch settlers from coming up the Hoosic (Hoosick) River from the

Hudson and establishing rights in Berkshire County. A replica of the old fort stands today. **FORT MORRISON,** at Colrain, also served as a defense against the French and Indians from 1754 to 1763, but all that remains is a stone to mark the site. **FORT HOOSAC,** near Williamstown, just west of Fort Massachusetts, was built in 1756 and first called **WEST HOOSAC BLOCKHOUSE,** named for the mountain range. A monument marks its site. **FORT ASHLEY,** at Pittsfield, was built during the French and Indian troubles. Its site is near Lake Onota.

FORT PHOENIX, at Fairhaven, on the east bank of the Acushnet River, an inlet from Buzzards Bay, was so named in 1798 at the time of a threatened war with France. It was built on the site of a battery maintained there during the Revolutionary War, and its builders considered that, like the mythical phoenix of ancient Egypt, it had arisen from the ashes. The British had plundered New Bedford, across the river, in 1778 despite the Fairhaven battery. In June of 1814, the small garrison of the fort under Lieutenant Selleck Osborn, saw little chance of fighting off the British with only a dozen iron cannon on its ramparts. But the fort was saved by a strange circumstance.

On a dark night, just before daylight, when the British armed ship *Nimrod* sailed in to attack, a solitary mail carrier, whose horse's feet clattered as he galloped across the Acushnet bridge and causeway, sounded his tin horn loudly. The British mistook the horn for a trumpet and the clatter on the bridge as the forerunner of an American force, and hastened to withdraw to a safe distance. The old fort was regarrisoned in the Civil War by the Home Guard of Fairhaven and New Bedford, but later fell into ruins.

FORT WASHINGTON, at Cambridge, was General Israel Putnam's headquarters during the siege of Boston in the Revolutionary War. It was to Cambridge that General Putnam, who had learned of the battle at Lexington, had hurried from his farm at Brookline, Connecticut, still in his work clothes. His troops erected a small earthworks that was named for General Washington, the site of which is now marked by a tablet near the City Hall.

FORT PICKERING was built at Marblehead in 1798 when war with France seemed certain, and was named for Timothy Pickering, then Secretary of State under President John Adams. It was an irregular work, occupying about an acre of ground and commanding Salem Harbor and the entrance to the North and South rivers. Not far from Fort Pickering, at the western end of the causeway leading to Winter Island, FORT LEE was erected during the War of 1812.

FORT WINTHROP was one of the early defenses of Boston Harbor. It was named in honor of Governor John Winthrop, first governor of Massachusetts. FORT STRONG, now a United States Military Post, on the east end of Long Island in Boston Harbor, was originally built by Governor Caleb Strong because of fear of invasion by the British in the War of 1812. The fort, completed on October 29, 1814, was never needed. FORT WARREN was another defense in the War of 1812, built on Georges Island, seven and a quarter miles southeast of Boston. It was named for Dr. Joseph Warren, who was killed at Bunker Hill, and became a military establishment in 1837. Other forts for the defense of Boston were FORT STANDISH, in the harbor; FORT BANKS, established in 1889 at Winthrop, and FORT RUCKMAN at Nahant.

FORT RODMAN, at the southern extremity of New Bedford at the top of Clark's Point in the Buzzards Bay area, and which antedates the Civil War, is one of the modern-day defenses of the Atlantic Coast. It was named for Thomas J. Rodman, general in the Ordnance Department, who invented the Rodman gun, a smoothbore, cast-iron cannon of large caliber.

CONNECTICUT

One of the Thirteen Original Colonies.

The plucky American garrison at **FORT GRISWOLD** had tried vainly to hold back the overwhelming British force. Finally, Lieutenant Colonel William Ledyard, in command of the 150 militiamen at this fort at Groton, and the 23 men at **FORT TRUMBULL,** across the Thames River at New London, surrendered on September 6, 1781.

As Colonel Ledyard handed his sword, hilt forward, to his British conqueror, a signal was received from Benedict Arnold, the American traitor then commanding the two attacking British regiments, from across the river. The signal was for a general massacre of the vanquished defenders. Ledyard was run through the body and killed by his own sword. Of the 160-odd men making up the garrison, all but 40 were killed or wounded. Benedict Arnold then burned the towns of New London and Groton and spread desolation and woe throughout the region. To commemorate the gallant defense of Fort Griswold and the terrible scene enacted there, the State of Connecticut erected a monument on Groton Heights in 1830.

Erection of the two forts had been begun in 1775. Fort Griswold, then but a blockhouse with embrasures, was named for Matthew Griswold, deputy governor of Connecticut. Fort Trumbull, a more imposing work, was named for Jonathan Trumbull, governor of the state. In addition to these two forts there was a smaller one on the summit of Town Hill, which became known as **FORT NONSENSE.**

After the Revolutionary War no attempt was made to rebuild Fort Griswold. But with the War of 1812 Fort Trumbull was reconstructed into a strong fort, with the old blockhouse inside its walls. The fort was often threatened but never attacked during this war. The present Fort Trumbull, begun in 1839, was built of millstone granite. Later, being outmoded as a coastal defense fortification, it served as United States Coast Guard Patrol Headquarters for the district.

FORT SAYBROOK, at the mouth of the Connecticut River, was Connecticut's first fort. It was built in 1635 by Governor John Winthrop, Jr., and named in honor of Lord Saye and Sele and Lord Brooke, who had helped him obtain a royal charter to occupy this piece of land on the New England shore. The British of Saybrook Colony had hardly erected earthworks before a Dutch ship sailed into the harbor. The fort hoisted the Union Jack, and the Dutch ship weighed anchor and sailed away. Lion Gardiner, Engineer and Master of Works of Fortifications, was engaged to make this fort a defense comparable to European fortifications, with ramparts, salients, bastions, and barracks, and other recognized elements. He never completed the task. Fort Saybrook saw little fighting, and fell into disuse. During the Revolutionary War an attempt was made to repair it, but it never seemed to have been ready for action. During the War of 1812 it was again partially restored and renamed **FORT FENWICK,** after Colonel George Fenwick, who had been head of the Saybrook Colony at its founding. After this war the activities of the fort ended. The mound on which Gardiner had placed his guns remained until 1871, when it was used as part of the fill for the tracks of the Connecticut Valley Railroad between Saybrook Junction and Saybrook Point.

In competition with Fort Saybrook as the first fort was the **HOUSE OF HOPE** at Hartford, which Jacob van Curler, in 1633, under orders of the governor of New Amsterdam, built as a fort and mounted with two guns. Today the site is known as Dutch Point.

FORT DECATUR was erected in the summer of 1813 by Commodore Stephen Decatur, when he sought refuge a few miles up the Thames River from the blockading British fleet in Long Island Sound. Decatur had his flagship, the United States frigate *United States;* the United States sloop of war *Hornet,* and the British frigate *Macedonian,* which he had captured. He ordered earthworks thrown up on Dragon Hill, a few miles north of Groton, and cannon moved there and manned. However, anxious to get to sea, he was ready on one dark night to run the blockade when he saw mysterious blue lights flashing from the eastern hills. As this was repeated thereafter whenever Decatur planned to move, it was determined that these lights were signals to the British fleet. Thereafter, British sympathizers were called "Blue Lights." Decatur was not able to get his squadron to sea during the remainder of the war. The site of his fortification is marked by a stone tablet.

PEQUOT HILL, at West Mystic, is one of several Indian forts in Connecticut. Mason Monument marks the spot where a fort of the Pequots was burned in 1637 by Captain John Mason, commander of a force of 77 men and 400 friendly Indians under Uncas, chief of the Mohegans. Of the 600 men, women, and children inside the long palisade, only seven escaped, while seven others were captured alive. The attack on the Pequots was made after they had raided the outskirts of coastal and river towns.

FORT SWAMP, east of Waterbury, was, according to legend, an Indian stronghold on an island in a deep swamp. Today Route 41 passes through the site of the fort. There are three former Indian defenses that are called **FORT HILL** in the state. One is at Thompson, which was used by the Nipmuck Indians against attacks by the Narraganset. Another is at the old Indian town of Mohegan, where a few Mohegans of mixed blood still live. The fort here, of which only a few foundation stones mark the site, was built by the Mohegan chief Uncas, on a hill commanding a view of distant hills to the north, of the Thames River to the south, as well as New London and Long Island Sound. **FORT HILL** at East Hartford was an old Podunk Indian stronghold.

FORT HILL, at Woodstock, the site of which is on a steep forested bluff, served as a refuge for women and children in the early

settlement days during Indian raids. A wooden sign marks the spot.

FORT HALE, or **LITTLE FORT,** on Black Rock, New Haven, two miles from the end of Long Wharf, was the scene of a fight between British and Colonials in July, 1779. Here the Americans had a battery of three guns with which they annoyed the British until they were finally driven off the rock. The fort was named for Nathan Hale, the American spy who was executed by Lord Howe, and who made immortal his last words: "I only regret that I have but one life to lose for my country."

FORT H. G. WRIGHT, a United States Military Post on Fisher's Island, eight miles from New London, is headquarters of the coast defenses of Long Island. The fort was named for Horatio Gates Wright, Connecticut-born Union Army general in the Civil War.

RHODE ISLAND

One of the Thirteen Original Colonies.

A few weeks before the Declaration of Independence fired the American people to fight and die for liberty, a large body of men marched from Newport to Brenton's Point on Aquineck Isle and began the construction of a fort, called **CASTLE HILL,** to protect the entrance to the harbor. This fort, later to be known as **FORT ADAMS,** was not completed.

Early in December, 1776, a British fleet with 6,000 troops on board appeared off Newport. The fort was abandoned, and Newport was taken over by the British. They occupied the town for three years, and when they left in October, 1779, they burned the barracks they had erected at Brenton's Point, where the American battery had been.

The site was not used for military purposes until 1793 when Congress, in anticipation of a war with France, took measures to protect the entrance to Narragansett Bay. Major Anne Louis de Tousard was assigned to build the fort, and on July 4, 1799, it was named Fort Adams and dedicated by President John Adams. This stronghold consisted of an enclosed work of masonry, indented for guns, with a brick magazine and barracks for one company. While additional guns were added during the War of 1812, the fort was neglected until 1824, when a Board of Engineers condemned it. Lieutenant Colonel Joseph G. Totten, chief engineer of the Army, that same year began reconstruction of the fort, making provision for almost 500 pieces of artillery. A permanent garrison was established in 1842 and has been maintained ever since. Modern fortification began in 1896. The fort covers 137 acres.

FORT NECK LOT, at Charlestown, is one of the state's oldest forts. The three-quarter-acre tract is now a state park and is owned by the Rhode Island Historical Society. At one time it was a stronghold of the Niantic Indians, being known as **FORT NINIGRET,** after the Niantic chief, or sachem. The belief today is that the original fort was built by early Dutch settlers, as bastions and other evidences of military engineering skill have been uncovered. It was here that Captain John Mason of Connecticut and his small band halted for one night during their dreary march through Pequot Indian country, and it was here that Mason persuaded the ancient sachem Ninigret to join him in the war against their common enemy, the Indians under King Philip.

QUEEN'S FORT is an authentic Indian fortification. It was named so in the belief that it was the stronghold of the Narraganset squaw sachem, Matantuck or Quaiapen. The ruins of the fort, west of Wickford Junction, consist of a low wall of rocks crudely piled together on a hilltop directly between North Kingston and Exeter. The Narraganset abandoned it in 1676, after they were defeated in King Philip's War, and Matantuck was killed after her capture by the British.

FORT WOLCOTT, on Goat Island in Newport Harbor, is on the site of an earlier fortification known as **FORT ANNA.** Fort Anna later was called **FORT GEORGE,** then **FORT LIBERTY;** during the Revolution it was named **FORT WASHINGTON.** This island in former days was a hangout for pirates, twenty-six of whom were captured and hanged at Gravelly Point in 1723. It is now the home of the United States Naval Torpedo Station.

FORT DUMPLINGS, at the southern tip of Conanicut Island, is one of the most interesting of the many points fortified about Newport during the Revolution. The fort, at first consisting of an earthworks and battery erected by the Americans in 1776, was given the unique name because the area is covered with huge boulders that at a distance resemble dumplings. It was also called **FORT CONANICUT.** It was abandoned to the British during the Revolution when they took over Newport in 1776. In 1800 a stone tower, still standing today, was erected, and mounted eight guns. Modern fortification began in 1896, and the fort was called **FORT WETHERELL** in honor of Captain Alexander Wetherell, who was killed in the Spanish-American War.

BEAVER HEAD FORT and **BEAVER TAIL FORT** were two American strongholds on Conanicut Island during the Revolution, so named as this part of the island southwest of Mackerel Cove was called The Beaver because of its shape. The British occupied both forts in 1776, and what remains of Beaver Head Fort is believed to be of British construction. On the east side of this island is **ELDRED'S ONE-GUN BATTERY,** manned by spunky Captain John Eldred, who took shots at British ships. One day a shot passed through the mainsail of a ship, and a landing party seized the gun and spiked it.

BONNETT POINT FORT was erected in 1777 by Americans on the site of North Kingston. The Colonials rebuilt it twice during the Revolution, and during the War of 1812 a battery was stationed there. During the Civil War it was rumored that the famous Confederate cruiser *Alabama* was anchored in Narragansett Bay, and the fort was hurriedly strengthened. On its site has been established a gay summer colony.

FOX HILL FORT, at Providence, was under the command of Brigadier-General Esek Hopkins at the beginning of the Revolution. This fort was armed with six 18-pounders and four of smaller caliber. In December, 1775, Hopkins was commissioned commander in chief of the Continental Navy, with four ships and three sloops. **FORT INDEPENDENCE,** on Robin Hill at Providence, has been restored and the area converted into a park. Erected in 1775, it was connected by earthworks with another fort on Sassafras Hill. In 1812 these forts were strengthened by a third, **FORT WILLIAM HENRY,** at the southeast extremity of Field's Point. All have disappeared except Fort Independence.

FORT HILL, on what was once called Hog Pen Point in East Providence, was erected in 1775 and maintained until after the War of 1812. Only the remains of the earthworks are to be seen.

GREEN END FORT was built by the British in 1777 at Middletown, during their occupation of Newport. The fort, from whose ramparts a fine view of the ocean can be had, is in a good state of preservation. **FORT BUTTS,** built by the British at Portsmouth in 1777, was occupied by the Americans as an island base for the Continental Army under General John Sullivan in the Battle of Rhode Island, August 29, 1778.

American light dragoon, 1778

FORT BARTON, built on a high hill at Tiverton, was the vantage point where Generals John Sullivan, Nathanael Greene, and Lafayette in August, 1778, watched the retreat of the Continental forces from the Battle of Rhode Island at Portsmouth, fought on the hills of that city. Failure to expel the British at that time was blamed on lack of cooperation from the French fleet. The fort, of which little is left, was named for Colonel William Barton, who on the night of July 9, 1777, captured British General Richard Prescott, in Portsmouth.

American militiaman, 1776

Minuteman

Among the Narragansett Bay area defenses at a later date were: **FORT GREBLE,** named for John T. Greble, who was killed in the Civil War, and erected by the Government in 1863 on Dutch Island; **FORT GETTY,** named for General George Washington Getty, on the west side of Conanicut Island in 1900–1909; and **FORT PHILIP KEARNEY,** named for the general, Philip Kearny (*sic*), at Kingston, overlooking the bay. This latter fort reversed the usual order of things. Instead of being the site of a village or city, it was built in 1905 on the site of a former village.

NEW YORK

One of the Thirteen Original Colonies.

The British flag flew defiantly over Fort George on lower Manhattan, New York City, on that cold clear afternoon of Tuesday, November 25, 1783. The redcoats had nailed their ensign to the high staff before leaving. The cleats of the flagpole had been removed and the pole greased. The British wanted to show the Yankees that their absence was only for a time. They would be back. But the Americans thought otherwise, and determined to haul the flag down.

"I'll get it down!" cried a young man. He was John Van Arsdale, a sixteen-year-old sailor. He took cleats, hammer and nails, and some sand. He renailed the cleats to the pole step by step, and covered the grease with sand. As the crowd watched, the young sailor ascended the pole. Soon he reached the top, tore off the flag, and nailed there in its stead the Stars and Stripes. There were loud huzzas. Fort George and New York once more were American after a British occupancy of seven years.

FORT GEORGE, originally named **FORT AMSTERDAM,** was built by the Dutch in 1615. The British changed its name to **FORT JAMES** to honor the Duke of York (later King James II) when they seized the colony in 1664. In 1673 it was renamed **FORT WILLIAM HENDRICK** when the Dutch retook it. It passed into British hands again and was known successively as **FORT WILLIAM, FORT ANNE,** and finally as Fort George, in honor of King George III. On the site of the old fort, at the foot of Broadway, today stands the United States Custom House.

A year before the Dutch built Fort Amsterdam they erected **FORT NASSAU** on Castle Island (Van Rensselaer Island), now a part of the Port of Albany. Henry Hudson had indicated the spot when he sailed there in the *Half Moon* five years earlier. A spring freshet destroyed the fort, and in 1617 a new one, **FORT ORANGE,** was built on the west bank of the Hudson River on the present site of Albany.

47

FORT SAINTE MARIE DE GENNENTAH, near the present Liverpool, marked the first settlement of the French in upper New York in 1656. The stockade has been reproduced with an exterior of unfinished logs and an interior of rough-hewn boards. It is near the spot where the powerful Iroquois Confederacy is reputed to have been founded by Hiawatha and Dekenawidah.

FORT NIAGARA, at the mouth of the Niagara River, in its restored form, marks a historic spot. Here Robert Cavelier de La Salle built a house in 1669, and a fortified trading post, **FORT CONTI,** ten years later. After some years it was rebuilt as **FORT DENONVILLE** by the French governor general of that name, and in 1725–1726 Joseph Gaspard Chausse-Gros de Lery reconstructed it and named it Fort Niagara. It was recognized not only as the most important military stronghold on the Great Lakes but also as the greatest trading post. Captured by the British in the French and Indian War, it was held by them throughout the Revolution and turned over to the United States in 1796. The British again captured it in the War of 1812, and later returned it under the Treaty of Ghent. The restoration of this historic pile was completed

Fort Niagara

in 1934 at a cost of $600,000. The old French fort plans were followed, even to the drawbridge, which is hoisted by the weight of rocks.

FORT CRAILO, at Rensselaer, is noted as the birthplace of the song "Yankee Doodle." Built as a Dutch stronghold in 1704, it fell into the hands of the British. In 1758, when provincial militia were drilling there in preparation for an attack on Fort Ticonderoga, Dr. Richard Shuckburgh, a British Army surgeon, sought to poke fun at them by writing the derisive words of "Yankee Doodle." In the Revolution the Colonials took it as a marching song. The fort has been restored as a public museum, even to a building known as the Yankee Doodle House.

FORT HUNTER, now a village near Amsterdam, was built by the British Governor Hunter, in 1711, as one of a chain of British defenses against the French and Indians. During the Revolution the remains of the fort were cleared away and used as a stockade around Queen Anne's Episcopal Chapel, with a blockhouse at each corner. This was one of several so-called fort-churches in New York. The chapel was torn down in 1820 to make way for the Erie Canal, but the parsonage has been preserved.

FORT HERKIMER, near Mohawk, was another fortified church. The stockaded fort, begun in 1730 by the Dutch, was expanded to include the Reformed Dutch Church building during the Revolution. It was named for Johan Herkimer, father of General Nicholas Herkimer of the Continental Army. On August 1, 1778, Tory-Indian raiders scourged the neighborhood, but no lives were lost, thanks to a Ranger scout, Adam Helmer, who ran twenty-two miles between **FORT DAYTON** (at Herkimer) and Fort Herkimer, warning the settlers. This famous run is faithfully dramatized in Walter D. Edmonds's *Drums Along the Mohawk.*

FORT ST. FRÉDÉRIC, near the Lake Champlain Bridge, on Crown Point peninsula, a five-pointed star-shaped structure, was built by the French in 1731 as a prospective capital of their territory from the Connecticut River to Lake Ontario. In colonial days it was from here that French, Indians, and half-breeds set forth on scalping parties, and the very name of its location, Crown Point, struck terror in the breasts of the peaceful settlers. The French blew up the fort and retreated into Canada before Sir Jeffrey Amherst in 1759. Amherst viewed the peninsula as an important place for a fortification, and began, but did not complete, **FORT AMHERST,** later to be known as **FORT CROWN POINT** when it was completed at a cost of $10,000,000. The Green Mountain Boys occupied it during the Revolution for a time, but it was abandoned and never used again.

FORT JOHNSON, built at a village by that name near Amsterdam, was one of the houses of Sir William Johnson, the remarkable Irishman known as the Empire Builder, and a man of great influence among the Indians of the Six Nations. At the time of the French and Indian War he was made sole superintendent of Indian affairs. As many as 1,000 Indians camped about his palisaded home at one time. Johnson married Molly Brant, sister of the famous Chief Joseph Brant. During the Revolution patriots melted down the lead roof, which had been brought from London, to make bullets. The gray-stone two-story structure is now the home of the Montgomery County Historical Society.

FORT TICONDEROGA is one of the most famous and best-known forts in the United States. It was constructed by the French in 1755 on the neck of land between Lake George and Lake Champlain and named first **FORT VAUDREUIL,** then **FORT CARILLON.** Four years later, Sir Jeffrey Amherst captured the stronghold and named it Fort Ticonderoga, from the Indian word *Cheonderoga,* "between two waters." In May, 1775, Colonel Ethan Allen and his Green Mountain Boys captured the fort from the British, but were forced to abandon it upon the approach of General Burgoyne. In the meantime General Henry Knox, chief commander of Washington's artillery, had transported the guns of the fort to Boston, which enabled Washington to drive out the British there. The historic fort is now owned by the Pell family, whose ancestor, William Ferris Pell, bought it in 1820 from Columbia and Union College to which it had been ceded by the state. Reconstruction work has been carried on for more than half a century. The West Barracks, on the Place d'Armes, has been fully restored. Here were the headquarters of Captain de la Place on the morning of May 9, 1775, when he was surprised by the loud demand for surrender from Colonel Ethan Allen, "In the name of the Great Jehovah and the Continental Congress," or, as the more popular version has it, "Come out, you damned old rat." The barracks is now a museum.

FORT STANWIX was built at a cost of $266,400 by the British in 1758 to guard their portage between the Mohawk River and Wood Creek. It was named for General John Stanwix, who erected it on the place where Rome now stands. In 1768 Sir William Johnson brought 2,000 Indians here, and a treaty was signed by which, for $50,600, the English were entitled to what are now great parts of New York, Pennsylvania, West Virginia, and Kentucky. During the Revolutionary War the patriots rebuilt the fort from a heap of ruins, and changed its name to FORT SCHUYLER, in honor of General Philip Schuyler. It was here, in August, 1777, that the Stars and Stripes first waved over an American fortification. Congress a month before had authorized the new flag, and the garrison made it from a newspaper description, using a woman's red petticoat, a soldier's white shirt, and a captain's blue military cloak. Fighting beneath this flag, the Americans repulsed Colonel Barry St. Leger's 1,400 British, Tories, Hessians, and Indians who besieged the fort. When the fort was rebuilt at a later date, it was once more called Fort Stanwix.

The French and Indian troubles in New York that finally flared into a full-fledged war in 1756 caused the building of many forts. Sir William Johnson built three or more. Among them was FORT ONTARIO, at Oswego, in 1755, where he lived for a time. Today the old fort, pentagonal in shape, is on a military reservation. There were also FORT HENDRICK, at Canajoharie, in 1756, named for his old friend "King" Hendrick, a Mohawk chief who had been killed the year before at Lake George; and FORT WILLIAM HENRY, also built in 1756 at the southern edge of Lake George. It was captured two years later by Montcalm, and the massacre of the garrison is vividly described in Cooper's *The Last of the Mohicans.* Ruins of the fort may be seen on the grounds of the Fort William Henry Hotel in the town of Lake George.

Among numerous other forts of this period were: **FORT LA PRÉSENTATION,** built at Ogdensburg in 1749 by Abbé François Picquet; **FORT WAGNER,** near the Palatine Bridge, erected in 1750 by Peter Wagner of the Palatine Regiment; and **FORT KLOCK,** a heavy story-and-a-half fortified house, built by Johannes Klock near St. Johnsville. There was also **FORT EDWARD,** on what was known as the "Great Carrying Place," at the Hudson River end of the portage between that river and Lake Champlain. It was first named **FORT LYMAN,** after Phineas Lyman, the builder, in 1755. Burgoyne occupied it briefly in 1777, and called it **FORT EDWARD** after the Duke of York. The town of Fort Edward stands on the site. **FORT GAGE,** near Lake George, was named for General Thomas Gage, second in command of the British troops in the French and Indian War. Here Lord Howe won an athletic contest when he "jumped the stick" at 6 feet 6 inches.

FORT SCHUYLER was built in 1758 by the British on what is now the main street of Utica, and was named for Colonel (later General) Philip Schuyler. Schuyler, a prominent man, was the father of the wife of Alexander Hamilton. This fort was noted for the treaty signed with the Indians in 1788 by Governor George Clinton. After the signing, an Indian chief began crowding the governor on the log upon which both sat. The governor moved away, but when the Indian pushed him to the edge of the log he demanded to know why. Said the Indian: "Just so white man crowd poor Indian. Keep crowding. By-an'-by him clear off. Where poor Indian then?"

FORT SCHLOSSER was built on the site of two older French forts at the head of the rapids above Niagara Falls. It was named for Captain Joseph Schlosser, a German officer in the British Army, who supervised construction of the fort in 1760. In the War of 1812 the British burned the fort. The old French chimney from one of the former French forts has been built into the fort's mess hall, which now stands on the grounds of the Carborundum Company.

GRENADIER'S FORT, one of the defenses of Crown Point, was constructed by the British general, Jeffrey Amherst, in 1759 when he drove the French from Lake Champlain. The site is occupied by the Champlain Memorial Lighthouse. General Amherst also began, but did not finish, **FORT GEORGE,** at the south end of Lake George. Revolutionary troops occupied it twice in the war with England.

The Revolutionary War produced many forts in this state. **FORT ANN** was one of the series of fortifications between the Hudson River watershed and Lake Champlain. The Battle of Fort Ann was fought here on July 8, 1777. The present town is named for the fort.

FORT PLAIN, considered one of the best fortifications in the Mohawk Valley, was built in 1776 to protect settlers from Indians. It was near the present town of Fort Plain. **FORT CUMMINGS,** at Honeoye, was the base of operations for Generals John Sullivan and James Clinton in 1779 when they attacked the Seneca Indians and broke their power forever. The site is marked by a bronze tablet in the center of the village. **FORT MARTINUS DECKER,** at Port Jervis, was built in 1779, and named for the builder, as a protection against Indians. The walls still are standing. **FORT GOLGOTHA,** at Huntington, Long Island, was erected during the Revolution by British soldiers, who converted an old cemetery into a fortification and, with grim humor, named it Fort Golgotha.

Several important forts were built around West Point in the Revolution. The first of these was **FORT CONSTITUTION,** on Constitution Island, now a part of the West Point Reservation. Later General George Clinton erected **FORT MONTGOMERY,** and, to keep the British from sailing up the Hudson, stretched a huge chain between the fort and the base of Anthony's Nose, a promontory on the east side of the stream (named for Anthony Corlear, Peter Stuyvesant's trumpeter). After a fierce engagement in October, 1777, the British hacked the chain in two and sailed up the river. The fort was named for General Richard Montgomery, killed in the attack on Quebec. A second chain, each link weighing 140 pounds, was stretched between Fort Constitution and West Point, and remained until the end of the war.

Another defense at West Point, on Mount Independence, was **FORT PUTNAM,** or **OLD PUT,** named for General Israel Putnam. A fourth was **FORT CLINTON,** near Fort Montgomery, on the west shore. It was named for General George Clinton, who was elected first governor of New York. Formerly this fortification was called **FORT ARNOLD,** but the name was changed when Benedict Arnold turned traitor. **FORT INDEPENDENCE** was built across the river, "in the shadow of Anthony's Nose." Remains of Forts Putnam, Constitution, and Clinton still are to be seen.

Governors Island in New York Harbor early was a garden spot, but during the Revolution the British fortified it. Later, in 1794, when a war with France threatened, **FORT JAY** was erected there. In 1799, when relations with France became more acute, there was a public clamor for a stronger fort. Students of Columbia College aided in the work with pick and shovel, and when the fort was finally completed in 1806 it was called **FORT COLUMBUS.** But in later years, this fort, which never saw active service, was again called Fort Jay, after John Jay who had negotiated Jay's Treaty with England.

American legionnaire, 1795

There were numerous forts in and around New York City. **FORT WASHINGTON** was an important military post during the Revolution, occupying the highest part of Manhattan overlooking the Hudson River. Its site is now the eastern terminus of the George Washington Bridge. Prior to its surrender to the British on November 16, 1776, Margaret Corbin became one of the heroines of the day when she took the place of her husband after he fell in battle and fought until her arm was torn off by a cannon ball.

CASTLE WILLIAMS, built just prior to the War of 1812, in the harbor of New York, stands as a quaint landmark.

About the time this was being built, a similar work was in erection just off the Battery in Manhattan, on a ledge of rocks now a part of the city itself. This was called FORT CLINTON (not to be confused with two other FORT CLINTONs—one in the northeastern section of Central Park and the other a Revolutionary War fort near West Point). Fort Clinton at the Battery, named for Governor De Witt Clinton, was sometimes called the Southwest Battery. In 1822 it was discontinued as a fortification, and two years later General Lafayette was officially welcomed there on his visit to the United States. The structure was later called Castle Garden, and it was there that P. T. Barnum staged the great triumph of Jenny Lind in 1850. Ten years later, one writer said: "It is neither a concert saloon, an opera house, nor a receptacle for needy immigrants; but the old whitewashed barn is devoted to the restaurant business on a very limited scale, as ice cream, lemonade, and sponge cake constitute the list of delicacies from which to select." Later it was transformed into the Municipal Aquarium, and more recently has been restored and named a historic site.

During the War of 1812 a little brick strongbox was erected just off the present-day FORT HAMILTON on Long Island. It was named FORT DIAMOND, but after Lafayette's visit to the United States in 1824, it was rechristened FORT LAFAYETTE. It later became the outpost of Fort Hamilton, built in 1831 to command the Narrows between upper and lower New York Bay. A few years earlier FORT WADSWORTH was erected across the Narrows on Staten Island, occupying a reservation of 221 acres. FORT SCHUYLER, built as one of the defenses to the northern entrance to New York Harbor, on Throgg's Neck, Long Island Sound, was started in 1833, but the United States Military Post was not established until 1856.

FORT BLUNDER, on Island Point, an island in Lake Champlain, was erected during the first part of the last century. It was replaced in 1819 by FORT MONTGOMERY, named for General Richard Montgomery, who fell before Quebec. A year earlier, his remains had been removed to New York City and reburied in front of St. Paul's Church. The work on Fort Montgomery was stopped when it was announced that the island belonged to Canada. But immediately after the boundary was established, in 1842, the fort was completed, but never garrisoned.

FORTs **MOREAU, BROWN,** and **SCOTT** were erected during the War of 1812 at Plattsburg. **FORT COVINGTON,** named for Brigadier General Leonard Covington, was built in 1812 at French Mills, which later became known as Fort Covington. **FORT FREY,** at Palatine Bridge, was erected in 1739 on the site of a log cabin built by Hendrick Frey. **FORT SALONGA,** on Long Island near Northport, was a British post captured by the Continentals in 1781. **FORT ALLEGHAN,** at Auburn, is believed to have been erected by prehistoric Mound Builders. **FORT TERRY** is a United States Military Reservation of 150 acres on Plum Island between Long Island Sound and Gardiners Bay.

One of the last forts built in New York was **FORT SLOCUM,** on David's Island off New Rochelle. Another was **FORT TOTTEN,** built in 1862 by General Joseph G. Totten, chief engineer of the United States Army during the Civil War, and named for him. It has a reservation of 136 acres on the East River at the western end of Long Island near Whitestone.

The Mideast States

VIRGINIA

DELAWARE

NEW JERSEY

MARYLAND

PENNSYLVANIA

OHIO

WEST VIRGINIA

KENTUCKY

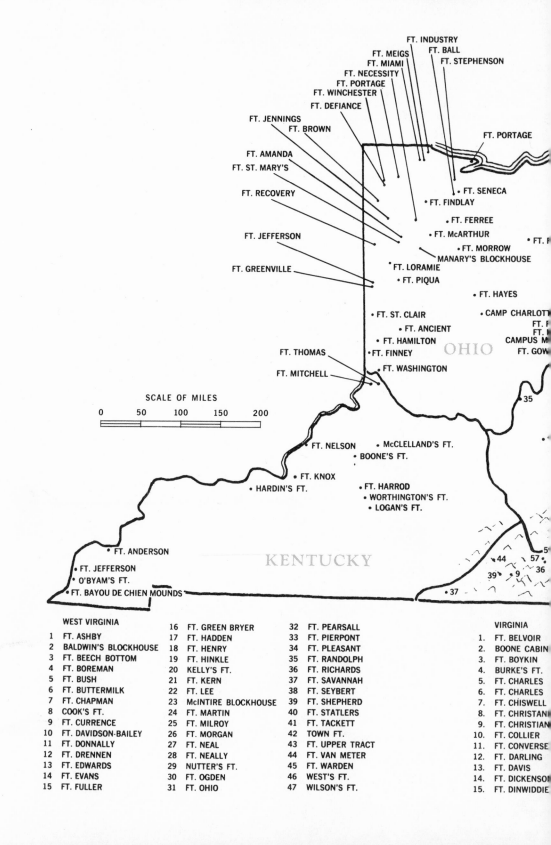

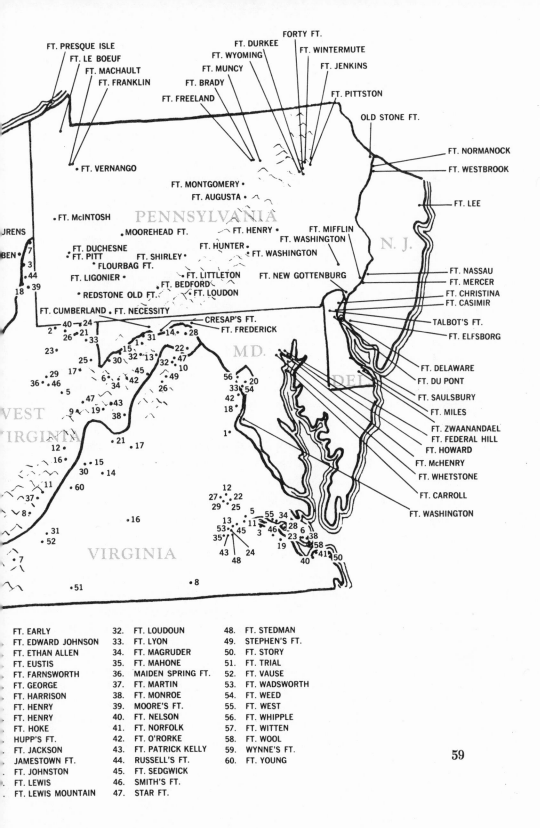

FT. PRESQUE ISLE
FT. LE BOEUF
FT. MACHAULT
FT. FRANKLIN
FT. DURKEE
FT. WYOMING
FORTY FT.
FT. WINTERMUTE
FT. MUNCY
FT. BRADY
FT. JENKINS
FT. FREELAND
FT. PITTSTON
OLD STONE FT.
FT. NORMANOCK
FT. WESTBROOK
• FT. VERNANGO
FT. MONTGOMERY •
FT. AUGUSTA •
FT. LEE
• FT. McINTOSH
PENNSYLVANIA
•MOOREHEAD FT.
FT. HENRY •
FT. MIFFLIN
FT. WASHINGTON
N. J.
FT. DUCHESNE
FT. PITT
FT. SHIRLEY •
FT. HUNTER •
FT. WASHINGTON
FLOURBAG FT.
FT. LIGONIER •
• FT. LITTLETON
FT. BEDFORD
• REDSTONE OLD FT.
FT. LOUDON
FT. NEW GOTTENBURG
FT. NASSAU
FT. MERCER
FT. CHRISTINA
FT. CASIMIR
FT. CUMBERLAND • FT. NECESSITY
CRESAP'S FT.
FT. FREDERICK
TALBOT'S FT.
FT. ELFSBORG
MD.
DEL.
FT. DELAWARE
FT. DU PONT
FT. SAULSBURY
FT. MILES
WEST
VIRGINIA
FT. ZWAANANDAEL
FT. FEDERAL HILL
FT. HOWARD
FT. McHENRY
FT. WHETSTONE
FT. CARROLL
FT. WASHINGTON
VIRGINIA

FT. EARLY   32. FT. LOUDOUN   48. FT. STEDMAN
FT. EDWARD JOHNSON   33. FT. LYON   49. STEPHEN'S FT.
FT. ETHAN ALLEN   34. FT. MAGRUDER   50. FT. STORY
FT. EUSTIS   35. FT. MAHONE   51. FT. TRIAL
FT. FARNSWORTH   36. MAIDEN SPRING FT.   52. FT. VAUSE
FT. GEORGE   37. FT. MARTIN   53. FT. WADSWORTH
FT. HARRISON   38. FT. MONROE   54. FT. WEED
FT. HENRY   39. MOORE'S FT.   55. FT. WEST
FT. HENRY   40. FT. NELSON   56. FT. WHIPPLE
FT. HOKE   41. FT. NORFOLK   57. FT. WITTEN
HUPP'S FT.   42. FT. O'RORKE   58. FT. WOOL
FT. JACKSON   43. FT. PATRICK KELLY   59. WYNNE'S FT.
JAMESTOWN FT.   44. RUSSELL'S FT.   60. FT. YOUNG
FT. JOHNSTON   45. FT. SEDGWICK
FT. LEWIS   46. SMITH'S FT.
FT. LEWIS MOUNTAIN   47. STAR FT.

59

VIRGINIA

One of the Thirteen Original Colonies.

FORT MONROE, sometimes called **FORTRESS MONROE,** at Old Point Comfort, satisfied the popular conception of a mighty stronghold of defense more completely than any other establishment in the United States.

It guards, or did at one time, the most vital points of entrance in this country, menacing hostile approach to the very capital of the country. It is at the southern limit of the western shore of Chesapeake Bay, on a long, narrow peninsula. Its walls encircle the greater part of 280 acres.

Sir Christopher Newport's band of adventurers paused here in 1607, exchanged greetings with the Kecoughtan Indians, named the point to the eastward Point Comfort, and continued on to Jamestown. In 1609 the Jamestown settlers built the defense they called **ALGERNOURNE FORT** when they feared an attack by Spaniards. This was a simple stockade without stone or brick, with fifty men, women, and boys and seven cannon, and was named for Lord Algernon (Algernourne) Percie, one of the directors of the Virginia Company. In 1630–1632 the defense was rebuilt by Colonel Samuel Mathews, and in 1727–1730 a new fortification was erected and called **FORT GEORGE,** in honor of King George II, who took the throne in 1727. This fort, which had double walls of brick, was destroyed by the "Great Gust" of 1749. Later, during the siege of Yorktown, Count de Grasse strengthened the defenses of the area by placing batteries on the Point. Construction of the present fort began in 1819 and was completed in 1847. It was named for President James Monroe.

Edgar Allan Poe, who had enlisted in the Army in Boston under the name of E. A. Perry, served at Fort Monroe in 1828–1829. Chief Black Hawk of Illinois was held prisoner here after the Black Hawk War. On the night of February 2, 1865, a steamer from Washington, D.C., anchored in Hampton Roads, bringing President Lincoln for

an informal peace conference with the Confederate commissioners, headed by an old friend and fellow congressman, Alexander Stephens, Confederate vice president under Jefferson Davis. The conference solved nothing. Though Davis was confined for two years in the fort on a charge of treason, he was released without ever being tried. Fort Monroe is now the home of the Army Coast Artillery Post and Coast Artillery School.

On May 13, 1607, Sir Christopher Newport, in command of the three ships, *Sarah Constant, Goodspeed,* and *Discovery,* shortly after visiting Point Comfort, landed at Jamestown Island, and his 105 English adventurers set to work at once to build **JAMESTOWN FORT,** the first permanent English settlement in the United States. In 1861 the Confederates built another **JAMESTOWN FORT** on the site, but a year later it was occupied by Union troops. Today, this fort is part of the Colonial National Historical Park. Two years after the landing at Jamestown, Captain Francis West purchased a site a distance up the James River and erected **FORT WEST.** In 1637 a trading post was established there. After an Indian massacre in 1644, **FORT CHARLES,** named for Charles I, was built at the head of navigation. **SMITH'S FORT,** named for Captain John Smith, but shown on his map as the **"NEW FORT,"** was also built in 1609 on the south bank of the James River near present-day Surry. Close to the house built by Thomas Rolfe, son of Pocahontas and John Rolfe, are to be seen remnants of this old fort. The following year, when the Kecoughtan Indians ceased to be friendly, Sir Thomas Gates, after driving them away, built two stockades on Hampton's Rivulet, naming them **FORT HENRY** and **FORT CHARLES** for the sons of James I. These were probably on the site of the present town of Hampton. A red-brick residence at Mountain View McKenzie Street, opposite the north end of South Street in Hampton, is believed to have been built partly from materials from the fort and from a stone building of Captain John Flood, the first commander.

Another **FORT HENRY** was erected on the site of Petersburg in 1645 at the falls of the Appomattox River. In the following year the fort was turned over to Abraham Wood for three years on the condition that he keep ten men there for protection. Wood established a trading post.

FORT CHRISTANNA, near the present Lawrenceville, was built by Governor Spotswood in 1714, and given a name combining those of the Saviour and Britain's Queen. Spotswood located the friendly Saponi Indians, one of the eastern Siouan tribes, near the fort for protection against their mutual enemy, the Tuscarora. These Indians, now extinct, became known as the "Fort Christanna tribes." An ancient, unmounted cannon, one of five in the stockade, today marks the site of the fort.

FORT YOUNG was the beginning of the present town of Covington. After it was erected in the middle of the eighteenth century, a settlement called Murry's Store grew around it. In 1819 town lots were laid out, and the settlement was named for its oldest resident, Peter Covington.

FORT VAUSE was on the site of the present town of Shawsville. Built in 1754 by Captain Ephraim Vause, it was later attacked by Indians, who burned the stockade and carried away Vause's wife, two daughters, and three servants. The Council of War at Augusta Courthouse, Staunton, ordered the stockade rebuilt.

At the beginning of the French and Indian War, Lieutenant Colonel George Washington, then only twenty-three years old, was placed in command of a project for a chain of forts to guard the Virginia frontier. The first of these, erected in 1755, was **FORT DINWIDDIE,** named for the governor of Virginia, and built in the lowlands of the Jackson River, near the present Warm Springs. Another of these forts was **FORT LOUDOUN,** at Winchester. This fortification was named for John Campbell, Fourth Earl of Loudoun, commander in chief of the British forces in America. Franklin said of him, "He is like little St. George on the signboards, always on horseback, but never goes forward." **FORT DICKENSON,** near the present Millboro Springs and also near the George Washington National Forest, was a third of such forts. Another was **FORT TRIAL,** near the present Stanleytown, built in 1756.

Besides these, dozens of forts and fortified houses were erected in Virginia as protection against Indians. There was **HUPP'S FORT,** a barnlike stone structure at Strasburg, which was built in 1775. **FORT LEWIS MOUNTAIN** was a fort and village of the same name. The stockade was built by Major Andrew Lewis in his intended expedition against the Cherokee. Near Bath Alum Springs, Charles Lewis, son of the founder of Staunton, built a stockade around his home and called it **FORT LEWIS**; others called it "Lewis's Hog Pen."

FORT CHISWELL, near Pulaski, was built in the fall of 1760 under the direction of William Byrd III, who named it for John Chiswell, owner of the nearby lead mines. The site is marked by a pyramid of boulders. There was also **WYNNE'S FORT,** built by William Wynne near Pocahontas. **FORT WITTEN,** near Tazewell, marks the first settlement in this section of Clinch Valley. It was built in 1767 by Thomas Witten, and has been reconstructed.

BOONE CABIN-FORT, some seventeen miles from Bluefield, was built by Daniel Boone and several companions on a hunting expedition in 1767–1768. The spot was later occupied by a log house where Tazewell County was organized and the first court held. Today a brick farmhouse stands on the site. **FORT MARTIN** was erected near Jonesville by settlers whose leader was Joseph Martin, an officer of militia who also had a wild reputation as a gambler. **MOORE'S FORT,** built on the Clinch River in the 1770's, is the site of the town of St. Paul. **MAIDEN SPRING FORT,** erected in 1772 by Reese Bowen, was not far from Tazewell. **FORT CHRISTIAN,** near Lebanon, was built in 1774 by Daniel Smith, surveyor and captain of militia.

On a plateau known as Burke's Garden, near Tazewell, was **BURKE'S FORT,** built in 1774. **FORT GEORGE,** an early refuge in Indian attacks, near McDowell in the Shenandoah Mountains, was named for King George III. Its outlines are well preserved, and clearly outlined are two bastions, a hole for the powder magazine, and a trenchlike tunnel by which water could be brought from the Cowpasture River. **STEPHEN'S FORT,** at Middletown, a small whitewashed hexagonal building, was erected before the Revolution.

RUSSELL'S FORT, at Dickensonville, was built by William Russell, Indian fighter and Revolutionary officer, in 1774. Later Russell married Elizabeth Henry Campbell, sister of Patrick Henry, and widow of General William Campbell.

FORT NELSON was erected by Virginians in 1776 on the Elizabeth River just below Portsmouth, on Windmill Point, to defend Portsmouth, Norfolk, and the Navy Yard at Gosport from British attack. It was named for General Thomas Nelson of Virginia. On May 9, 1779, it was garrisoned with 150 men under Major Thomas Matthews, who on the approach of Admiral George Collier, commander of the British fleet, and General Edward Mathew, commanding the land forces, abandoned the fort, leaving the American flag flying, and retreated to Dismal Swamp. The British landed and burned the fort and the Marine Yard, and seized Portsmouth and Norfolk. In the War of 1812, when the British again attempted to take Portsmouth, the guns of Fort Nelson and nearby Fort Norfolk drove them off. On June 22, 1813, in a second attack made on Craney Island, a bombardment from the fort sank several vessels and routed the enemy.

British field artillery officer, 1812

FORT NORFOLK, on the east, or opposite, side of the Elizabeth River from Fort Nelson, was built in 1794 by the State of Virginia but was sold in the following year to the Government. It aided in the repulse of the British attacks during the War of 1812. The garrison abandoned it upon Virginia's secession during the Civil War, and it was held until 1862 by the Confederates until Norfolk was evacuated. The old fort stands at the west end of Front Street in Norfolk and is district headquarters of the United States Engineers and an ammunition storage place.

FORT STORY, at Virginia Beach, is one of the defense systems guarding the naval base, shipyards, and ports of Hampton Roads, as well as the water approach to Washington. Detachments from the Coast Artillery Base at Fort Monroe man the long-range coast defense and antiaircraft batteries.

FORT WOOL, erected on a man-made island in mid-channel in Hampton Roads, was first built as **FORT CALHOUN.** Work began in 1830 but was not completed until the Civil War broke out in 1861. On May 9th of the following year, the Union forces captured the fort and renamed it in honor of General John E. Wool, department commander of the Department of Virginia. During the First World War defense nets were spread from the fort's foundations to trap enemy submarines.

FORT BELVOIR, at Fredericksburg, at one time called **FORT HUMPHREYS,** was named for Belvoir Mansion, which stood on these grounds. The mansion was gutted by fire in 1783 and completely demolished by the British in 1814. Today it is a military reservation of the United States Corps of Engineers.

FORT BOYKIN, near Shoal Bay, and on a bluff overlooking two bends in the James River, is composed of earthworks in the form of a seven-pointed star. The remains of this interesting fort are grass-covered, with almost hidden gun emplacements and an earthen bank that was once a bombproof powder magazine. Fortifications are believed to have been first erected here during the Revolutionary War; but the fort was built during the War of 1812; and later, during the Civil War, it was enlarged. Sidney Lanier, the poet, was stationed here in 1863, and it was here that he began his war novel, *Tiger-Lilies.*

FORT WHIPPLE, now known as **FORT MYER,** at Washington, D.C., was one of the strongest of a cordon of 127 forts erected to defend Washington during the Civil War. In 1861 the land now constituting Arlington Cemetery, on the old Arlington Estate, was occupied by Union forces. Fort Whipple, named for General Amiel

Thirty-two-pounder Federal cannon

W. Whipple, chief engineer for General Irvin McDowell, commanded the first Federal forces gathered in Washington. The fort was not completed until near the close of the Civil War, and was never garrisoned. The grass-covered ramparts are to be seen in the southwestern part of Arlington Cemetery. Today it is a typical Army post where the Chief of Staff resides in a red-brick mansion. It was on the parade ground that the Wright brothers, after experiments at Kitty Hawk, North Carolina, and Dayton, Ohio, held their first public demonstrations. The fort had been renamed Fort Myer in 1881 to honor General Albert J. Myer, creator of the Army Signal Corps, then known as the Signal Bureau.

Ruins of other forts for the southern defense of the Capital during the Civil War are to be found along the wooded parkway, Route U.S. 1. They are **FORT FARNSWORTH,** near Huntington Creek; **FORT WEED, FORT LYON,** and **FORT O'RORKE.** Fort Weed was named for General Stephen H. Weed, killed at Gettysburg, and Fort Lyon for General William Haines Lyon, killed at the Battle of Chickamauga.

FORT STEDMAN was one of a line of Federal forts and entrenchments around Petersburg. One of the most horrific slaughters of the Civil War took place here when the Federal troops sought to capture the fort. A tunnel had been built beneath the stronghold, and a huge quantity of powder stored there was set off. Several hundred Confederate soldiers were killed, but when the Federal troops sought to follow up their advantage they became confused on the broken ground, which became a death trap as the Confederates, who had re-formed, poured in their deadly fire for thirty minutes. Today "The Crater," as it is called, can be seen, a huge hole in the ground, ten feet or more in depth and about two hundred in diameter.

FORT MAHONE, at Petersburg, a Confederate fortification, was named for General William Mahone, whose division occupied it in 1864. This fort fell on April 2, 1865, during Grant's attack. At the time of his siege Grant used a Federal outpost, **FORT PATRICK KELLY,** whose breastworks are well preserved at the junction of U.S. 301 and County 609 outside Petersburg. **FORT WADSWORTH** was another Union fort built during the Union campaign on Petersburg. It was named for General James S. Wadsworth, who was killed on May 6, 1864, in the Battle of the Wilderness. Grant also built **FORT DAVIS,** a unit for the left flank of his army. **FORT SEDGWICK,** too, was erected as the Union lines were extended to the left in the early summer of 1864. It was named for General John Sedgwick, who was killed at the Battle of Spotsylvania Courthouse. This fort received the nickname **FORT HELL** because of the tremendous amount of ammunition used there.

FORT DARLING, near Richmond, on Drewrys Bluff, high above the James River, enabled the Confederate forces to drive back a Union fleet, including the ironclad *Monitor,* on May 15, 1862. The fort has been partially restored. At the time of Grant's campaign against Richmond, the city was ringed with forts. **FORT HARRISON,** to the southeast of the city, is now a park headquarters and museum. Within the three-mile radius of Richmond were **FORT**s **JACKSON** and **JOHNSTON. FORT HOKE,** in the Richmond National Battlefield Park, was one of the important outer defenses. This fort has been restored with sandbags and gabions.

STAR FORT, on a wooded hill near Winchester, was built by Federal troops in 1862 but abandoned by them a few months later. During the third Battle of Winchester, on September 19, 1864, the Federal cavalry captured these works, turned the Confederate left flank, and captured the town. **FORT COLLIER,** from which Confederate fortifications formed a semicircle around Winchester, was abandoned during the third Battle of Winchester.

FORT MAGRUDER, at Williamsburg, was where the Battle of Williamsburg was fought on May 5, 1862.

FORT CONVERSE, at Hopewell, whose site is on the grounds of a United States Reformatory, was used by Union forces. General Butler stationed Negro troops here during the Civil War to guard his pontoon bridges.

FORT EDWARD JOHNSON, near Churchville, on a crest of the Shenandoah Mountains, was occupied by General Edward Johnson's Confederate command of 3,000 troops in February, 1862.

Cavalryman, Civil War

FORT EARLY was at Lynchburg. At the northeast corner of Fort and Vernon avenues is to be seen the restored square earthworks originally built during the Lynchburg Campaign. Confederate forces under General Jubal A. Early repulsed General Hunter's attack here in June, 1864.

FORT ETHAN ALLEN, at Cherrydale, was erected during the Civil War to guard the approaches to Chain Ridge.

FORT EUSTIS, near Hilton Village in Warwick County, was used as a cantonment during World War I and later as an artillery post.

DELAWARE

One of the Thirteen Original Colonies.

Peter Minuit, as the first Director-General of New Netherland, had purchased Manhattan Island from the Indians for trinkets valued at $24, but in 1631 he had a parting of the ways with the Dutch West India Company. Restless and adventuresome, he entered into negotiations with Queen Christina of Sweden, to found "New Sweden" in America.

In March of 1638, Minuit, with two Swedish vessels, sailed up the Delaware River and landed at The Rocks, now at the foot of East Seventh Street in Wilmington, Delaware. Here he established **FORT CHRISTINA,** named for the young Queen of Sweden, and formed the first permanent settlement of Europeans in Delaware. Minuit sailed away that year and was lost in a hurricane in the West Indies.

But the Dutch were determined to have the Delaware River trade, usurped by the Swedes. In 1655 Peter Stuyvesant, governor for the Dutch West India Company, surrounded the fort and hamlet and took over without bloodshed. He renamed it **FORT ALTENA.** The reign of the Dutch lasted only until 1665, when Sir Robert Carr stationed British soldiers at the fort, and the Swedes swore allegiance to James, Duke of York. The Swedish, Dutch, and Finnish planters were not disturbed.

The old fort fell into ruins, and it was not until the War of 1812, when, in order to protect the Delaware from the British, James A. Bayard, first named to represent the state in the United States Senate, joined the citizens in building **FORT UNION** on the site. This was the fourth time the place had been fortified; but, as before, there was never any fighting.

FORT ZWAANANDAEL (Swaanendael), established in 1631 at the present site of Lewes, marked the first settlement by the Dutch in Delaware. Dutch patroons, in partnership with the navigator David Pieter De Vries, erected the fort, but Indians destroyed it within a year, and the colony was abandoned. In 1909 the state erected the De Vries Monument to mark the site.

FORT CASIMIR, at New Castle, was built by Peter Stuyvesant in 1651, four years before he captured Fort Christina. It was erected on Sand Hook, a point of land, long since washed away, beyond the end of the present Chestnut Street in New Castle. In the three decades following the building of this fort, and until William Penn established his province, it had five changes of sovereignty and two additional changes of government. Johan Classon Rising, assistant governor of "New Sweden," took it over on Trinity Sunday, May 21, 1654, and renamed it **FORT TREFOLDDIGHET** (Trinity), but Stuyvesant had it back within little more than a year when he conquered all of New Sweden, and restored the old name.

Colonel Richard Nicholls, the Duke of York's Deputy Governor of New York and the Province of Delaware, in October, 1664, visited New Amstel (named for a suburb of Amsterdam) when the English took over and called it New Castle, for William Cavendish, the Earl of Newcastle-upon-Tyne in England.

TALBOT'S FORT, at Christiana, west of New Castle, was built in 1684 by Colonel George Talbot, a cousin of the third Baron (or

Lord) Baltimore, as a defense of the latter's claim to territory along the Delaware River as a portion of the 1632 Maryland Grant. The fort was garrisoned for two years by Maryland soldiers during the bitter dispute with William Penn over the Northern Boundary. Baron Baltimore's Charter was overthrown by a Protestant Revolt in 1689.

FORT DELAWARE, on Pea Patch Island in the Delaware River, a mile from Delaware City, was built as one of the most ambitious projects of the United States Government. The 178-acre island was named during Colonial days when it was said that a boat loaded with peas ran aground and its cargo sprouted in the sandy loam. An earthwork was erected here in 1813, but was dismantled in 1821 and replaced by a masonry fort. This was destroyed by fire in 1832.

Meanwhile a controversy raged as to whether the island belonged to New Jersey or Delaware; but when the trouble was finally settled in Delaware's favor, Congress in 1847 passed an appropriation of $1,000,000 to construct the largest modern fort in the country.

Dragoon, 1851

When the fort was only partially completed, Congress had to provide another million. The fort, pentagon-shaped in size, with walls of solid granite, was not completed until two years before the start of the Civil War. Though it mounted 131 guns, it served mainly as a prison during the Civil War. By August, 1863, it held 12,500 Confederate prisoners. All those captured at Gettysburg, including General James J. Archer, were imprisoned there. Among its political prisoners were such notables as Burton H. Harrison, private secretary to Jefferson Davis, president of the Confederate States, and Governor Francis R. Lubbock of Texas. Some 2,700 prisoners died during their incarceration, and most were buried at Finn's Point, just across the river in New Jersey.

This grim, bleak gray mass was further enlarged, and emplacements for three 2-inch disappearing guns were built during the Spanish-American War, at a cost of more than $500,000. Finally, in 1944, the fort was declared surplus property by the Government and turned over to the State of Delaware. It is now within the jurisdiction of the Delaware Park Commission, and the Fort Delaware Society assists in its preservation and restoration as a tourist attraction. Like some other great forts of the nation, its guns never were fired in combat.

FORT DU PONT, opposite Pea Patch Island in New Castle County, stands on a reservation of 173 acres. It first bore the name of **FORT REYNOLDS,** in commemoration of General Reynolds who was killed at Gettysburg, but it was renamed for Admiral Samuel F. du Pont in 1896. In 1945 it was turned over to the state and made into the Governor Bacon Health Center. Under the jurisdiction of the original fort, which was headquarters of harbor defenses of the Delaware River and Bay, were the forts Delaware and Saulsbury.

FORT SAULSBURY, on lower Delaware Bay, near Slaughter Beach, was built in 1896, and in World War I was established as a United States Coast Artillery defense unit. It was named for Senator Willard Saulsbury. It was deactivated in 1946 and is now privately owned. The importance of guarding Cape Henlopen as an entrance to Delaware Bay was realized by the Colonials, who in 1725 erected a lighthouse on the cape under the brow of Sand Hill. In 1767 a 45-foot hexagonal stone tower, painted white and containing the Cape Henlopen Light, succeeded this structure. During the Revolution the light was extinguished in the hope that British men-of-war would be wrecked on the shore. But the British landed one day and burned the inside of the tower. Later, **FORT MILES,** named for General Nelson A. Miles, was erected here as a coastal defense work. It was declared surplus property on July 1, 1962.

NEW JERSEY

One of the Thirteen Original Colonies.

The Indians called him "The Big Tub." Johan Björnsson Printz weighed four hundred pounds, and as governor of New Sweden in America he was a big man in another sense, too. In 1643 he arrived in the Delaware River and built a fort on the New Jersey side below the Varkens Kill, where Salem stands today, to control the trade and river traffic. He named it **FORT ELFSBORG.** As the river narrows at this point, no Dutch ship could pass out of range of the Swedish guns, and Governor Printz forced each one to haul down her colors while her cargo was inspected. This angered the Dutch, who had been in this section first. As a result, on May 30, 1655, Peter Stuyvesant with seven ships and more than six hundred men anchored before the fort. But he found it in ruins. The Swedes already had burned it down, some say because they could no longer stand the swarms of mosquitoes. They had nicknamed the settlement Myggenborg, or Mosquito Castle.

Governor Printz divided his time between Fort Elfsborg and **FORT NEW GOTTENBURG** across the river near Essington, Pennsylvania.

The first fort in New Jersey along the Delaware was **FORT NASSAU.** It was built by the Dutch in 1624 near the site of the present-day city of Gloucester, a few miles below Philadelphia. Henry Hudson, an Englishman engaged by the Dutch East India Company, had sailed into Delaware Bay in 1609, and Captain Cornelius Jacobsen Mey had entered the river in 1614. It was he who, ten years later, erected Fort Nassau, for the Dutch West India Company, naming it for Nassau in Holland.

Cape May at the lower tip of New Jersey was named for Captain Mey. After the Swedes had set up Fort Elfsborg down the river, the friction between the Dutch and Swedes finally came to a climax when Peter Stuyvesant took over all Swedish forts along the Delaware, thus bringing to an end the Swedish phase of Colonial history.

FORT LEE stood on the site of the town of Fort Lee, at the western end of the Washington Bridge over the Hudson River.

Early on the morning of November 20, 1776, the British general Cornwallis crossed the Hudson from Dobbs Ferry to Closter's Landing on the New Jersey side, five miles above the fort, with a force six thousand strong, including artillery. Stealthily the troops climbed a steep, rocky pathway up a gorge in the Palisades. General Nathanael Greene of the Continental forces was still asleep. A farmer who had observed the British advance rushed into the fort and awoke General Greene.

In the morning twilight Greene had just time hastily to withdraw his garrison of two thousand men. But cannon, tents, stores, and camp equipage were left behind. Greene barely escaped capture. General George Washington, whose army was camped a few miles west, covered Greene's retreat so well that less than a hundred stragglers were captured by the British.

This was a severe blow to the Continental forces. Washington, standing on the brow of the Palisades at Fort Lee just three days before, in company with Thomas Paine, author of *Common Sense*, had observed the British capture of Fort Washington directly across the river in New York and had seen the British colors hoisted in triumph. The British at once changed the name to **FORT KNYP-HAUSEN,** after General Baron Knyphausen, whose German troops had aided in the capture.

The site of Fort Lee is marked by a monument, erected in 1908. The fort was named for English-born General Charles Lee, who as an officer in the Continental Army was said to have been ambitious to replace George Washington. The town of Fort Lee was the center of the early moving-picture industry.

There were many forts, including fortified homes, for 104 miles up and down the road, from Esopus (Kingston) to the Mines Holes in the Water Gap. They were mainly for defense against Indians. Among these were **FORT WESTBROOK** on the Delaware near what is now Montague. It was named for Johannes Westbrook, an early settler, and its site is marked today by a few stones. Another was **FORT NORMANOCK,** also on the Delaware and named for Normanock (an Indian word for Fish or Fishing Place) Island to the west in the Delaware River.

FORT MERCER on the Delaware River directly across from Fort Mifflin, Pennsylvania, was built in the latter part of 1777 on what was termed Red Bank. It was here that the garrison of Fort Mifflin escaped to safety during the heavy bombardment of their fort by the British. Fort Mercer, named for General Hugh Mercer, who was killed earlier in 1777 at the battle of Princeton, was but little more than earthen embankments and a ditch covered by an abatis. Its site is in the Red Bank National Park near Woodbury.

MARYLAND

One of the Thirteen Original Colonies.

Attorney Francis Scott Key, held for security reasons on board His Majesty's Ship *Tonnant*, at early dawn of September 14, 1814, gazed at the far-distant Fort McHenry. Fluttering in the breeze above the fort he could see the American flag. " 'Tis the Star-Spangled Banner," he murmured joyfully. "It's still there!"

Key, who had come aboard the ship in an effort to obtain the release of his friend Dr. William Beanes, began to scribble on the back of an envelope. He called his poem "The Defense of Fort McHenry," later to be retitled "The Star-Spangled Banner," and it began "O Say, can you see through the dawn's early light . . ." He crossed out the word "through," substituted "by," and continued writing the lines of America's National Anthem.

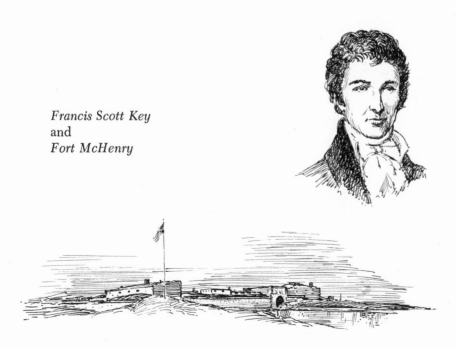

Francis Scott Key
and
Fort McHenry

FORT McHENRY, a star-shaped fortification on what was Whetstone Point in the Patapsco River, had undergone a terrific bombardment by the British fleet for twenty-five hours during which the British sent over some 1,880 shells and rockets, but her defenders, under Major George Armistead, had withstood the attack, and so saved Baltimore in the War of 1812.

Fort McHenry stands near the site of **FORT WHETSTONE,** erected during the Revolutionary War. In 1776 a battery was stationed in a crude fort of mud and logs, and a boom was stretched across the river to Lazaretto, a small projection of land on the north side of the stream. In 1794 the Federal Government appropriated $20,000 for the erection of a permanent fortification to be named for James McHenry, one of Washington's private secretaries and Secretary of War at the time. At the beginning of the War of 1812 the fort was strengthened.

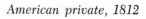

American private, 1812

Fort McHenry again saw action during the Civil War. On April 19, 1861, citizens of Baltimore, after a brush with Federal troops, paraded the streets and shouted, "Capture Fort McHenry!" But the fort was saved when it was reported that eight hundred Federal troops had arrived; and many historians believed this also saved Maryland from seceding from the Union. That same year Francis Key Howard, grandson of Francis Scott Key, was arrested and held a prisoner in the fort with the mayor of Baltimore and members of the assembly, who were suspected of being southern sympathizers. Howard later was removed to Fortress Monroe, where he was held during the war.

Until 1900 the fort was an infantry post, when it was abandoned by the Government as useless because of modern artillery. Fifteen years later the grounds were leased to the City of Baltimore for a park, but during World War I the Government reclaimed it and converted it into a hospital. In 1925 it was made a National Park.

As a result of the mob action in Baltimore in 1861, **FORT FEDERAL HILL,** on a commanding eminence overlooking the city and harbor, was built a month later. Fifty guns were mounted there.

The spot on North Point, on the Patapsco River seventeen miles below Baltimore, where five thousand British soldiers, under General Robert Ross, landed on September 12, 1814, and began their northern march to attack Baltimore, is the location of **FORT HOW-ARD.** General Ross had said, "I'll eat dinner in Baltimore or in Hell." He was killed and his army defeated. Built in 1900 as the chief coastal artillery defense for Baltimore, Fort Howard was named for Colonel John Eager Howard of the Revolution.

One of the most interesting fortifications in the country is **FORT WASHINGTON,** built about the time the City of Washington was laid out as the Capital of the United States. Known then as **FORT WARBURTON,** its major function was the protection of Washington. Fort Warburton, on the Maryland side of the Potomac River a few miles below Alexandria, Virginia, received its name from the estate upon which it was built. Warburton Manor, patented in 1661, was the home of Edward Digges, governor of Virginia from 1652 until 1689. His descendants lived there during the time the fort was built.

Major Charles L'Enfant, who laid out the City of Washington, also designed the fort, which was situated on a high promontory above the great bend of the Potomac so that it commanded a view up and down the river for many miles.

A British squadron appeared before Fort Warburton on August 27, 1814, three days after the capture and burning of Washington. The commander of the fort at once blew up and abandoned the fort without firing a shot.

The name was changed to Fort Washington in 1815. The fort was abandoned by the Government in 1940 after the river parkway was completed, but the structure has been preserved. The grounds have been made into Fort Washington Park.

CRESAP'S FORT, built in 1740 by Thomas Cresap, the first white settler at what is now Oldtown in Allegheny County, was one of the oldest fortified structures and trading posts in Maryland. George Washington, sixteen-year-old surveyor for Lord Fairfax, mentioned this place in his journal in 1748. He had forded the Potomac River and intended to spend but one night there, but he remained four days because of the floods. Cresap was a commissary during the French and Indian War, and General Braddock's troops camped at the fort in May, 1755. French and Indians finally drove Cresap out and today only the ruins of a stone chimney stand.

Field officer at Cresap's Fort, 1755

FORT FREDERICK was built in 1756, during the French and Indian War, and was named for Frederick Calvert, sixth Lord of Baltimore. It has now been restored on the Potomac River near Clear Spring and is a state park. The fort is square-shaped with bastions at each corner of the seventeen-foot stone walls. The fort was garrisoned during the Civil War but never attacked.

FORT CUMBERLAND, on the Potomac River on the site of the present town of Cumberland, was ordered built by Lieutenant Governor Robert Dinwiddie of Virginia at the beginning of the French and Indian War in 1754. It had formerly been **FORT MOUNT PLEASANT,** a fortified trading post established by the Ohio Company of which Lawrence and Augustine Washington, older brothers of George Washington, were shareholders. Usually referred to as "the post at Wills Creek," at the outbreak of the trouble with France it was enlarged into a log fort and storage magazine capable of holding provisions for some fourteen hundred men over a six-month period. Governor Dinwiddie named it for the Duke of Cumberland, Captain-General of the British Army and son of George II. It was here that George Washington, Lieutenant Colonel of the Virginia Militia, retreated after his capitulation to the French at Fort Necessity, Pennsylvania, on July 4, 1754.

FORT CARROLL was built in 1848 on a man-made island in the middle of the Patapsco River below Baltimore under the supervision of Robert E. Lee, then a brevet colonel of engineers in the United States Army. It was intended as a full military post but was never completed. The stone walls, considered a menace to navigation, today are supplied with warning lights, bells and horns.

PENNSYLVANIA

One of the Thirteen Original Colonies.

They had been fighting all day in a heavy rain. Around eight o'clock in the evening, Lieutenant Colonel George Washington heard the French commander, Captain Louis Coulon de Villiers, call for a truce. Washington, with only four hundred men, was determined to hold out in the small fort he had built, and which he called **FORT NECESSITY**, against the combined force of more than a thousand French and Indians. At first he hesitated to accept De Villiers's request for a parley, but finally agreed. The next day, July 4, 1754, he signed a capitulation that allowed his men to leave the fort with all the honors of war. The stockade was burned by De Villiers.

This fort, unique in that it was circular in form, with a house in the center and a ditch around the outside, was erected by Washington in what was called Great Meadows, a section of swampy land ten miles from what is now Somerfield. It was unique, too, in that it was here that the French and Indian War, the fourth intercolonial war between the English and French, can be said to have begun. Horace Walpole, in describing Washington's attack on the French a few days earlier and the resulting action at Fort Necessity, said, "A volley fired by a young Virginian in the backwoods of America set the world on fire."

As Fort Necessity had always been represented on maps of the period as square, which was the usual symbol for a fort, when it was decided to reconstruct the fort it was assumed it was of this shape. However, on digging several feet below the surface the ends of the original posts were revealed, showing the fort had been round. So today it has been restored to its formed circular shape and stands in the Fort Necessity National Battlefield Site, two acres in extent and entirely surrounded by the Fort Necessity State Park, a 311-acre recreational area, including a 234½-acre tract purchased by George Washington in 1769 and owned by him until his death.

The bloody French and Indian War was responsible for the creation of more than half the forts on Pennsylvania soil. It was a struggle for control of the upper Ohio River Valley. The French believed the British by possession of the land would deprive them of the valuable fur trade and prevent communications between Canada and Louisiana.

In the summer of 1753 a French force under Sieur Marin from

Montreal established **FORT PRESQUE ISLE** at what is now Erie, under the sheltering arm of the peninsula, as the first of a chain of strongholds. The French in the latter part of the French and Indian War abandoned the fort and burned it to the ground. Colonel Henry Bouquet rebuilt another near the site, but in Pontiac's War in 1763 this was captured and burned by the Indians. A blockhouse was erected here in 1795. It was a year later that Mad Anthony Wayne died there.

The second fort established by the French in 1753 was **FORT LE BŒUF** at what is now Waterford. Washington visited this fort with a message from Governor Dinwiddie of Virginia warning the French they were on English territory. But the warning was ignored. The French abandoned it in 1759, and it was occupied by the British. But four years later Indians under Pontiac captured the fort and destroyed it.

The French next seized the British trading post at Vernango (now Franklin) and converted it into a stronghold which they named **FORT MACHAULT.** After it was abandoned by the French in 1759, the British built **FORT VERNANGO** nearby in 1760; but Pontiac destroyed it too, three years later, gaining entrance to the fort by a ruse. The Indians, apparently friendly, had been playing lacrosse outside the fort, and chased a ball that fell inside the fort. In 1787 a third fort was built at Franklin, called **FORT FRANK-LIN,** but this was abandoned when comparative peace came to the frontier.

During February, 1754, Captain William Trent and seventy men began to erect a small fort and trading post for the Ohio Company at a spot recommended by George Washington at the fork of the Monongahela and Allegheny rivers. But the fort was captured and destroyed by Le Mercier before it was completed. The French then built a larger fort near the point of land and called it **FORT DU-QUESNE** for the governor general of Canada. In 1755 General Braddock lost his life in an attempt to capture it, but in 1758 Brigadier General John Forbes did capture the fort. Forbes built a new fortification on the Monongahela side of the present city of Pittsburgh south of the present West Street and between West and

Liberty streets. The stone bombproof magazine stood until 1852, when the Pennsylvania Railroad built its terminal there.

In 1764 Colonel Henry Bouquet erected **FORT PITT** on the site of present-day Pittsburgh. It stands today on Walnut Street midway between the Monongahela and Allegheny rivers. The blockhouse, or more properly the redoubt, was purchased by private parties in the early days of Pittsburgh. In 1894 it was deeded to the Pennsylvania Chapter of the Daughters of the American Revolution, who reconstructed it and have maintained it. The historic fort is 16 feet wide and 22 feet high, of brick covered with clapboards and a double layer of logs, and contains 32 portholes.

The fort had served as provisioning place for settlers on their way down the Ohio River.

The English built their share of forts. **FORT AUGUSTA,** near Northumberland, was erected in 1755. It was of solid construction, as can be seen today in the remains of the underground powder magazine. While French and Indians did not attack the fort, it served in later years as an important outpost as a base for north- and west-bound pioneers. While in command in 1779, Colonel Samuel Hunter ordered settlers to flee when the vicinity of **FORT BRADY,** built at Muncy by Captain John Brady, was overrun by Indians. This was known as the "Big Runaway."

FORT LOUDON, at the present town of Fort Loudon, was built in 1756 by Colonel John Armstrong, and named for John Campbell, fourth Earl of Loudoun, who briefly commanded Colonial forces. In 1765, ten years before the Battle of Lexington, settlers disguised as Indians captured a quantity of "King's Goods," on its way to the Ohio forks. The British of the fort captured eight of the "Indians," but the Colonials captured enough British soldiers to make an exchange of prisoners. Later, three hundred of the settlers forced the British to evacuate the fort.

FORT BEDFORD, at Bedford on the Raystown Branch of the Juniata River, is said to have been the first British fort in America taken by what were termed "American rebels." It was built in 1758 by Brigadier General John Forbes as **FORT RAYSTOWN,** but a year later it was renamed Fort Bedford after the Duke of Bedford.

It was constructed of eighteen-foot logs and surrounded by water defenses, the river and deep moats. While the fort was considered by the British to be impregnable, in 1759 Captain James Smith of the Sideling Hill Volunteers, who had forced the British to evacuate Fort Loudon, captured Fort Bedford with only eighteen men when admission was obtained by a ruse.

Other British forts during the French and Indian troubles include **FORT SHIRLEY,** at Shirleysburg, where Conrad Weiser, Indian interpreter and provisional agent, conferred in 1754 with chiefs of the Iroquois, Shawnee and Delaware. **FORT LITTLETON,** at the present town of Fort Littleton, was named for Sir George Littleton. Built in 1756, it was near Gobbler's Knob, a high spot used as a lookout for scouts from the fort who signaled to each other by imitating the turkey's gobble. **FORT HUNTER,** at Rockville, was at what is now the eastern terminus of the Rockville Bridge over the Susquehanna River. Built in 1756, its exact spot is now occupied by the Fort Hunter Museum. An unusual fortification and key defense in the line of frontier strongholds from the Delaware to the Susquehanna in this period was **FORT HENRY.** It was near Bethel on the summit of Round Head, up which led a natural stairway called Shower Steps. The fort's stone walls formed the shape of a half moon.

FORT LIGONIER, termed the first English fort west of the Alleghenies, was built on the site of the present-day Ligonier, and named for Sir John Ligonier, commander in chief of the British Army. Brigadier General John Forbes, selected to take the French Fort Duquesne, erected Fort Ligonier in 1758 and remained there until his forces had rested and reprovisioned. He then marched against Fort Duquesne and captured it on November 25, 1758. The fort then served as a place of refuge for settlers during the Indian wars and, with Fort Pitt, was the only stronghold that did not fall during the Pontiac War of 1763. It was officially abandoned in 1765. Daughters of the American Revolution marked the site of the fort on Loyalhanna Street in Ligonier with a small monument.

FLOURBAG FORT, near Jeanette, in the Bushy Run Battlefield Park, gained its unique name in August, 1763, when Colonel Henry

Bouquet with five hundred men made a stand against Chief Pontiac and his Indians. The colonists had to use bags filled with flour for barricades. Bouquet was on his way to raise Pontiac's siege of Fort Pitt, twenty miles away, and in the two-day battle the Indians were defeated and sued for peace.

REDSTONE OLD FORT, on the Monongahela River at the present town of Brownsville, was a welcome sight to thousands of westward-bound emigrants in the early days as it was the end of the weary journey overland, and they could now continue by water to Kentucky and points south. It was also an outfitting point. Said to have been an early Indian fortification, the site was chosen in 1758 by Colonel James Burd as his stockade.

FORT DURKEE, on the present site of Wilkes-Barre, was built in the summer of 1769 by a small band of settlers who came into the Wyoming Valley from Connecticut. The fort was named for their leader, John Durkee, veteran of the French and Indian War, who was called the "bold bean-hiller of Norwich." The establishment of this fort brought on the Pennamite-Yankee War, a conflict between original Pennsylvania settlers and the newly arrived Connecticut Yankees.

Being short of cannon during the battle, the Yankees tried to fashion one from a tree trunk by hollowing it out and banding it with iron. But when they fired a heavy charge in it, the cannon blew up in splinters, and one of the iron hoops later was found a quarter of a mile distant, across the Susquehanna.

In 1771 the proprietary government of Pennsylvania erected **FORT WYOMING,** but the Connecticut settlers captured it in the same year. In the following year the Yankees built **FORT PITTS-TON** at the present town of Pittston, named for William Pitt, British statesman and friend of the Colonies. The first part of the war ended in two years, with the Yankees in control of the valley. At the beginning of the Revolution the Continental Congress ordered both sides to stop fighting. In July, 1778, Indians and Tories attacked and left Wilkes-Barre in ruins. By the Decree of Trenton the Wyoming Valley was given to the Pennsylvanians, and the Yankees burned the newly erected town. In 1800 Connecticut withdrew all claims to the territory.

FORTY FORT at the present town of Forty Fort, near Wyoming, was named for the first forty settlers from Connecticut. When Colonel John Butler's Tory Raiders and Indians swept into the valley in the summer of 1778 and captured **FORT WINTERMUTE** at Exeter and **FORT JENKINS** at West Pittston a few miles up and on the other side of the Susquehanna River, the settlers sought safety in Forty Fort. However, the fort surrendered on July 5, and, despite the promises of Colonel Butler, the Iroquois allies murdered three hundred men, women and children. Forts Wintermute and Jenkins had been erected by settlers of those names from New York.

FORT MIFFLIN, on Mud Island in the Delaware River within the corporate limits of Philadelphia, was the scene of one of the heaviest bombardments of the Revolutionary War, when it held off the attack of the combined British naval and land forces until it was almost reduced to rubble. Called **MUD FORT** at the time, it was garrisoned with 300 men and had 20 cannon. The British, who had placed batteries on Province Island, 400 yards away, laid down a heavy fire for six days. The garrison of the fort escaped across the river to Fort Mercer in New Jersey. Plans for the original Mud Fort were made in 1771 by Captain John Montrésor, a British engineer, but the fort had not been finished by the start of the Revolution. The Committee of Safety ordered it completed in 1777. The British evacuated the fort after they withdrew from Philadelphia. The ground on which the fort stood was deeded to the Government in 1795 and the fort renamed Fort Mifflin after Thomas Mifflin, Washington's aide-de-camp and first governor of Pennsylvania. In 1798 work began to rebuild the fort of stone from plans by Major L'Enfant, who designed the City of Washington. The Government dismantled the fort in 1904, and in 1915 it was made a National Monument. Fifteen years later it was restored from the plans of L'Enfant.

FORT McINTOSH was built in June, 1778, at the mouth of Big Beaver Creek, thirty miles northwest of Pittsburgh, by orders of General Lachlan McIntosh, who headed an expedition against Indian allies of the British. The fort, which was the first built on the right bank of the Ohio River, was erected under supervision of Chevelier de Cambray, a French engineer, and built of strong stockades furnished with bastions, and mounted one 6-pounder.

Other forts erected during the Revolution included **FORT RICE** at McEwensville, which was built by Frederick William Rice in 1779–1780 and later named **FORT MONTGOMERY** in honor of General Richard Montgomery, who was killed in attempting to take Quebec. This small fort had thick walls with conical-shaped loopholes, which gave a wide firing range. **FORT MUNCY,** near Muncy, was a log structure, built, destroyed, and rebuilt—all in the year 1778. Later it was again destroyed by British and Indians, but was once more rebuilt in 1782. **FORT FREELAND** at Muncy was a stockade built in 1778 around a mill owned by Jacob Freeland. The fort was taken in 1779 by British and Indians, and 108 settlers were killed and captured. **MOOREHEAD FORT** at the town of Indiana was a small stone blockhouse built in 1781 by Fergus Moorehead. Today it is covered with concrete and used to store farm implements. **FORT WASHINGTON,** a small redoubt of earth, at Valley Forge, has been carefully preserved. It stands near the Memorial Arch erected by the Government to the memory of the men and officers who shared the privations of the terrible winter of 1777–1778.

There is another **FORT WASHINGTON** in Pennsylvania, at Harrisburg. This marked the northernmost point of the Confederate invasion during the Civil War, in 1863, when General Robert E. Lee led his army to Gettysburg, where, on July 1–3, he suffered defeat. Panic had been created by the Confederate invasion, and embankments were thrown up on the eminence of Washington Heights.

FORT NEW GOTTENBURG, at Tinicum Island in the Delaware River, near Essington, was built in 1643 by Johan Printz, a Swede, and his colonists. The fort was erected after Printz had built Fort Ellsborg downriver on the New Jersey shore. He erected it of stout hemlock logs near the water's edge and mounted four brass cannon on its walls. Printz, the four-hundred-pound governor of New Sweden, also erected a palatial dwelling of hewn white cedar logs. Fine lumber for the interior and fireplace bricks were imported from Sweden.

OLD STONE FORT, at Matamoras, was erected in 1740 by Simon Westfaeil, one of the first Dutch settlers in that region. It was a structure of one and one-half stories.

OHIO

Admitted to the Union in 1803 as the seventeenth state.

As General Henry Proctor with 400 British soldiers and several hundred Indians, and Tecumseh with some 2,000 of his own Indians, approached **FORT STEPHENSON** on the west side of the Sandusky River where Fremont now stands, General William Henry Harrison, in command of the Northwest Army, sent an urgent message for the fort's garrison to withdraw. But Major George Croghan, twenty-one-year-old Regular Army officer and nephew of George Rogers Clark, hastily scribbled a reply that ended with: "We have determined to maintain this place, and by heavens! we can."

General Harrison angrily relieved Major Croghan of his command, but before the British and Indians attacked, this insubordination was overlooked. For Croghan, a Kentuckian, did "maintain this place." With a garrison of 160 men and one 6-pounder, affectionately called "Old Betsy," on August 2, 1813, he beat off repeated attacks by the enemy, shifting his single cannon from blockhouse to blockhouse, and relying on his corps of Kentucky sharpshooters. It was one of the notable victories of the War of 1812, and Croghan later received a gold medal from Congress. The British suffered 120 killed and wounded, while only one man was killed and seven wounded in the fort.

The site of the fort is now Fremont's Birchard Library Park, and "Old Betsy," the old iron cannon, is still to be seen there.

In this campaign, which had its climax when General Harrison defeated the British on the Thames River in Canada, and the great chief Tecumseh was killed, Harrison built numerous forts in Ohio.

FORT MEIGS, at what is now Perrysburg, on the lower rapids of the Maumee River, was built in 1813 and named in honor of Governor Return Jonathan Meigs of Ohio. British and their Indian allies besieged it unsuccessfully during the spring and summer of 1813, and it became known as the "Gibraltar of the Northwest." Today remnants of the fort remain and are marked by a granite shaft 61 feet high.

FORT AMANDA, near the source of the Auglaize River and not far from Wapakoneta, was built by Colonel John Poague and named for his wife. **FORT BALL,** another early fort of this war, was built at Tiffin and named for Major James V. Ball. The bronze figure of "The Indian Maiden" marks the spot.

FORT FERREE was established in what is now the Wyandot County courtyard at Upper Sandusky. Colonel William Jennings built **FORT JENNINGS** on the Ottawa River not far from Kalida. Another quaint little fort was **MANARY'S BLOCKHOUSE,** built by Captain James Manary three miles north of Bellefontaine. In 1823 a war veteran bought the structure, plugged up the rifle ports, and lived there. In 1924 the structure was removed to Lakeview and made into a museum.

In the beginning of this war, General William Hull had marched up through Ohio to a disgraceful defeat at Detroit. Along what was known as Hull's Trace (or Road) he had established several forts. One was **FORT McARTHUR** on the Scioto River near the present town of Kenton. This fort, named for Colonel Duncan McArthur, has completely disappeared. Hull's Trace is marked by large stones.

Three days out of Fort McArthur the army stopped and erected **FORT NECESSITY,** named because of the dire need for it. Rains, swamp, and black mud hampered the progress of the army. Later, **FORT FINDLAY,** now a town by that name, and the county seat of Hancock County, was built by Colonel Findlay. Here Hull received a mysterious communication from the War Department on June 24 telling him to hasten to Detroit. Although it was dated June 18, 1812, no mention of the declaration of war made on that date was in the letter. It was not until July 2 that Hull received through the ordinary mail another letter dated June 18, telling him the country was at war with England.

When General Harrison took over command of the Army of the Northwest and worked his way northward to Canada, he built a number of other forts and reconstructed some old ones.

FORT SENECA was one of these, and its site is known today as Old Fort, a rural trading center near Tiffin. **FORT WINCHESTER** was built on the Auglaize River some eighty yards above old Fort Defiance (now a town) on the Maumee River. It was named for General James Winchester, whose Kentucky troops were massacred at Frenchtown after their surrender to the British and Indians.

FORT PORTAGE, eighteen miles south of Fort Meigs on the Maumee River, was built by General Hull on his march to Detroit. General Harrison also built a **FORT PORTAGE** in the fall of 1813 when he embarked; but this structure was merely an enclosure.

FORT BROWN was erected sixteen miles south of Fort Defiance.

FORT MORROW, midway between Marion and Delaware, was built in 1812 to protect settlers from Indians. It consisted of a half-acre enclosure with two blockhouses.

FORT ST. MARYS, at the site of the present town of St. Marys, once known as Girty's Town for the notorious renegade Simon Girty, was headquarters and supply depot for Generals Harmar, Wayne, and Harrison at various times. At the north of the Pioneer Portage, on the St. Marys River, this was the most important fort in this section. On September 18, 1818, a treaty was signed here between the Wyandot, Shawnee, Ottawa, and the Government, which opened large tracts of land to white settlers. A local government was established at the town of St. Marys.

FORT GOWER, at the mouth of the Hocking River at Hockingport, was built in 1774 by Lord Dunmore during Dunmore's War with the Indians of Ohio. Today a marker indicates the site. After finishing this fort, Lord Dunmore and his army marched up the Hocking Valley to Pickaway Plains, where they established **CAMP CHARLOTTE** and forced the Indians to sign a treaty that named the Ohio River as their southern boundary.

FORT LAURENS, near Bolivar, in what is now Fort Laurens State Park, was erected on the Tuscarawas River in the fall of 1778 by General Lachlan McIntosh. General McIntosh named it in honor of his friend Henry Laurens, president of the Continental Congress. It was the only fort in Ohio during the Revolutionary War. General McIntosh built it as a winter quarters in his plans to take Detroit. He left the fort in charge of Colonel John Gibson and 150 men, and it later was attacked by Simon Girty, the renegade, and his Indians in February, 1779. General McIntosh relieved the beleaguered fort by returning with 500 soldiers. The fort was abandoned in August, 1779.

FORT HARMAR, across the Muskingum River from Marietta, on a site now occupied by a school building, was erected in 1785 by Major John Doughty, a subordinate of General Josiah Harmar, for whom the pentagonal stockade was named. General Harmar, then Indian agent for the Northwest Territory, and later commander in chief of the Army, mounted an attack against the Miami Indians in 1789 and was defeated, after which he resigned his post.

FORT FINNEY on the Great Miami River, not far from the Indiana state line and near Cleves, was established in 1785 so that the provisions of the treaty of Fort McIntosh (Pennsylvania) could be conducted between the Government and representatives of the Wyandot, Delaware, and Shawnee Indians. Fort Finney was named for a Regular Army officer. By the treaty the Indians ceded two-thirds of Ohio to the Federal Government. General George Rogers Clark and others summoned chiefs of the tribes after the fort was built. All came but the Shawnee, who later showed up with the black belt of wampum, which meant war. Clark angrily threw the belt on the floor, and the next day a white belt, denoting peace, was brought.

FORT STEUBEN, at Steubenville, was built in 1787 to protect a section of Government land in east central Ohio. It was named for Baron Frederick von Steuben, who aided the colonists in the Revolution. The fort was burned in 1790.

CAMPUS MARTIUS, a stockade fort, was built at the mouth of the Muskingum River by General Rufus Putnam and forty-eight veterans of Washington's Army, who landed at Marietta to settle lands of the Ohio Company. Completed in 1788, it was built entirely of logs, and Putnam termed it "the strongest fortification in the

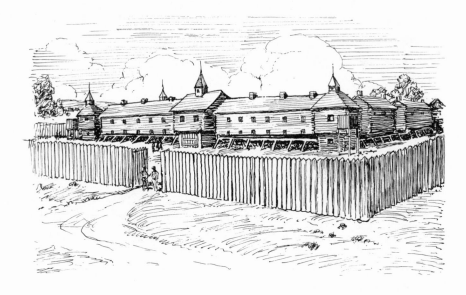

Campus Martius

territory of the United States—the handsomest pile of buildings on this side of the Allegheny Mountains." The fort was a regular parallelogram, with an exterior line of 720 feet with a strong blockhouse at each corner. It stood through all the Indian wars of that period, but was dismantled in 1795, and the logs were used to build homes of settlers. Marietta was built on the site. Today the Campus Martius Memorial State Museum, enclosing the two-story house of General Putnam, stands at Second and Washington streets in Marietta.

FORT FRYE was built in 1791 by nineteen adventurers from Marietta who had settled two years earlier at Beverly. After the Big Bottom Massacre on the Muskingum River, the fort, a triangular stockade, was erected. It was abandoned in 1794.

FORT WASHINGTON was erected on the site of a blockhouse built by Ensign Luce within the limits of the present city of Cincinnati. The fort was constructed under the supervision of Major John Doughty in 1790, and when Arthur St. Clair, first governor of the Northwest Territory, organized the County of Hamilton, he decreed the little village of Cincinnati, which grew up around the fort, the county seat. In 1792 Congress reserved fifteen acres around the fort for use of the garrison, and it was here that General Mad Anthony Wayne trained his Indian fighters. At East Third Street, between Broad and Ludlow streets, is a miniature reproduction in stone of one of the five blockhouses that were a part of the original 480-foot-square fort.

Fort Washington

FORT HAMILTON, on the site of the present city of Hamilton, was erected as an outpost of Fort Washington when in 1791 General St. Clair notified Indians of his arrival by firing a salvo from two pieces of artillery. A few weeks after it was completed, it became a refuge of settlers from a surprise Indian raid. In General Wayne's campaign it was a garrisoned post and trade headquarters. In 1803, when Ohio became a state, the settlement was named for the fort. The site today is marked by a miniature concrete reproduction of the fort.

FORT ST. CLAIR, near the present town of Eaton, was one of a series of forts constructed between Fort Washington and the headwaters of the Maumee River. It was completed in 1792 and in the fall of that year the stockade was attacked by 250 Indians under Little Turtle. The Indians were routed after a desperate battle in which six of the defenders were killed. They were later buried under the Whispering Oak. Today the grounds form Fort St. Clair State Park.

FORT JEFFERSON, near the present town of Greenville, was built by General Arthur St. Clair in 1791. Twelve days after the fort was finished, he moved north to a place on the east branch of the Wabash River, where General Wayne later re-established Fort Recovery. Chief Little Turtle attacked the army here and put them to flight, with astonishing casualties of nine hundred men lost or disabled. Fort Jefferson State Park is on the site of the old fort.

FORT RECOVERY, on the site of General St. Clair's disastrous defeat of 1791, was erected by General Mad Anthony Wayne two years later after his "recovery of the area." On the east branch of the Wabash River at Celina, with its entrance on Wayne Street, the fort has been reconstructed under the auspices of the Ohio State Archaeological and Historical Society. It has overhanging tower rooms at each of the corners and encloses a well used by Wayne's garrison. The fort is entirely of wood, even to pegs and hinges, with firing platforms. The area is known as Fort Recovery Park, and southwest of the fort itself is the Fort Recovery Museum. It is notable that Wayne's troops were the 3rd Infantry, organized in 1784, and the organization exists today as the 1st Battle Group of the 3rd

Infantry, which composes the Capital's ceremonial honor guards. One of their duties is to guard the tomb of the Unknown Soldier in Arlington National Cemetery.

FORT PIQUA, near Piqua, was formerly a stockade built by the French in 1752 and rebuilt by General Wayne in 1793 in his Indian campaign. Earthworks still are visible.

Other forts built or rebuilt by General Wayne in his determined campaign against the Indians included **FORT LORAMIE,** at the headwaters of the Great Miami River near the shore of Lake Loramie. In 1769 a trading post was operated here by Peter Loramie, hence the name given the fort. The fort was destroyed during the War of 1812.

FORT INDUSTRY was built by Wayne on the present site of Toledo. The Battle of Fallen Timbers, in which the Indians suffered their final defeat, was fought a few miles southwest of the present city of Toledo. As a safeguard against the British at Fort Miami, Wayne erected the fort a short time after the battle in 1794. Here, on July 4, 1805, a treaty was made with the Indians by which they gave up title to the so-called Firelands, named after the Revolutionary War when Connecticut awarded 500,000 acres of her western lands to citizens whose villages had been burned by British troops. Today the site of Fort Industry is marked by a bronze tablet.

FORT DEFIANCE, on the site of the town of Defiance, at the junction of the Maumee and Auglaize rivers, was built by General Wayne in 1794, two weeks before he defeated the Indians at Fallen Timbers. In giving the name to the fort, General Wayne said: "I DEFY the English, the Indians, and all the devils in hell to take it!" When General William Henry Harrison arrived there during the War of 1812, he found Wayne's old fort in ruins, so he built a larger and stronger fort on a height above on the banks of the Auglaize and named it Fort Winchester for the officer in charge.

FORT MIAMI, on the present site of Maumee, was built in 1764 by the British where a French trading post had stood since 1693. General Wayne was angered at the continued presence of the British at Fort Miami, and three days after the Battle of Fallen

Timbers his victorious army marched to the fort, and pitched camp. The Americans destroyed all British storehouses, and fired fields and gardens, but the fort was not attacked. In the spring of 1813 Colonel Dudley, with a force of 800 Kentuckians on the way to relieve Fort Meigs, was ambushed and all but 140 slain near the fort. Tecumseh stopped the massacre. Earthen walls are all that remain of this fort, which the British did not relinquish until 1817—two years after the close of the War of 1812.

FORT GREENVILLE, at the present town of Greenville, was built by General Wayne during the winter of 1793–1794. Here he remained to plan his campaign against the hostile Indian tribes, which came to a climax at the Battle of Fallen Timbers in August, 1794. The fort was named for Nathanael Greene and was a sturdy stockade with comfortable quarters for officers and men, covering fifty acres. Following his successful battle Wayne returned to Fort Greenville to await peace overtures from the defeated chieftains. It was not until June, 1795, that they began to arrive—1,130 chiefs and warriors, including such famous names as Little Turtle, Blue Jacket, The Sun, Little Beaver, Tarhe the Crane, and Red Pole. On August 3 the treaty was signed, giving the Indians about one-fourth of what later was to become Ohio. Fort Greenville was abandoned and burned after the treaty, but in 1805 a site adjoining the spot where the fort stood became headquarters for Tecumseh and his brother, The Prophet, who thus founded their town on the white man's side of the Greenville Treaty Line. But in 1814 another treaty was signed with the Indians whereby they relinquished this territory.

FORT FIZZLE, near Killbuck, was the scene of the Holmes County Rebellion in the winter of 1863. Some Northerners, called Peace Democrats or Copperheads, rose against the enforcement of the Draft Act and attempted to rescue four men. Soldiers took up their position in a fortified place and fought off the rebels. Lewis (Lew) Wallace, author of *Ben Hur* and a soldier, dubbed the place "Fort Fizzle."

FORT HAYES, at Columbus, had its beginning as an arsenal during the Civil War. Named for President Rutherford B. Hayes during World War I, it had been known as Columbus Barracks, and garrisoned as a military post since 1863.

FORT ANCIENT was a prehistoric Indian fortification in Warren County. It is now a state park covering about one hundred acres.

WEST VIRGINIA

Admitted to the Union in 1863 as the thirty-fifth state.

Betty Zane, unaccustomed to the horrors of Indian warfare, had just returned home from Philadelphia, where she had completed her education, when a band of Shawnee under the white renegade Simon Girty attacked Fort Henry in the latter part of August, 1774. Twenty-three of the forty-two men in the fort were slain at the first attack, and the Indians settled down to starve the garrison into submission. The powder supply became low. Colonel Ebenezer Zane, brother of Betty, and one of the founders of the town of Wheeling, called for volunteers to bring a keg from his house 150 yards away. The men all offered to go, but Betty rushed forward and said, " 'Tis better a maid than a man should die." The gates were opened, and she ran for the house. The Indians, surprised, withheld their fire and shouted in derision, "A squaw!" But when she came out of the house with the keg of powder, the savages gave angry cries and opened fire. Although bullets pierced her skirt, Betty arrived safely with the powder. The garrison held out until a company of men under Major Samuel McCulloch of nearby **FORT VAN METER** arrived. McCulloch, a noted Indian fighter, was cut off before he could enter the fort with his men and pursued to the crest of Wheeling Hill, where he urged his horse over a 150-foot precipice to make his escape. This spot became known as McCulloch's leap. Elizabeth (Betty) Zane McLaughlin Clarke died in 1823

at her home across the Ohio River from Wheeling, after many had forgotten her heroic act.

FORT HENRY, second to Fort Pitt, Pennsylvania, in importance during the early days of Ohio River traffic, was erected as **FORT FINCASTLE** in 1774. Fort Fincastle was built during Dunmore's War and named in honor of Lord Dunmore, royal governor of Virginia whose title was Viscount Fincastle. It was an oblong structure of pickets pointed at the top with bastions and sentry boxes at the angles. It enclosed about one-half acre of land where there were log barracks, a storehouse, a well, and cabins. It was characteristic of forts of that section. The site of the fort, which had been renamed in honor of Patrick Henry, first governor of Virginia, in 1776, is marked by a bronze plaque on Main Street between Eleventh and Ohio streets, in Wheeling. Fort Henry was unsuccessfully attacked by Indians and British on September 10, 1782, in what historians claim was "the last battle of the American Revolution."

Women saved two other forts of that period, according to legend. When **FORT LEE,** the site of Charles Town, was besieged by Indians in 1789, "Mad Ann" Bailey volunteered to go to Fort Savannah, one hundred miles distant, for powder. "Mad Ann," a cockney-speaking Englishwoman, had worn the garb of an Indian scout since her first husband was slain at the Battle of Point Pleasant. She made the round trip to Fort Savannah, eluding the Indians, in three days and brought back the powder. The site of Fort Lee, built in 1788 and named for Governor Henry Lee of Virginia, is marked by a plaque in front of 1202 E. Kanawha Boulevard, Charles Town, and Mad Ann's heroism is told in a poem, "A Legend of Kanawha," by Charles Robb. Another historic character, Daniel Boone, had lived near the fort.

FORT EVANS, at Big Spring near Martinsburg, which was built in 1755 by John Evans, was saved the next year by his resourceful wife, Polly. Indians attacked the stronghold during the absence of the men, and Polly, in her deepest voice, began to shout orders, as if directing a large force. But her only "soldiers" were women. The Indians, however, hearing the gruff commands, thought better of

their attack and, after a few shots on both sides, the attackers withdrew.

Indian troubles accounted for the erection of the majority of forts in West Virginia. As settlers began to build homes in the northeastern section of the state, the powerful Delaware chief Killbuck in 1753 declared a "death claim" on every foot of land between the Blue Ridge Mountains and the Ohio River. One of the first forts built was **FORT PEARSALL,** on the site of the present town of Romney. It was named for Job and John Pearsall, early settlers in the region. A few years after it was built, George Washington, engaged in erecting a string of forts in that section, reported that the settlers were leaving. But when Killbuck and his followers gave up the struggle, the settlers began to return.

FORT SEYBERT, named for Captain Seybert, on the site of the present town of Fort Seybert, and built in 1758 as a refuge against Indians, was destroyed in the same year by Chief Killbuck and his allies. They also leveled **FORT UPPER TRACT,** in South Branch Valley, that year. But after the destruction of these forts, John Justus Hinkle and his four sons built **FORT HINKLE,** near Riverton in German Valley, as a refuge for residents of South Branch Valley.

FORT ASHBY, on the site of the present town of Fort Ashby, has the distinction today of being the sole survivor of a chain of twenty-three forts built under the direction of George Washington in 1755. The fort, named for its second commander, Colonel John Ashby, is owned today by the Mineral County Court. That which remains consists of a story-and-a-half cabin of hand-hewn logs, secured with dovetail joints at the corners, and half-doors with original latches and locks on wrought-iron hinges. Troops were raised here at the time President Washington suppressed the "Whisky Rebellion" in 1791.

FORT SAVANNAH, on the site of the present town of Lewisburg, was erected in 1755 under orders of British General Braddock in the French and Indian War. In 1774 General Andrew Lewis assembled a thousand militiamen at the fort, renamed it **FORT UNION,** and marched against the Indians in the Battle of Point Pleasant. This battle, on October 10, 1774, brought an end to what was termed "Lord Dunmore's War," and the Indians sued for peace.

Chief Cornstalk of the Shawnee, who had been a leader of the Indian allies in the Battle of Point Pleasant, was killed at **FORT RANDOLPH,** at Point Pleasant, three years later. He had come to warn the colonists of an impending Indian uprising. But he was arrested with his two sons and all were slain. In 1896 a monument to Cornstalk was erected in the courthouse yard at Point Pleasant. Fort Randolph had been built in 1776 on the site of **FORT BLAIR,** erected in 1770 and later burned by Ohio Indians.

In May of 1778, the year following the slaying of Cornstalk, a large band of Indians, bent on avenging his death, attacked **FORT DONNALLY,** near Richlands. The fort had been warned by a messenger from Fort Randolph, and in turn sent a call for help to Fort Savannah. During the second day of the siege a force arrived, and the Indians were beaten off. This battle was considered second only to that at Point Pleasant, as it ended Indian attacks in Greenbrier Valley. Fort Donnally had been built by Andrew Donnally prior to 1771, and was named for him.

FORT EDWARDS, at the town of Capon Bridge on the bank of the Cacapon River, was built in the late 1740's after George Washington had surveyed three tracts of land for David, Joseph, and Thomas Edwards. In 1756 Washington garrisoned this fort, but his men suffered defeat by Indians.

Many forts in West Virginia, or what was then Virginia, were "private" forts erected by settlers, for in those times a man's house was his fort. FORT OHIO, on the south bank of the Potomac River opposite Fort Cumberland in Maryland, was the first Indian trading post and the first of a chain of forts erected by the Ohio Company in 1747 to encourage settlement in the Ohio section. The fort was on the site of the present town of Ridgeley, a residential suburb of Cumberland, Maryland.

TOWN FORT, five miles from Moorefield, was built in the 1750's for the protection of settlers unable to reach Forts Pleasant and Buttermilk. FORT PLEASANT was at Old Fields, some thirty miles from Keyser. FORT BUTTERMILK was built by Captain Thomas Waggoner on a farm between the Maryland line and Petersburg, near Old Fields.

FORT OGDEN, near Difficult Hill along U.S. 50, was one of Washington's chain of forts established in 1755.

FORT GREEN BRYER was a small stockade erected by General Andrew Lewis in 1755. Pocahontas County Courthouse in Huntersville stands on the site of the old fort. Here Lewis organized his company for the Battle of Point Pleasant.

FORT NEALLY, about two miles out of Martinsburg (four miles from Fort Evans), was taken by Indians in 1756. They killed the members of the garrison and took women and children captives.

WEST'S FORT was erected in 1770 by Edmund West and two sons on the site of the present town of Jane Lew. In 1779 the fort was burned by Indians. The settlers fled to Buckhannon. Some returned in 1790 and built FORT BEECH.

FORT BEECH BOTTOM was built on the site of the present town of Beechbottom in 1775. It was mainly a shelter for the settlers.

FORT WARDEN, on the site of the town of Wardensville, was a

small stockade built by Jacob Warden; it was burned by Indians in 1758.

FORT MORGAN and **FORT KERN** were built by Zackquill Morgan at the mouth of Deckers Creek on the Monongahela River in 1767. This is now Morgantown.

FORT PIERPONT was erected by John Pierpont in 1769, a son-in-law of Zackquill Morgan, on the site of the town of Easton.

NUTTER'S FORT, now the town of Nutter Fort, near Clarksburg, was erected in 1772 by settlers on West Fork River, opposite the mouth of Elk Creek.

FORT DRENNEN, near Edray in Tygarts Valley, was named for Thomas Drennen, who settled here in 1774. His wife was killed during an Indian attack and his son taken captive. Years later he found his son, who had been ransomed by the Indians to a trader.

FORT RICHARDS, also known as **LOWTHER'S FORT,** was erected in 1774 by Arnold Richards south of Clarksburg. It was also named after Colonel William Lowther, Indian fighter, Revolutionary War soldier, and leader of settlers in the region.

FORT CHAPMAN, on the site occupied by the town of New Cumberland, was erected in 1784. **FORT BUSH,** between Hodgesville and Buckhannon, was built in 1773 by John Bush. **BALDWIN'S BLOCKHOUSE,** at Blacksville, was built in the 1770's. **KELLY'S FORT,** on the site of Cedar Grove, was built by William Morris in 1774, but named for Walter Kelly, who was killed by Indians.

FORT NEAL, now the location of Parkersburg, was erected by Captain James Neal in 1785. On the south bank of the Little Kanawha, near the mouth, the Daughters of the American Revolution have marked the spot with a bronze tablet. **FORT SHEPHERD,** on Wheeling Creek, not far from Wheeling, was built in 1777 by David Shepherd. **FORT TACKETT** was erected at what is now St. Albans in 1787 by General Andrew Lewis and John Tackett. Three years later it was attacked by Indians and almost all the people were killed.

FORT STATLERS, northwest of Westover, was erected in 1770 and used as a fort until the end of the Indian troubles in 1794, and then as a school and church until 1850.

McINTIRE BLOCKHOUSE, on the Monongahela River, across from Enterprise, was built by John McIntire in 1773.

WILSON'S FORT, near Beverly, was erected in 1774 by Captain Benjamin Wilson, who was with Braddock on his disastrous campaign against the French and Indians. After the war he was given command of all military forces in northwestern Virginia. The fort was in Tygarts Valley, and a monument marks the site.

FORT MARTIN, near Maidsville, was erected by Colonel Charles Martin, about 1773. FORT DAVIDSON-BAILEY, at Bluefield, was erected in 1777 by John Davidson and Richard Bailey.

FORT HADDEN was at Elkwater in Tygarts Valley, where the town occupies the site of the fort erected by the Hadden family in 1774. During the Civil War Colonel John Augustine Washington, aide-de-camp to Robert E. Lee, and grandnephew to George Washington, was killed here on September 13, 1861.

FORT CURRENCE is the site of the town of Mill Creek, and was built in 1774 by William Currence, who operated a grist mill there.

COOK'S FORT, near Greenville, was erected in 1770 by Captain John Cook, and covered more than an acre with its four blockhouses. It was one of the largest frontier forts.

FORT FULLER, at Keyser, was a Union stronghold in the Civil War, on the site of Potomac State School and West Virginia University. This fort saw much fighting. Between 1861 and 1865 the town changed hands fourteen times. FORT BOREMAN, in Nemesis Park, Parkersburg, on the summit of Mount Logan, was erected in 1863 to protect the city from Confederates. FORT MILROY, on the summit of White Top Mountain, along the Cheat River, was used by Union troops during the War Between the States.

KENTUCKY

Admitted to the Union in 1792 as the fifteenth state.

The situation looked bad for Daniel Boone and his garrison of fifty men. The Canadian officer Captain Duquesne, in command of five hundred Indians, demanded the surrender of **BOONE'S FORT,** on the western bank of the Kentucky River on September 9, 1778. Boone called together his men and said: "If we surrender, our lives and those of our women and children might be spared, but we would lose all our property. If we resist and are overcome it will mean the death of every one of us. What shall we do?" "Defend the fort till the last!" cried the men. Captain Duquesne was chagrined, and sought to gain by a trick what he might not accomplish by force. He asked for a parley. Boone, with eight others, went out of the fort and met the officer. Indian warriors seized them. Boone and his companions fought them off and fled back to the fort. The siege began, but after nine days the Indians left, never to return. The fort had been attacked twice before. Once Boone's daughter and two other girls were captured by Indians, but Boone and a party pursued them for forty-five miles and rescued the girls. Boone had built his fort on the site of Boonesboro, not far from where Lexington is today, in the spring of 1775. The fort consisted of a number of log houses in an oblong square. The corner ones were larger and were used as blockhouses.

A granite monument of Daniel Boone is on the site of the old fort.

Boone's Fort with **FORT HARROD** and Logan's Fort were the first defenses erected by the early settlers of Kentucky. Fort Harrod was built earlier by James Harrod and thirty men as a palisaded village in 1774 much on the order of Boone's Fort, with the houses forming the walls and their roofs sloping inward. It was here that George Rogers Clark first came from Virginia and conceived the idea of wresting the old Northwest from the British. It was here, too, that the first white child was born in Kentucky. The old fort on the site of Harrodsburg in Mercer County has been faithfully reconstructed.

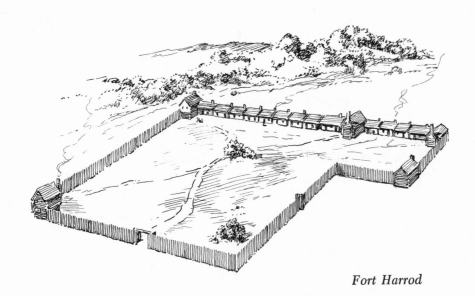

Fort Harrod

LOGAN'S FORT was erected about a mile west of the present town of Stanford in Lincoln County by Colonel Benjamin Logan and others. When Indians could not capture the fort, they named it "Standing Fort." The name became contracted and was soon pronounced "Stanford," and thus the town received its name from the fort.

McCLELLAND'S FORT, on the site of the present Georgetown, twelve miles north of Lexington, was named for John McClelland, who was wounded there in an attack by Indians on December 29, 1776. McClelland died a week later of his wounds.

HARDIN'S FORT, on the site of the present-day Hardinsburg, seat of Breckinridge County, was built in 1780 by William Hardin, soldier and frontiersman and a member of one of the first families to settle in Kentucky. Hardin was known to Indians as "Big Bill."

WORTHINGTON'S FORT, four miles west of the present Danville, was built in 1779 by Captain Edward Worthington. Worthington had been wounded at McClelland's Fort in the attack there and had moved to Harrodsburg and later to the place where he erected his fort. He had been one of Clark's officers in the Northwest Campaign.

George Rogers Clark, after expelling the British from the Northwest, erected two important forts. One was **FORT NELSON,** named for General Thomas Nelson, who would later be governor of Virginia. This fort was built on the site of present-day Louisville, under the direction of Captain William Linn, and completed on Christmas Day, 1779. Clark later established headquarters in the fort, which also served as courthouse and jail. A slab of granite with a bronze tablet commemorates the fort on the northwest corner of Seventh and Main streets, Louisville.

The other fort built by Clark in Kentucky was **FORT JEFFERSON,** five miles below the mouth of the Ohio River at a place called the Iron Banks on the Mississippi. The fort was named for Thomas Jefferson, then governor of Virginia.

A settlement nearby was called Clarksville. The French had a fort here as early as 1702, and the English had planned a later one. The United States Government created a military post here in 1804 when Federal troops were rushed to this point at the time of the Aaron Burr conspiracy. In 1814, when the British burned Washington, real-estate speculators proclaimed Clarksville the approximate center of the nation and agitated to have the national Capital established there. Their efforts were not successful, but the new

name they gave the town, Columbus, remained. The first violation of Kentucky's neutrality in the Civil War occurred here when General Leonidas Polk of the Confederate Army seized and heavily fortified the bluff at Iron Banks. He stretched a chain more than a mile long across the Mississippi River to Belmont to prevent the passage of Union gunboats. The bluff was fortified with 140 guns, arranged at four elevations. When General U. S. Grant captured Forts Henry and Donelson, and was victor at Shiloh, the fort at Columbus was evacuated. During World War I the place was once more fortified. In 1927 high water forced citizens to leave, and the Red Cross established a new town to the east. All land was given to the State of Kentucky and converted into the Columbus-Belmont Memorial State Park. A blockhouse similar to one erected by George Rogers Clark has been reconstructed here.

FORT ANDERSON, at Paducah, was established by General U. S. Grant when he took possession of the town in 1861. The fort became an important depot of supply for the Union Army. In 1864 General Lew Wallace, who was later to write *Ben Hur,* was in command for a time.

FORT MITCHELL, at Bromley near Covington, across the river from Cincinnati, was built by Professor Ormsby Mitchell in 1862 and named for him. The fort actually consisted of a series of earthworks reaching from the Ohio River at Bromley west to the banks of the Licking River, and to the Ohio near where Fort Thomas later stood.

FORT THOMAS, on a bluff overlooking the Ohio River, three miles from Newport and four miles from Cincinnati, was established in 1887 when the site was selected by General Philip H. Sheridan. The 280-acre military post cost $4,000,000, and was named for General George H. Thomas, the "Rock of Chickamauga."

FORT KNOX was established in 1917 when the Government purchased the site, including the town of Stithton. It became a training camp in 1917 in World War I and was named for General Henry Knox, first Secretary of War under President Washington. In 1936 the Treasury Department built the Gold Bullion Depository here to store 9,000,000 pounds of Federal gold reserve.

FORT BAYOU DE CHIEN MOUNDS, near Hickman, consists of seven large mounds that average 15 to 20 feet in height, 50 to 100 feet in diameter, and are grouped closely within a space of five acres. These mounds, believed to have been built long ago by the so-called Mound Builders for defense, are on an elevated plateau rising 10 to 15 feet above the surrounding plain. Nearby is Indian Hill, sometimes termed O'BYAM'S FORT, an Indian fortification believed to be one of the most ancient mounds in the Mississippi Valley.

The Southeast States

ALABAMA

GEORGIA

FLORIDA

SOUTH CAROLINA

NORTH CAROLINA

TENNESSEE

MISSISSIPPI

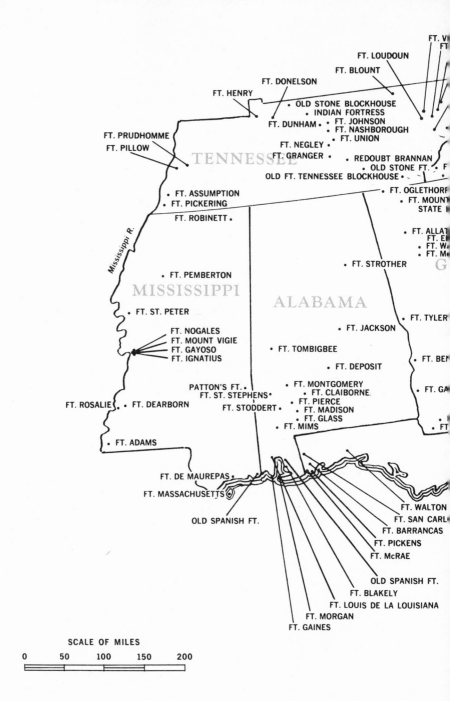

FT. V
FT

FT. LOUDOUN

FT. BLOUNT

FT. DONELSON

FT. HENRY

• OLD STONE BLOCKHOUSE
• INDIAN FORTRESS
FT. DUNHAM • • FT. JOHNSON
• FT. NASHBOROUGH
FT. NEGLEY • • FT. UNION
FT. GRANGER •
• REDOUBT BRANNAN
• OLD STONE FT. • F
OLD FT. TENNESSEE BLOCKHOUSE • •

FT. PRUDHOMME
FT. PILLOW

TENNESSEE

• FT. OGLETHORP
• FT. MOUNT
STATE

• FT. ASSUMPTION
• FT. PICKERING

FT. ROBINETT •

• FT. ALLAT
FT. E
• FT. W
• FT. M

Mississippi R.

• FT. STROTHER   G

• FT. PEMBERTON

MISSISSIPPI

ALABAMA

• FT. ST. PETER

• FT. TYLER

FT. NOGALES
FT. MOUNT VIGIE
FT. GAYOSO
FT. IGNATIUS

• FT. JACKSON

• FT. TOMBIGBEE

• FT. BEP

• FT. DEPOSIT

• FT. GA

PATTON'S FT. •
FT. ST. STEPHENS •

• FT. MONTGOMERY
• FT. CLAIBORNE.
• FT. PIERCE
FT. STODDERT •   • FT. MADISON
• FT. GLASS
• FT. MIMS

FT. ROSALIE • FT. DEARBORN

• FT

• FT. ADAMS

FT. DE MAUREPAS •

FT. MASSACHUSETTS

OLD SPANISH FT.

FT. WALTON
FT. SAN CARL
FT. BARRANCAS
FT. PICKENS
FT. McRAE

OLD SPANISH FT.
FT. BLAKELY
FT. LOUIS DE LA LOUISIANA
FT. MORGAN
FT. GAINES

SCALE OF MILES

0   50   100   150   200

112

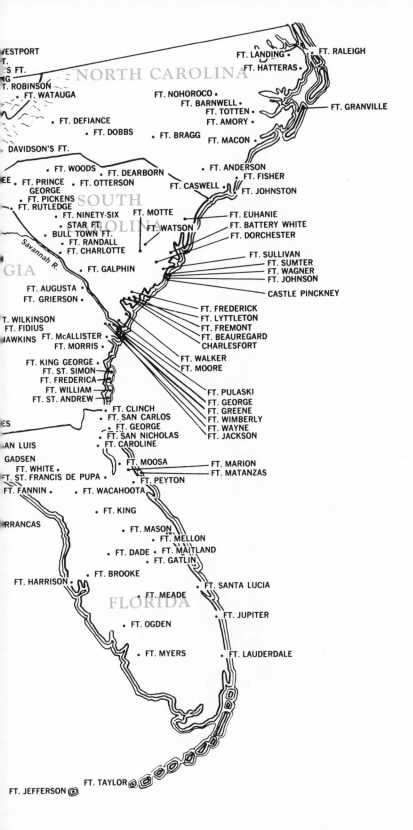

ESTPORT
T.
S FT.
IG
T. ROBINSON
• FT. WATAUGA

NORTH CAROLINA

FT. LANDING •
FT. HATTERAS •

• FT. RALEIGH

FT. NOHOROCO •
FT. BARNWELL •
FT. TOTTEN •
FT. AMORY •

• FT. DEFIANCE

• FT. DOBBS   • FT. BRAGG
FT. MACON •

DAVIDSON'S FT.

FT. GRANVILLE

• FT. WOODS   • FT. DEARBORN
EE • FT. PRINCE • FT. OTTERSON   FT. CASWELL • f
GEORGE
• FT. PICKENS SOUTH
FT. RUTLEDGE
• FT. NINETY-SIX   FT. MOTTE
• STAR FT.
• BULL TOWN FT.   FT. WATSON
• FT. RANDALL
• FT. CHARLOTTE

• FT. ANDERSON
FT. FISHER
FT. JOHNSTON

FT. EUHANIE
FT. BATTERY WHITE
FT. DORCHESTER

Savannah R.

GIA   • FT. GALPHIN

FT. SULLIVAN
FT. SUMTER
FT. WAGNER
FT. JOHNSON

FT. AUGUSTA •
FT. GRIERSON •

CASTLE PINCKNEY

T. WILKINSON
FT. FIDIUS
AWKINS FT. McALLISTER •
FT. MORRIS •

FT. FREDERICK
FT. LYTTLETON
FT. FREMONT
FT. BEAUREGARD
CHARLESFORT

FT. KING GEORGE •
FT. ST. SIMON
FT. FREDERICA
FT. WILLIAM
FT. ST. ANDREW

FT. WALKER
FT. MOORE

• FT. CLINCH
• FT. SAN CARLOS
• FT. GEORGE
• FT. SAN NICHOLAS
• FT. CAROLINE

FT. PULASKI
FT. GEORGE
FT. GREENE
FT. WIMBERLY
FT. WAYNE
FT. JACKSON

ES

AN LUIS
GADSEN
FT. WHITE •
T. ST. FRANCIS DE PUPA •
FT. FANNIN •   • FT. WACAHOOTA

• FT. MOOSA
• FT. PEYTON

FT. MARION
FT. MATANZAS

• FT. KING

RRANCAS

• FT. MASON
• FT. MELLON
• FT. DADE • FT. MAITLAND
• FT. GATLIN

FT. HARRISON •   • FT. BROOKE

• FT. SANTA LUCIA

• FT. MEADE

FLORIDA

• FT. JUPITER

• FT. OGDEN

• FT. MYERS   • FT. LAUDERDALE

113

FT. TAYLOR
FT. JEFFERSON

ALABAMA

Admitted to the Union in 1819 as the twenty-second state.

At seven-thirty on the morning of August 5, 1864, the Ironclad *Tecumseh* was well up with Fort Morgan on Mobile Point at the entrance of Mobile Bay, drawing slowly by when suddenly she reeled to port and went down with almost every soul on board. The *Tecumseh* had struck a mine.

"What's the matter?" was shouted from the flagship *Hartford* to the *Brooklyn* just ahead.

"Torpedoes!" came the reply.

"Damn the torpedoes!" cried Admiral David Glasgow Farragut from the *Hartford's* bridge. "Go ahead!"

And go ahead the Union fleet did, to gain the sheltering waters of Mobile Bay. Here for seventeen days Fort Morgan was subjected to a terrific shelling until it finally surrendered, with the citadel destroyed and the walls nearly blown to bits.

Admiral David Glasgow Farragut

FORT MORGAN, a five-star fort named in honor of General David Morgan, commander of the Louisiana Militia at the Battle of New Orleans in the War of 1812, was built originally of brick. It was refurbished and regarrisoned during the Spanish-American War, as well as at the opening of World War I.

Since 1955 Fort Morgan has been under the Fort Morgan Historical Commission. Members of this commission are appointed by the governor, and include representatives of the United Daughters of the Confederacy, the Daughters of Colonial Wars, and the Daughters of the American Revolution. Today it is a part of Fort Morgan State Park. Here also are the ruins of FORT SEROF, built by Spanish colonists under Tristan de Luna in 1559.

Fort Morgan had been erected on the site of an equally historic defense work, FORT BOWYER. This fort, named for Lieutenant Colonel James Bowyer, was built by General James Wilkinson in 1813 when he expelled the remaining Spanish from the Mobile area. In 1814 General Andrew Jackson, who was on his way to New Orleans, stopped at Fort Bowyer and left there a force under Major William Lawrence. Shortly afterward the British fleet attacked the fort but was severely repulsed. After Jackson had defeated the British at New Orleans, they again attacked Fort Bowyer during their retreat, and this time, on February 11, 1815, captured it. But shortly afterward, on learning of the termination of the war by the Treaty of Ghent, drawn up on December 24, 1814, they gave up the fort.

FORT GAINES, on Dauphin Island across the entrance to Mobile Bay from Fort Morgan, had surrendered to Admiral Farragut early in the battle in 1864. This fort had been built on the eastern point of the island in 1822 and named for General Edmund P. Gaines. Today it is a state monument.

FORT LOUIS DE LA LOUISIANA, named in honor of King Louis XIV, or, as it also was called, FORT LOUIS DE LA MOBILE, was established by the French on the Mobile River at Twenty-seven Mile Bluff, and here Bienville, who had been appointed Governor of Louisiana, moved the seat of French government from Fort Maurepas, near Biloxi, Mississippi. Henri de Tonti, lieutenant of

La Salle, and known as the "Man of the Iron Hand," because of the metal replacement for his lost hand, died here in 1704 and was buried in an unmarked grave. That same year twenty-three so-called "cassette girls," orphans from Canada to whom the government had given little trunks, or "cassettes," arrived and were promptly married—all but one, who was said to have been "coy and hard to please." In 1711, after several disastrous floods, this fort was moved south to the present site of Mobile, and in 1720 its name was changed to **FORT CONDÉ DE LA MOBILE** to honor the French General Condé.

After the French and Indian War, Mobile was turned over to the English, as were other French possessions. Fort Condé de la Mobile was renamed **FORT CHARLOTTE,** for Charlotte Sophia, former Princess of Mecklenburg-Strelitz, who two years before had married King George III. In 1780 the Spanish seized the fort and held it, and called it **FORT CARLOTTA.** In 1813 General Wilkinson ousted the Spanish government and garrisoned the fort with United States troops. General Jackson reconditioned it in 1814, but this historic fort had seen the end of its fighting days.

This fort stood in the block of what now is bounded by Royal, Church, St. Emanuel, and Theater streets. In 1819 it was blown up, and the debris was the first fill in the marsh near Royal Street.

Bernardo de Gálvez, who seized Mobile in 1780, some time later built a fort on the northeast shore of Mobile Bay. This has been called **OLD SPANISH FORT**, and, with **FORT BLAKELY,** Confederate earthworks built in 1865, was the last stronghold in that section to stand against invading Union troops.

FORT JACKSON, on the Coosa River four miles above its junction with the Tallapoosa, was built in 1814 by General Andrew Jackson. The old French **FORT TOULOUSE,** which had been established exactly a century before by Antoine de la Mothe Cadillac, was the site of Jackson's new fort, which was composed of a strong blockhouse and outer walls. It was here, on August 9, 1814, that Jackson made his notable treaty of peace with the Creeks.

FORT MIMS, a stockade thirty-five miles north of Mobile, is where occurred, on August 30, 1813, the massacre of nearly four

hundred men, women, and children, by the Creek Indians under their half-breed chief, Weatherford. This stockade, covering an acre, had been built with the house of Samuel Mims, an old and wealthy inhabitant, as the center. At the time of the Indian attack the fort was garrisoned by two hundred militiamen. Only a few persons escaped. "Remember Fort Mims!" became the battle cry of soldiers under General Andrew Jackson during the Creek War. A monument, erected by the United Daughters of the Confederacy, marks the approximate site of Fort Mims.

FORT TOMBIGBEE, on the Tombigbee River in Sumter County, was erected in 1735 by Bienville as a supply depot and permanent trading post. At the close of the French and Indian War, the English were ceded the fort, and renamed it **FORT YORK.** When the Spaniards took over the region in 1783, they rebuilt the post and called it **FORT CONFEDERACIÓN.** In 1802, when Americans occupied the fort, one of the treaties by which the United States took over the Choctaw Indian lands was negotiated here. A marker on the site placed by the Colonial Dames of America carries the inscription: "Here Civilization and Savagery Met and the Wilderness Beheld the Glory of France."

FORT ST. STEPHENS, on a high bluff near the present town of Saint Stephens on the west bank of the Tombigbee River, was built around 1714 by the French, and held later by the Spaniards. The Spanish garrison was relieved in 1799 by United States troops. George S. Gaines, Alabama pioneer, was appointed Indian agent at St. Stephens and was so liked by the Choctaw that he prevented them joining Tecumseh in the War of 1812 and persuaded them to aid the United States against the Creeks.

FORT STODDERT was established in 1799 by United States troops on the west side of the Mobile River, forty-four miles above its entrance into Mobile Bay. It was four miles east of the arsenal at Mount Vernon. It was at this fort that Aaron Burr, charged with treason against the United States, was held before being sent to Richmond for trial. He had been arrested on February 19, 1807, by First Lieutenant Edmund P. Gaines, commandant of the fort, who found him disguised as a Mississippi boatman. In 1887, Geronimo, the Apache chief, and several hundred of his followers were brought as prisoners to this fort. Geronimo was soon removed to Fort Sill, Indian Territory, where he died, but the other Indians were kept at Fort Stoddert for seven years.

FORT MADISON, located in the eastern section of Clarke County not far from the Alabama River, was a place of refuge for settlers who flocked here following the Fort Mims massacre. It was just 225 yards north of **FORT GLASS.** The two forts were said to have held more than a thousand settlers and soldiers after the Fort Mims tragedy.

Fort Madison, named for President James Madison, contained almost an acre of ground, being 60 yards square. A trench 3 feet in depth was dug around the area, and logs of pine trees about 15 feet in length were placed upright in the trench, side by side, thus making a wall 12 feet high. Portholes were cut at convenient distances. It was typical of stockades of the 1813 period. They were lighted at night by means of pitch pine placed on platforms covered with earth. At Fort Madison this lighting system was improved by Captain Samuel Dale, Alabama's great Indian fighter, and one of the outstanding heroes of this war. Refusing to evacuate the fort, and swearing to defend the women and children under his care, he illuminated the fort by attaching burning pitch wood to 50-foot poles; he spread wet clay on the roofs of the blockhouses to keep them from catching fire from Indian fire arrows, and had women dressed in their husbands' clothes parade in the enclosure to fool Indian spies. The Indians did not attack.

Alabama was dotted with forts, or stockades with the name "fort," during the Creek Indian War. There was **FORT CLAIBORNE,** in Monroe County on the Alabama River, named for General F. L. Claiborne, who built it; **FORT DEPOSIT,** now the name of a town, established by General Jackson; **FORT MONTGOMERY,** not far from Fort Stoddert, and also **FORT PIERCE,** in the same section. **FORT STROTHER,** erected by Jackson on the Coosa River at the Ten Islands, was his base during the Creek campaign.

GEORGIA

One of the Thirteen Original Colonies.

On the morning of April 10, 1862, the Union forces opened fire on **FORT PULASKI** with thirty-six siege guns, heavy rifled cannon and mortars. The fort, on Cockspur Island, guarding the entrance of the Savannah River, had refused to surrender, and for thirty hours Federal guns hurled metal at this historical fortification. It was gallantly defended until April 12th, when, so battered as to be untenable, the fort was surrendered by Colonel Charles H. Olmstead, the Confederate commander. Three hundred and eighty-five officers and men were captured, as well as large quantities of ammunition and supplies. Two eastern walls of the huge fort were destroyed; the officers' quarters were damaged and the powder magazines endangered.

This victory enabled the Union forces to close the port of Savannah against blockade runners. These vessels, which carried vast quantities of arms, ammunition, and other supplies to the Confederates, received in exchange quantities of cotton and tobacco that

Heavy mortar

were taken to England. Though Great Britain had expressed her neutrality at the opening of the war, Confederates were permitted to have privateer vessels built and supplied there, while swift-sailing British merchant steam vessels, constructed for this purpose, were permitted to carry on an exchange with the South by running the blockade of southern ports.

Fort Pulaski had been occupied by troops sent by Governor Joseph E. Brown of Georgia on January 3, 1861, when he learned that Federal soldiers planned to reinforce Fort Sumter. Since Georgia had not seceded at this time, this was considered by the Government to be an act of treason; Southerners considered it an act of patriotism.

Fort Pulaski is now a National Monument. The 537 acres on Cockspur Island enclose one of the best-preserved fortresses constructed for coast defense during the first half of the nineteenth century. Facing seaward at the entrance to the Savannah River, it is encircled by two moats spanned by drawbridges. The gateway is protected by a portcullis and the guns by casemates. On the ground between the moats are breastworks or crescent-shaped mounds known as demilunes (half moons).

Pulaski was actually the third fort erected on the island. The first was **FORT GEORGE,** a small blockhouse structure built in 1761. American patriots tore it down in 1776. **FORT GREENE,** also a small structure, was built in 1794. A hurricane swept it away in 1804.

In 1816, at the invitation of President James Monroe, Napoleon's chief engineer, Simon Bernard, came to the United States and became senior member of the Board of Engineers, constructing a new system of coast defense. He made first drafts of Fort Pulaski, and actual construction began in 1829. Lieutenant Robert E. Lee, a recent graduate of West Point, assisted in a preliminary survey. The fort was named for Casimir Pulaski, a Polish nobleman who fought with the Americans in the Revolution and was mortally wounded in the siege of Savannah.

FORT WIMBERLY, on the Isle of Hope south of Savannah, was built in the early 1700's by Governor Oglethorpe to guard the narrows of the Skiaway River. He selected a tract of land situated strategically on the Inland Waterway leading south to Spanish territory. This land belonged to Noble Jones, who was given command of the small wooden fort. In 1741 the wooden structure was replaced by one made of "tabby," a concrete of ground oyster shells and sand mixed with water. The fort was about thirty feet square, with an armament of four brass cannon. Mary Jones, wife of the captain, once successfully defended the fort from a sudden attack by Spanish and Indians. In the Civil War a Confederate battalion stationed there prevented Federal ships from passing along the Inland Water Route. Today ruined walls eight feet high may still be seen.

FORT WAYNE, whose site in Savannah today is occupied by the Municipal Gas plant, was built in 1762 and named for General Mad Anthony Wayne. The British captured the fort in 1779 and strengthened it. Americans rebuilt it during the War of 1812 at the time that British Admiral George Cockburn was marauding on the southern coast, seizing slaves and property and reselling at a profit. The massive buttressed brick walls, encircling a high bluff and overlooking what was once a marshy plain, still appear formidable with their old black cannon pointing seaward.

FORT JACKSON was built during the War of 1812 on the Savannah River, two miles south of Savannah. Confederates seized it in March, 1861, and the flag flew over the customhouse until Savannah was taken by the Union forces.

FORT McALLISTER, built by Confederate forces at the start of the Civil War on the Great Ogeechee River, twelve miles south of Savannah and opposite Genesis Point, was one of the principal defenses of this city, and withstood attacks by Union forces during 1862 and 1863. However, on December 13, 1864, General William B. Hazen captured the fort after a gallant defense by its commander Major George Anderson. The fall of Fort McAllister was the final event of Sherman's march to the sea. After this defeat and the occupation of Savannah by the Federals, the Confederate forces withdrew.

FORT MORRIS was established at Sunbury, south of Savannah, in 1776. The two hundred Continental troops garrisoned there offered spirited resistance to the British in several attacks, but in 1779 the fort was finally taken and Sunbury virtually destroyed by British General Sir George Prevost with two thousand troops and Indians. The fall of the fort was a final blow to Republican power in eastern Georgia. Today the ruins of this fort are overgrown with wild myrtle and cedar trees.

FORT KING GEORGE was erected near Darien at the mouth of the Altamaha River in 1721 to protect the colonists from the encroachments of the French and Spanish. It was named for King George I of England and garrisoned by His Majesty's Independent Company. This was the first English settlement on Georgia land. Fire almost completely destroyed the fort in 1727, and although it was rebuilt the garrison was withdrawn and sent to South Carolina on the urgent appeal of the colonists there. In 1938 the legislature purchased the site for the Fort King George Memorial Park.

FORT MOUNTAIN STATE PARK was believed to have been built in 1540 by De Soto just east of the present town of Chatsworth in the northwestern section of the state on a peak in the Cohutta Mountains. Today a United States Forest Service lookout tower stands on the site. Encircling the crest is a low stone wall, 12 feet thick and 2 feet high, and ancient pits are to be seen at regular intervals.

FORT AUGUSTA was built by Governor Oglethorpe around 1735 after he had laid out the town of Augusta, naming it for the mother of King George III. In 1780 this was the seat of government, but soon afterward the fort and town were taken by the Tory Lieutenant Colonels Brown and Grierson. Fort Augusta was renamed **FORT CORNWALLIS,** after the British general, and Colonel James Grierson built **FORT GRIERSON** nearby. Colonials captured both forts, but the British retook them. Then, in June, 1781, Colonel "Light-Horse Harry" Lee first took Fort Grierson and then, with the aid of a Maham tower, a log structure that enabled riflemen to fire down into the fort, which Lee had used effectively at Forts Watson and Ninety-Six in South Carolina, he subdued the garrison and forced the British to surrender.

The site of Fort Augusta (Cornwallis) is today marked by a Celtic

cross placed in the churchyard of St. Paul's Episcopal Church by the Colonial Dames. The place where Fort Grierson stood at Eleventh and Reynolds streets is indicated by a granite marker with a bronze plate.

FORT WILLIAM was built by Governor Oglethorpe on Cumberland Island in 1736 to command the entrance to the St. Marys River.

Also on this island, off the southeastern coast of the state, was erected **FORT ST. ANDREW,** as well as a battery on the western side to protect inland navigation. In the early days Fort William successfully resisted an attack of twenty-eight Spanish vessels and a large land force. This island later became the refuge of outlaws and smugglers.

FORT FREDERICA, on St. Simon Island, was built in 1736 by Governor Oglethorpe, for colonial expansion as well as for defense. The fort and the little town that grew up there were named in honor of Frederick, the only son of King George II of England. The site of the fort, now a national monument, was on a bluff ten feet above the high-water mark of the southern branch of the Altamaha River, known locally as the Frederica River. It was at a strategic point commanding the curve of the stream. Within a short time this small fort was replaced with a four-bastioned fortification with tabby walls, made from oyster shells and sand. The little town itself was located behind the fort in the shape of a crescent. Today all that remains of the old fort are two small tabby chambers surmounted by a low parapet.

FORT ST. SIMON, built about the same time on the eastern tip of St. Simon Island, played an important role with Fort Frederica in breaking the Spanish hold on Georgia territory. On June 28, 1742, a Spanish fleet of 51 ships carrying 5,000 men under Don Manuel de Montiano anchored off St. Simon Bar. On July 5, 36 of these vessels sailed into the harbor, and Oglethorpe was forced to retreat to Fort Oglethorpe after spiking the guns of Fort St. Simon. The Spanish swarmed over the island, and on July 7 Oglethorpe met them at Grenadier Marsh, where so many of the Spaniards were slain that the engagement became known as the Battle of Bloody Marsh.

FORT EDWARDS, in Watkinsville, was a blockhouse erected in 1789 as defense against the Cherokee Indians. Later, it was covered inside and out with wide boards, and greatly enlarged. In 1801 it became a tavern, and today is the Eagle Hotel, opposite the courthouse.

FORT FIDIUS, at Milledgeville, near what is called Rock Landing on the Oconee River, was established in 1793, nine years prior to the time this town became the capital of Georgia. It had the largest garrison of Federal troops south of the Ohio River. **FORT WILKINSON,** named for General James Wilkinson, was built three years later, a few miles north of Fort Fidius. It was here that in 1802 representatives of thirty-two Creek towns signed the Indian treaty of 1802 that ceded the lands of this section to the State of Georgia.

FORT HAWKINS, upon the site of which Macon was built, was constructed in 1806 on the Ocmulgee River, thirty-five miles west southwest of Milledgeville. Its main purpose was to protect the state against Indian insurrection, and served as a meeting place for Federal agents and the Creek. During the War of 1812 this fort was the assembling place for troops who were equipped and sent to the aid of General Andrew Jackson prior to the Battle of New Orleans. The site of this important fort is marked by a blockhouse, built in 1938 by the Nathaniel Macon Chapter of the Daughters of the American Revolution. Plans also were drawn up to reconstruct the fort, which was originally named for Benjamin Hawkins, Government Indian agent. The stockade, enclosing 14 acres, was made of hewn posts, 14 inches thick, sunk 4 feet into the ground. Every other post had a round hole through which a musket barrel could be thrust. Inside the stockade were two long blockhouses, 23 feet square, consisting of two stories on a stone basement, the upper floors projecting outward over the lower. Smaller log houses were used as living quarters and trading rooms.

FORT SCOTT, on the bank of the Flint River near the Georgia-Florida line, was built in 1816 as headquarters for the first Seminole War. General Edmund P. Gaines was in charge of the war against the Indians and fugitive slaves who had joined them, until General

Andrew Jackson arrived and invaded their territory in Florida—an act that nearly brought on a war with Spain. **FORT HUGHES,** not far from Fort Scott, was near the town of Bainbridge. This was mainly an earthwork used by General Jackson's troops during the Seminole War in the territory of the Flint and Chattahoochee rivers. Still another fort on Georgia soil was **FORT GAINES** in Clay County, on a bluff overlooking the Chattahoochee. The fort was named for General Gaines, and today the town of Fort Gaines, seat of Clay County, occupies the site.

FORT WALKER, a Civil War fort in Atlanta, was built on the crown of the hill near the Atlanta Avenue and Boulevard entrance to Grant Park. This commanding position was held by a Confederate battery during the siege and battle of Atlanta in 1864. The fort was named in honor of William T. Walker, Confederate general killed in the battle of Atlanta.

FORT McPHERSON, a United States military post now located four miles south of Atlanta, formerly was on the site of the present-day Spelman College. The college acquired the grounds and buildings of the old fort in 1883, and the fort was moved in 1885. The fort was named for Union General James Birdseye McPherson, killed in the Battle of Atlanta.

FORT ALLATOONA, at Allatoona, had the distinction of being saved in 1864 by the first effective use of signals perfected by General Albert J. Myer, who had organized the United States Signal Corps the year before. As Confederate forces were pressing on the Union-held fort, General William Tecumseh Sherman, who was posted on the summit of Kennesaw Mountain, had a signal sent to the fort commander, "Hold out for relief is approaching." The besieged fort held until relief came and the Confederates withdrew. The incident inspired the evangelist Philip Paul Bliss to write his religious song "Hold the Fort, for I Am Coming."

FORT TYLER, on a hill at West Point, erected to save the city from the fire of Federal guns in the Civil War, held out for several hours on Easter Sunday, April 16, 1865. The fort was named for Confederate General Robert C. Tyler, who was killed in the battle. Ruins of the fort are to be seen today.

FORT OGLETHORPE, a United States Military Post near Dodge, eleven miles from Chattanooga, was established in 1903 as a military reservation of 810 acres, and named for James E. Oglethorpe, founder of Georgia.

FORT BENNING, nine miles from Columbus, was ·established during World War I and named for Confederate General Henry L. Benning of Columbus.

FLORIDA

Admitted to the Union in 1845 as the twenty-seventh state.

Garrison duty was becoming very boring to the soldiers in **FORT SAN CARLOS DE BARRANCAS.** Guard duty, drill, and various duties about the fort were broken only by leave to Pensacola, some six miles away. Then one day a stranger—a man who insisted that his name did not matter—called upon the commanding officer. He had a vellum document, yellow with age, and upon it in faded brown ink was a plan of the fort. One corner of the part showing the parade was marked with a cross.

"What do you make of this?" asked the commandant.

"It is here that the Spanish treasure is buried," said the man, placing a finger on the cross.

"What treasure?" asked the commandant.

"The treasure left behind by the Spaniards at one time when they were forced to evacuate this fort to the French or to the English. This should be evident from the mellowed age of this chart—it was drawn many, many years ago."

The commandant gave his consent to dig at the place marked by the cross. This helped relieve the monotony of garrison life, and everyone pitched in. After a time a pickax struck a rotten wooden

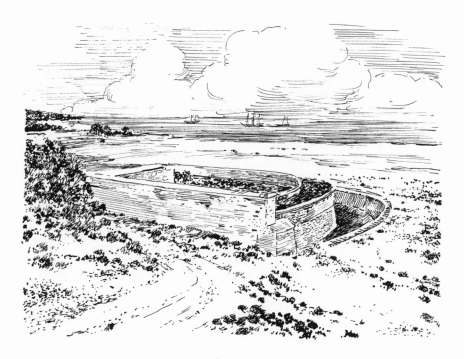

Ruins of Fort San Carlos de Barrancas

board, which when torn away showed that it was the cover of a well. At the bottom of the well was a mass of watery mud. As this was cleared away, the top of an old rusty iron chest came to view. But darkness brought an end to the day's work, and everyone went to bed in great excitement and in anticipation of what the next day would bring.

Early next morning the men were back at work. Nothing could be seen of the chest. The stirring up of the earth and water had caused it to sink so deep in the unstable soil that although the men worked for days they could not again uncover the chest. It was lost forever.

This little fort has a long and interesting history. It first was built as a wooden fortification by the Spaniards in 1698 and named for Charles (Carlos) II of Spain. It was destroyed by the French in 1719 but rebuilt the following year. Then in 1771 the British built a fort here. Between 1783 and 1796, after England had returned Florida to Spain, it was rebuilt of brick after the Spanish had destroyed the British structure. In 1814, when General Andrew Jackson invaded Florida, the British, who had been allowed by Spain to occupy the fort, blew it up before fleeing. These are the ruins that have been restored today, and Fort San Carlos is now a National Park.

FORT BARRANCAS, a military post in the harbor of Pensacola, is a U-shaped fort built between 1839 and 1844. It was held by Confederates from early in 1861 to 1862. Large bricks were used in the construction, but some granite was employed for stair treads, gun mounts, and at the main entrance. The fort is well preserved because open joints had been left in the building to take care of settling. A dry moat is on the north and west sides. This fort rises abruptly behind old Fort San Carlos and is connected with it by a brick tunnel. The drawbridge at the entrance still has the iron operating mechanism and chains. The fort derived its name from the type of ground it was built upon—the Spanish word *barrancas* meaning "broken," or "a high hill" or "bluff."

FORT PICKENS, located on the western tip of Santa Rosa Island, commanded the eastern entrance of Pensacola Harbor, opposite Fort Barrancas. It was built as defense to the harbor and the United States Navy Yard at Warrington. Named for General Andrew Pickens of the Revolutionary War, it was constructed under the supervision of Captain William H. Chase, United States Engineer, in 1834. Later, as a Confederate general, Chase was ordered to capture the fort he had built, but failed. It was one of the "star forts," pentagonal in shape, which became popular in coastal defense after the War of 1812, with a bastion at each of the five corners. A curved granite stairway has a rail of wrought iron. In the fort are cells in which Geronimo, the Chiricahua Apache chief, and his entire band of 340 were imprisoned in 1886. Fort Pickens, at the time of its building the second largest fort in the United States, had the distinction of being one of the few that remained in Union hands throughout the Civil War.

FORT McRAE, built on the opposite side of the channel on a peninsula opposite Fort Pickens, and erected shortly after this fort, had a short life. Sweeping tides and pounding surf destroyed it.

Portions of the old brick foundations are to be seen at low tide, and the center of the parade grounds, where the flagpole stood in 1852, is now covered by thirty feet of water in the ship channel.

FORT JEFFERSON, off southern Florida on one of the group of low-lying coral and sand bars of the Dry Tortugas, was a massive structure covering 16 acres. This fort was started in 1846 to guard the straits of Florida, and was built with considerable difficulty and expense. It became one of the largest masonry fortifications in the Western Hemisphere. The foundations are on coral rock ten feet below sea level. The 40,000,000 bricks used cost $1 per brick for transportation alone. The fort is surrounded by high thick walls and a moat 70 feet wide that was said to have been filled with sharks—hence the spot was called Shark Island. It is a hexagonal, three-tiered, casemated fortification. Large-caliber guns were mounted—243 of them—but not one was ever fired in anger. It became a Federal prison in 1863. Dr. Samuel A. Mudd, sentenced to life in connection with the assassination of President Lincoln, served four years here before he was pardoned. He had not previously known Lincoln's assassin, John Wilkes Booth, but merely had set the actor's broken leg. It was from off here that the battleship *Maine* sailed to her fate at Havana during the Spanish-American War. This gigantic pile was declared a National Monument by President Theodore Roosevelt.

FORT TAYLOR, sixty miles east of Fort Jefferson, was built during the Mexican War (1846–1848) at Key West. It was held by Union forces during the Civil War.

FORT MARION, at St. Augustine, the oldest fort in the United States, was originally built by the Spanish on Matanzas Bay. Called by them **CASTILLO DE SAN MARCOS,** the fort followed designs by the famous French military engineer Vauban, and was started in 1672. It was not completed until 1756, and seven years later it fell to the British, who occupied it for twenty years, renaming it **FORT ST. MARKS.** The Spanish again gained possession of the fort and restored the old name, but in 1825, when Florida became United States territory, the fort was called Fort Marion, in honor of General Francis Marion (the Swamp Fox) of South Carolina. During the Second Seminole War it was used as a prison and the Seminole chiefs Osceola, Coacoochee, and Hillis Hadjo were confined here. The last two escaped, but Osceola later died at Fort Moultrie, South Carolina.

This historic fort, which cost some $30,000,000 and caused the King of Spain to exclaim: "Its curtains and bastions must be of solid silver," was built of gray coquina (shell marl) blocks quarried on Anastasia Island with outer walls 12 feet thick at the base and tapering to 7 feet at the top. The fort has several remarkable architectural features, chief of which is a broad ramp upon which cannon were dragged to the terreplein (top of the rampart), the ramp itself being supported by an elliptical arch without a keystone. Granite arcs, upon which American guns were turned, still remain; there is also a hot-shot oven where cannon balls were heated white hot before being rammed into the cannon, so they might set fire to enemy ships. Fort Marion was declared a National Monument in 1924 and in 1942 restored its original name.

Fort Marion

FORT CAROLINE, on St. Johns River near Jacksonville, was built in 1564 by René de Laudonnière, French explorer, as one of the first strongholds in America. The fort was triangular in shape with the base of the triangle on the riverfront. It was constructed chiefly of earth from a deep moat surrounding it, the earth faced with bundles of sticks to form fascines. Soon after its completion the colony was joined by Jean Ribaut and his company of French Huguenots. The Spanish, who settled St. Augustine the following year, considered the fort a nest of pirates preying on the gold and silver of the Spanish galleons. Don Pedro Menendez de Aviles, in command of the Spanish at St. Augustine, attacked and destroyed the fort in 1865. Meantime Ribaut's ships were wrecked in a storm just south of St. Augustine and survivors were slaughtered by the Spanish. This spot was named *Matanzas,* the Spanish word meaning slaughter or massacre, and thus gave its name to the river and a fort later built there. The Spanish rebuilt Fort Caroline and re-named it **FORT SAN MATEO,** but in 1568 the French retook it and destroyed it. The site later was washed away by the river. To-day the Fort Caroline National Memorial stands on the river bank near the old fort site.

FORT MATANZAS, on Rattlesnake Island south of St. Augustine, was built by the Spaniards in 1736 near the site of the massacre of the French Huguenots from Fort Caroline. It obtained its name from the *matanzas* (slaughter) of the Frenchmen. The fort, a coquina (shell marl) structure 40 feet square and more than 30 feet high, replaced a tower erected there to prevent enemy ships moving up the Matanzas River. The Government established a reservation there in 1915, and it is now a National Monument.

FORT KING, at Ocala, which was established as a trading post in 1825 and two years later garrisoned and named Fort King, was the scene of the beginning of the Second Seminole War, and a great deal of the action took place in this vicinity. Wiley Thompson, Indian agent, sought to enforce the treaty, which provided for the emigration of the Indians to Indian Territory. Osceola defied him and pinned the treaty to the table with his scalping knife. "This is the only treaty I will ever make with the whites!" he cried. Later, he killed Thompson and Lieutenant Constantine Smith, and on the same day Major Francis L. Dade and 109 men were massacred nearby. This brought on the war, and the fort was military head-quarters for central Florida.

FORT DADE, at Bushnell, named for Major Francis L. Dade, was the scene of the massacre of December 28, 1835, when Major Dade and 109 men were killed by Seminoles. This fort was a breast-works of huge logs, and has been reproduced in concrete on the 80-acre reservation known as Dade Memorial Park. Major Dade had made a stand here on his way to Fort King. It is interesting to note that in the supplies of the soldiers were Cuban oranges. The dis-carded seeds took root and grew, and in 1846 William Miley laid out a homestead here and transplanted the seedlings, thus starting an orange crop for which Florida became famous.

FORT PEYTON, at Moultrie—a wooden fort and blockhouse—was built in 1836. This fort, nothing of which remains, takes its place in history because it was while Osceola and a party were on the way here to ask the release of the imprisoned Seminole chief, King Philip, that they were seized on orders of General Thomas S. Jesup, in command of the army in Florida, and taken prisoners to Fort Marion in St. Augustine. Osceola died a prisoner at Fort Moul-trie in South Carolina, and General Jesup was denounced by public opinion for breach of faith.

FORT JUPITER was erected during the Seminole War by settlers at the town of Jupiter. Here General Jesup imprisoned 678 Indians and Negroes until they were transported to western reservations. The fort was abandoned in 1842, and today the Jupiter Lighthouse occupies the site.

FORT LAUDERDALE, which gave the town of Fort Lauderdale its name, was built in 1837 during the Seminole War and named for its commander, Major William Lauderdale. FORT MAITLAND, at the town of Maitland named for the fort, was built during the war by Captain William S. Maitland. FORT MASON also gave its name to the town of Mason. The fort was erected by Major Richard Barnes Mason, during the Seminole War. FORT WACAHOOTA was built in the vicinity of Wacahoota during the war. No traces are left of this fort or of the Mission Francisco de Potano, established in the first part of the seventeenth century. **FORT WHITE,** at High Springs, was another Seminole War fort.

FORT WALTON, on the site of Fort Walton Beach east of Pensacola, was built in 1839 during the Seminole War. Later, Confederate soldiers who occupied the fort dug up skeletons and displayed them in a wooden shack. During a Federal attack shells from a gunboat destroyed the building and the relics.

FORT MYERS, at the city of Fort Myers, which grew up around it, was built in 1839 during the Indian troubles and named for Colonel Abraham C. Myers, then chief quartermaster in the Florida military district. **FORT MELLON,** at Sanford, was an early fort that gave its name to Mellonville but that later became Sanford. It is marked by a stone monument at Mellonville Avenue and Second Street in Sanford.

FORT MEADE, at the town by that name, was a Seminole War fort named for Lieutenant George Gordon Meade, who later gained prominence at the Battle of Gettysburg.

FORT CLINCH, near Fernandina at the northern end of Amelia Island, overlooking Cumberland Sound, was completed in 1861 and named for General D. L. Clinch, an officer in the Second Seminole War. It was seized by Confederates at the opening of the Civil War, but in March, 1862, they were forced to evacuate it on the approach of the Federal fleet. It was garrisoned during the Spanish-American War but saw no action. Today the fort stands on the 980 acres that compose Fort Clinch State Park. Its notable brickwork is well preserved. The inner wall is pierced with tunnels, while the outer is eight feet thick.

FORT OGDEN, now at the town of Fort Ogden, was built in 1841 on the site of an Indian fort of the same name. It stands near the Peace River and was selected because of huge cypress trees nearby, which were used to build fifty-five pirogues to invade Seminole territory deep in the Everglades.

FORT GADSDEN, up the Apalachicola River a short distance from Apalachicola Bay, was built on the ruins of **FORT BLOUNT** in 1818 by General Andrew Jackson during the First Seminole War.

He named it for his aide-de-camp, James Gadsden, who later was to negotiate the Gadsden Purchase. Fort Blount, also known as **NEGRO FORT,** was occupied by fugitive Negroes and Seminoles encouraged by the British. It was blown up on Jackson's orders in the summer of 1816. This provided a prelude to the Indian war. Captain Duncan McKrimmon, a Georgia militia officer stationed here, was captured by Seminole Indians and sentenced to be burned to death. But the pleading of the young Seminole girl Milly Francis, with her father, Chief Hillis Hadjo, known to the whites as the Prophet Francis, saved his life. Later he was sold to Spanish traders for a barrel of whisky. Milly was captured, and McKrimmon asked her to marry him, but she refused. She was taken to live near Fort Gibson, Oklahoma, and in 1844 was awarded the first Congressional Medal of Honor given a woman, and granted a pension of $96 a year for her act. The Milly Francis Monument was erected to this "Seminole Pocahontas" by faculty and students of the Bacone College in Oklahoma in 1933.

FORT ST. FRANCIS DE PUPA, at Green Cove Springs, was erected by the Spanish in 1737. It was destroyed by British troops under Governor Oglethorpe of Georgia in 1841. Only traces of earthen embankments remain.

FORT SANTA LUCIA, another Spanish fort, was built in 1568 by Pedro Menendez de Avilés at the present town of Jensen. The Indians killed so many soldiers that the garrison mutinied and, abandoning the fort, fled to St. Augustine. **FORT SAN LUIS,** at Tallahassee, was erected around 1640, and served as headquarters for seven missionary settlements. **FORT SAN CARLOS,** at Fernandina, was built by the Spanish in 1784. Crumbling walls are all that remain. **FORT SAN NICHOLAS,** on the St. Johns River at Jacksonville, was erected in 1740 by the Spanish governor, Don Manuel de Monteano, when threatened with attack by the British. It was burned in 1812 by the Patriots of Florida during their operations against St. Augustine. A gray stone marker indicates the site. **FORT MOOSA,** an outpost of St. Augustine, was built in the seventeenth century to provide a haven for escaped slaves from the Carolina plantations.

FORT GEORGE, on Fort George Island near the mouth of the St. Johns River, was built on the site where Spanish soldiers had a blockhouse prior to 1568. It was here that James Oglethorpe, English general and colonial leader of Georgia, made his temporary headquarters when he invaded Florida in 1736. The area today is owned by the Fort George Club.

FORT GATLIN, at Orlando, was established in 1837 during the Seminole War, but was abandoned in 1848. It was named for Dr. John S. Gatlin, assistant surgeon of the United States Army, who lost his life in the Dade massacre. Settlers built houses near the fort, and later incorporated the town of Orlando.

FORT HARRISON, established in 1841, also provided protection to settlers, and thus sprang up the city of Clearwater on the Gulf of Mexico. FORT FANNIN, at Fannin Springs, was built in 1838. Old stone ovens still remain on the fort site on a high bluff of the Suwanee River. FORT BROOKE, a log structure erected in 1823, marked the pioneer settlement of the Tampa region. It was named for Colonel George Brooke, the commander. His son, John Mercer Brooke, who was born in the fort, became chief of the Bureau of Ordnance and Hydrography in the Confederate Government, and refitted the *Merrimac* as an ironclad.

SOUTH CAROLINA

One of the Thirteen Original Colonies.

The cannon balls of the British fleet thudded into the soft palmetto logs of FORT SULLIVAN on June 28, 1776, but had little effect. However, one chance shot cut the flagstaff in two, and the flag of South Carolina fell to the ground. Sergeant William Jasper leaped from one of the embrasures, seized the ensign, carried it back, fixed it to a cannon sponge-staff, jumped on the parapet, stuck the staff into the sand, and then calmly returned to his duties. His comrades cheered.

The British failed in their attack on Charleston, and withdrew. Governor John Rutledge visited the fort the next day and, on learning of Jasper's heroism, took his own sword from his side and handed it to the sergeant. He offered him a lieutenant's commission.

"I am not fit to keep officers' company," modestly said Jasper. "I am but a sergeant."

A Whig lady of Charleston presented Jasper's regiment with a stand of colors made by her own hands. The next year, at Savannah, these colors were shot down in an assault, and in trying to replace them on the parapet of the redoubt Jasper was mortally wounded. But before he died he managed to plant the colors. Georgia joined with South Carolina in honoring Jasper. A county in Georgia and a square in Savannah bear his name.

The defeat of the British fleet saved the southern states from invasion. As a result the name of Fort Sullivan, which honored Captain Florence Sullivan of the ship *Carolina* which brought the first settlers to the island in 1672, was changed to that of **FORT MOULTRIE** to honor the brave commander, Colonel William Moultrie. The symbol of the white palmetto was added to the state's flag after the battle to commemorate the efficacy of the logs of the fort.

As Fort Moultrie this fort had a subsequent long and interesting history. Edgar Allan Poe, in the army under the name of E. A. Perry, served here in 1828 and wrote the poem "Israfel," and later utilized the local setting for his story *The Gold Bug*. It was here that the Seminole chief, Osceola, was imprisoned in 1835 after being treacherously arrested in Florida under a flag of truce. He died three years later, and was buried beside the gate, and a small marble shaft marks his grave.

In 1841 the present Fort Moultrie, a star-shaped structure of brownish brick, was started. In 1903 Army Headquarters at Washington decided to change the name of the fort to Fort Getty, in honor of a dead soldier, but such a chorus of indignation arose that the order was hastily withdrawn.

When South Carolina seceded from the Union in 1860, Major Robert Anderson, the commandant, spiked the guns of Fort Moultrie and moved his garrison to Fort Sumter. Confederate troops occupied the former fort. The bombardment of Fort Sumter from Fort Moultrie on April 12, 1861, which brought on the Civil War, was the first time in history that two forts so fought each other. They pounded away, one at the other for thirty-six hours, until Fort Sumter surrendered.

The first shots of the war actually were fired by Confederates at **FORT WAGNER** on Morris Island, three months before on the steamer *Star of the West,* which was bringing troops and supplies to Fort Sumter.

FORT SUMTER, now a National Monument, is on an island in midchannel between Fort Moultrie on the northeast and Fort Johnson on the southwest. This little stone fort, named for Thomas Sumter, of South Carolina, the "Gamecock" of the Revolution, was begun in 1828 by the United States Government on a sandy shallow. It was not fully completed at the time of the opening of the Civil War. After Major Anderson evacuated it, the Confederates occupied it, as well as other forts in the harbor, and it withstood three terrific bombardments by the Federals in 1863–1864.

In 1864 General Quincy A. Gillmore, Union commander of the Department of the South, employed one of the sensational guns of the Civil War against this fort, as well as against Charleston. It was a 200-pound Parrott gun placed in a marsh between James and Morris islands and affectionately nicknamed "The Swamp Angel." It almost demolished Fort Sumter and Fort Wagner and even hurled 150-pound shells into Charleston, five miles away. Still the Confederates held out.

As General William Tecumseh Sherman began his march through the interior of South Carolina, the fort was quietly evacuated on February 17, 1865. The next day the Stars and Stripes once more waved over Fort Sumter, and on April 14 of that year Major Anderson, then a retired brigadier general, had the satisfaction of raising once more the flag he had pulled down four years earlier. Henry Ward Beecher made a stirring address. That night President Abraham Lincoln was assassinated in Washington. Thus, the destiny of one of the greatest Presidents of this country was linked from first to last with this little stone fort in Charleston Harbor. The very day he assumed office, on March 4, 1861, the Fort Sumter situation was placed squarely before him, as the outgoing Secretary of War had that morning received a dispatch from Major Anderson telling that rations from Fort Moultrie would last but a few weeks, and the firing on the fort brought on the war that occupied the President during his entire term of office.

FORT JOHNSON, on James Island in Charleston Harbor, from whose battery the first shell was sent over Fort Sumter at 4:30 A.M., on April 12, 1861, is Charleston's oldest fortification. It was built by Governor Sir Nathaniel Johnson and named for him in 1704–1708. This fort was a fully garrisoned post of the British in 1765. Then, one night in 1775, it was quietly occupied by a group of Charleston's patriots who trained all its guns on a British sloop of war anchored in the harbor and carrying a cargo of the despised tax stamps. The next morning the ship prudently sailed back to England with its cargo. It was at this fort that Colonel William Moultrie, in command, first hoisted his blue banner. It was a flag with a blue field with three white crescents in the center, and was the first used by an American colony. It has been retained today as the flag of the State of South Carolina. Colonel Moultrie explained in his Memoirs: "As there was no national flag at this time, I was desired by the Council of Safety to have one made, upon which, as the state troops were clothed in blue, and the fort was garrisoned by the first and second regiments, who wore a silver crescent in the front of their caps, I had a large blue flag made, with a crescent in the center, to be in uniform with the troops. This was the first American flag displayed in the South." Fort Johnson's ruins are still to be seen.

Two other forts, built during the Civil War to guard Charleston, were located on Port Royal Sound. One was **FORT WALKER,** on Hilton Head, and the other, across the sound, was **FORT BEAU-REGARD** on Bay Point.

CASTLE PINCKNEY, located on an island in Charleston Harbor opposite Fort Sumter, was built in 1797 when there was a threat of war with France. It was named in honor of Charles Cotesworth Pinckney, American statesman and diplomat and a native of Charleston. The fort saw no action and later became a depot for buoy tenders. In 1924 it was made a National Monument.

FORT NINETY-SIX, at the town of Ninety-Six, was so named because it was calculated to be 96 miles from the frontier Fort Prince George. Here occurred the first bloodshed of the Revolution when 562 patriots, under Colonel Williamson, defeated a superior force of British in November, 1775. Later the British seized this fort and **STAR FORT** nearby. On May 12, 1781, General Nathanael Greene began a 37-day siege. While a tunnel was begun toward Star Fort under the direction of Thaddeus Kosciusko, Polish engineer with the Continental forces, a Maham tower was erected to be used against Fort Ninety-Six. This tower, the invention of Colonel Hezekiah Maham, was a structure that would elevate riflemen above the walls of the fort so they could fire down within the fort itself. But the approach of British reinforcements forced Greene to retire at this time.

The Maham tower, however, when used for the first time by

Maham tower

General Francis Marion, the "Swamp Fox," on April 23, 1781, against **FORT WATSON,** located on a bluff where the Congaree and Wateree rivers join to form a lake, proved highly successful. The British, unable to withstand the withering fire from sharpshooters on the high tower, surrendered. This fort had been built by Lieutenant Colonel John Watson Tadwell-Watson, and was named for him. He had copied it from the plan of Old World forts with a fosse, parapets, abatis, and cannon ports, and built it at the base of an old Indian mound.

FORT PRINCE GEORGE, near the present town of Pickens, was erected in 1753 by Governor James Glen as protection against Spanish and French invaders. This important fort was the gateway from South Carolina to the Cherokee country. The Cherokee Indians donated two thousand acres as a site for the fort. However, three years after the fort was built, the Cherokee, influenced by the French, became enemies, and many bloody battles were fought here. But finally the British began a thirty-day march through Cherokee territory, destroying settlements and cultivated fields. The Indians sued for peace. **FORT PICKENS,** named for General Andrew Pickens of the Revolutionary War, later was erected fourteen miles from the town of Pickens.

FORT CHARLOTTE was built in 1765 by the British where old Vienna later stood on the Savannah River just below present-day Mount Carmel. A buffer between Cherokee territory and South Carolina, it was among the first manned by Colonial troops during the Revolution. It was named for the wife of King George III. It gained its greatest notoriety after it had fallen into ruins. When dueling was outlawed in Georgia, it became the favorite spot where duelists met, as it was conveniently situated just across the Savannah River. Another fort, separating Cherokee country from that which the Indians had ceded to Governor Glen, was **FORT WOODS,** near Lyman, almost on the Old Boundary Line.

FORT MOORE, erected where earlier Savannah Town stood, on the Savannah River on a bluff near what was Sand Bar Ferry, was an important post. It was here that all Indian treaties were made until 1750.

FORT RUTLEDGE, at Clemson, was built in 1776 by General Andrew Williamson, then a colonel who called in one thousand inhabitants to oppose the Cherokee, who had been incited by the British. The fort, named for John Rutledge, one-time governor of South Carolina, sometimes was called **FORT SALVADOR,** for Captain Salvador, Williamson's Jewish-English guide who had been shot and scalped by Cherokee at the Indian village of Essenca. The site of this fort is now the home of Clemson Agricultural College. In the rear of the administration building the site of the original fort is marked by a small concrete fortification.

CHARLESFORT, on Parris Island, was built in 1562 by French Huguenots led by Jean Ribaut, a naval officer, and named for Charles IX of France. The Charlesfort Monument was erected in 1927 at a spot where excavations uncovered the cedar foundations of either Charlesfort or **FORT SAN MARCOS,** built by Spaniards in 1577. Today the United States Naval Station and Marine Training Center are located there.

BULL TOWN FORT, near Calhoun Falls in what was known as the Abbeyville District, was built before the Revolution. A low embankment of rocks and vine-covered timber is pointed out today as the ruins of this old fort. It was here that Langdon Cheves, one-time speaker of the House and Chief Commissioner at the Treaty of Ghent following the War of 1812, was born on September 17, 1776, during an Indian raid.

FORT MOTTE, some ten miles from St. Matthew, was the home of Mrs. Rebecca Motte during the Revolution. British officers took up quarters there, and an engineer added a fosse, earthworks, abatis, and a strong palisade to convert the place into a fort. When General Francis (Swamp Fox) Marion attacked the stronghold, Mrs. Motte agreed that her home should be burned rather than allow the British to remain. She provided a bow and fire-arrows that a sea captain had given her some years before. The place was set on fire, and the British fled.

FORT GALPHIN, also called **FORT DREADNOUGHT,** on Silver Bluff, was built on the Savannah River by the British in pre-Revolutionary days. It was named for George Galphin, British Indian agent. On May 21, 1781, Colonials, hearing that supplies intended for the Indians were stored there, attacked and captured the fort without loss of a man.

FORT DORCHESTER, near Summerville, marks the site of the old town of Dorchester, named by people who came from Dorchester, Massachusetts, and settled there in 1696. Later materials of the fort were carried away for other construction when after fifty years the fort and town were abandoned. A similar fate was in store for **FORT OTTERSON,** near Union, a fort built of stone during the early Indian troubles. Much material from the old fort was used for the building of nearby homes.

FORT DEARBORN, on an island in the Catawba River east of the town of Fort Lawn (a settlement named for the *Fort* family), was built in 1802 as an arsenal. It became a military post in the War of 1812. The ruins of this old fort, named for Secretary of War Henry Dearborn, are still to be seen.

FORT FREDERICK, a tabby (oyster shell concrete) structure, was built on Cat Island in 1731. Now only three sides remain, the fourth having been washed away by the sea. **FORT EUHANIE,** between Plantersville and Toddville at the Yauhannah Causeway and Bridge that spans the Pee Dee River, was a pre-Revolutionary fort and trading post. **FORT LYTTLETON,** two miles south of Beaufort, was built in 1758 during Spanish and Indian troubles, and was named for Governor William Henry Lyttleton.

FORT BATTERY WHITE, between Georgetown and Charleston, was a Confederate stronghold during the Civil War. Among the ruins is to be found an iron cannon with "1864" engraved on the breech. **FORT RANDALL,** another Confederate battery, was on Tilgham's Point near Little River.

FORT FREMONT, on the tip of St. Helena Island, largest of Beaufort County's sixty-five islands, was built with massive concrete bastions and gun emplacements during the Spanish-American War, but saw no action.

NORTH CAROLINA

One of the Thirteen Original Colonies.

When Governor John White, head of the second of Sir Walter Raleigh's expeditions to the "Citie of Ralegh in Virginia," arrived at Roanoke Island on July 22, 1587, he was confronted with a melancholy sight. The **NEW FORT IN VIRGINIA,** as it had been called, established there two years before, had been destroyed and the only trace of the men left to defend it was an unburied skeleton.

Governor White rebuilt the fort, named it **FORT RALEIGH,** and re-established the colony. The new colonists wisely determined to cultivate the friendship of the Indians. Manteo, one of two chiefs who had been taken to England by the earlier colonists and who was then living on Croatan Island, invited them to settle on his domain.

On August 13, in accord with Raleigh's instructions, Manteo was christened and declared "Lord of Roanoke and Dasamonquepeuc," the first and last peerage ever created on American soil. Five days later, Governor White's daughter, Eleanor, wife of Ananias Dare, gave birth to a daughter, who was named Virginia Dare. She was the first child of English parentage to be born in the New World. Another child was born to Dyonis and Margery Harvie shortly afterward.

Governor White, on August 27, at the earnest entreaty of the planters, sailed homeward to obtain supplies for the colony. It is interesting to note that on his way home he touched at Ireland, where he left some potatoes that he had brought from Virginia— the first of that kind ever seen in the Old World.

He did not come straight back to the colony at Fort Raleigh, for his greed caused him to pursue two Spanish ships in search of plunder. His own vessels were so battered by bad weather that he was forced to return to England, where he had to remain until 1590 because of Spanish war vessels in the English Channel.

When he did get back he found Roanoke a desolation, and there was no trace of the colony. Only on a tree trunk that formed a part of a hastily built palisade was carved the word CROATAN. It was supposed that the friendly Lord of Roanoke had saved the lives of the colonists and they had gone to Croatan Island. But White never found his daughter or grandchild, Virginia Dare, or any other of the colonists.

As the birthplace of English history in America, the old fort has been restored, as have been some of the colonists' log cabins. Today it is a National Historic Site.

FORT JOHNSTON, the second fort built in North Carolina, was named in honor of Governor Gabriel Johnston. Situated on a six-acre bluff, on the Cape Fear River near Wilmington, it was completed in 1764 as protection against Spanish pirates. In 1775 Royal Governor Josiah Martin took refuge here until patriots forced him to flee. The fort was destroyed. In 1794 the state ceded the site to the Government on condition that a new fort be built there. Confederates seized it in 1861 and held it until 1865, when Union forces captured it along with other forts at Wilmington, closing the last Confederate port of entry.

The brick masonry of the old fort is in good repair. It is now used by Army Engineers as a base for dredge crews and survey parties, as well as by the Lighthouse Service for crews working on lighthouses and buoys.

FORT FISHER, the bulwark of defense of Wilmington during the Civil War, remains as the largest earthwork fort in the former Confederacy. It is located on the peninsula north of the entrance of the Cape Fear River, called New Inlet. Started in 1861 this gigantic structure was not completed until 1864. It was named for Colonel Charles F. Fisher of Salisbury, who had been killed in the First Battle of Manassas. It extended from Cape Fear River all the way across the peninsula for half a mile and then south down the beach for a mile. Here occurred the most fiercely fought land and naval battles of the war. The Federal fleet alone fired 2,000,000 pounds of metal. The fort fell with Forts Johnston and Caswell. **FORT FISHER BEACH** is now on the site of this old fortification.

Fort Fisher

As a State Historic Site it is marked by a monument to both the northern and southern soldiers who fought in the battle. The remains of the fort are stretches of grass-grown earthworks. There is a museum at the Fort Fisher State Historic Site.

FORT CASWELL, guarding the mouth of the Cape Fear River near Southport, was constructed in 1825. It took its name from Richard Caswell, first governor of the State of North Carolina, and was garrisoned during the Civil War, Spanish-American War, and both world wars. It fell in 1865 along with Fort Fisher. It is now a part of the North Carolina Baptist Assembly grounds. A swimming pool fed by warm springs has been built within the well-preserved brick fortifications.

FORT ANDERSON was built, during the Civil War, diagonally across Brunswick Town, which had lain in ruins for almost a century. The fortification, named for General Richard H. Anderson of the Confederate Army who was wounded at Antietam, was constructed of sand and extended from the Cape Fear River to Orton Pond, a distance of more than a mile. It was here, after the fall of Fort Fisher, that the Confederate troops rallied and held out until, after a three-day bombardment in February, 1865, the fort was captured by the Union forces. The earthworks, with gun emplacements almost intact, stand today as a monument of the Civil War, and offer a vantage point for viewing the ruins of old Brunswick Town.

FORT MACON, at the entrance to the Beaufort Harbor, is a striking example of nineteenth-century military architecture. It was one of the many forts that formed a part of the national system of maritime defenses that grew out of the lack of protection during the War of 1812. It was erected in 1826–1834 and named for Nathaniel Macon, speaker of the House of Representatives and United States senator from Warren County. It replaced the earlier **FORT HAMPTON,** which was nearer the inlet and was washed away in a storm in 1815.

The court of this fort is pentagonal in shape, while the outer walls are in the form of a square. A deep moat, twenty-five feet wide, surrounds the fort, with a drawbridge on one side. Beneath the outer ramparts are dungeons, while domed rooms, arches, supports, and vaulted stairways illustrate some of the intricate brickwork of the period.

Fort Macon was designed to protect the harbor, and thus only a few guns could be brought to bear on the land approach, which enabled the Union troops in April, 1862, to capture the fort in a land attack. It was garrisoned during the Spanish-American War and the two world wars, but its fighting period ended with the Civil War. Restored in 1934–1936 by the Civilian Conservation Corps, the fort is now a State Park. A historical museum is inside.

FORT NOHOROCO, on Contentnea Creek at Snow Hill, the county seat of Greene County, was a palisaded stronghold of the Tuscarora Indians. It was here that Colonel James Moore finally defeated the Indians on March 25, 1713, after a two-year struggle. This powerful tribe then left for New York to join the Five Nations. Trouble with the Tuscarora began in 1711 after sixty years of colonization by the whites. Some historians claim that one of the main causes of the uprising was the practice of the whites in seizing young Indians and selling them into slavery. Today a marker on the spot commemorates the decisive battle.

FORT BARNWELL, at the small farming village of that name nine miles from Dover, was erected during the Tuscarora uprising and named for Colonel John (Tuscarora Jack) Barnwell, a South Carolinian appointed by Governor Edward Hyde to avenge the Tuscarora massacre in 1711 in which hundreds of colonists were killed.

FORT BUTLER, at Murphy, was set up in 1838 for the removal of the Cherokee Indians, who after many treaties had finally given up all lands in their territories—although 90 per cent of them objected. **FORT EMBREE,** on a hill southwest of Hayesville, was one of the collecting stockades.

FORT GRANVILLE, on Portsmouth Island at the northern tip of Core Banks, was erected in 1753 and named for Lord Granville, one of the Lords Proprietors to the original grant of the territory of Carolina. It was manned by Confederates during the Civil War and was fired by them upon the fall of Ocracoke. The Union forces maintained a prison and hospital here until after the war, but today there is no trace of fort, prison, or hospital.

FORT DOBBS was built of logs near the present Statesville in 1755, and named for Governor Arthur Dobbs. It was here that Colonel Hugh Waddell, hero of the French and Indian War, defeated the Cherokee, who had turned on their former English allies. A marker is at the site of the fort.

DAVIDSON'S FORT, at the present town of Old Fort, was built in 1776 as a shelter for pioneer settlers. **FORT DEFIANCE,** an early colonial fort in Happy Valley near Patterson, later gave its name to a big heavy-timbered farmhouse built by General William Lenoir, Revolutionary officer and leader at the Battle of Kings Mountain. **FORT LANDING,** near Columbia on the Alligator River, takes its name from an earlier fort on this site.

FORT HATTERAS, located on Cape Hatteras, was captured by the Union forces on August 27–29, 1861. The Federal fleet shelled the fort at will, using Dahlgren guns, whose range was greater than the smoothbore pieces of the Confederates.

The fall of this fort gave the Union forces an effective entrance into North Carolina.

FORT AMORY, not far from New Bern, a colonial capital, was erected by Federal troops in 1862 as part of a mile-long defense works between the Trent and Neuse rivers. Parts of its pentagonal earthen rampart and deep moat are still to be seen. FORT TOTTEN, at New Bern, also was erected by the Union forces when they seized the town. It was named for General Joseph G. Totten, Chief Engineer of the Federal Army. Trenches were built across the town to the Trent and Neuse rivers, with a fort at each end and one in the center.

FORT BRAGG, one of the largest United States Military reservations in the country, with an area of 130,000 square miles, was named for Confederate General Braxton Bragg. It was built in 1918–1922 and has long been known as the "Home of the Airborne." During the Revolutionary War this site was the headquarters of General Francis Marion, the "Swamp Fox."

TENNESSEE

Admitted to the Union in 1796 as the sixteenth state.

The great bear dogs inside Fort Nashborough began to growl and strain at their chains early on the morning of April 2, 1781. These huge animals, brought overland from the East, were trained to trail and fight bears. They hated Indians. When they began to act up, Colonel James Robertson said to his wife, "Must be Indians or bears around."

Just then a lookout from the blockhouse shouted, "Indians!"

Not far from the fort three painted savages suddenly appeared, fired several times at the fort, and then vanished.

Colonel Robertson at once organized a company of twenty men. They leaped on their horses and started in pursuit of the Indians.

When they gained the forest they could find no sign of the warriors. They rode on.

The Chickamauga Indians, lurking in great numbers in the forest,
allowed the white men to ride through their first lines. Then they
closed in on them from all sides. Colonel Robertson ordered his
men to dismount and use their horses as shields. But they were
trapped and it looked like certain death.

When the sound of rifle fire was heard at the fort, Mrs. Robertson realized how desperate the situation was, and how tragically it might end not only for their men but also for the women and children left in the fort. There were no men to send to help.

"Let loose the dogs!" she cried.

The mastiffs were released, and in a howling, snarling pack rushed out of the fort's gate. They ran for the Indians. Loud yells were heard. The warriors, taken by surprise and in deadly fear of the bear dogs, scattered. Colonel Robertson at once ordered his men back into the fort, calling off the dogs as he did so.

The next day the Indians, recovered from their fright, attacked the fort. But this time the garrison was ready for them. With a swivel cannon loaded with scrap iron, bits of chain and stones, the savages soon were repulsed.

FORT NASHBOROUGH, on a bluff overlooking the Cumberland River, on the site of the city of Nashville, was built by Colonel Robertson and his hardy band of pioneers in 1780. Others came in the boat *Adventure* under the command of Colonel John Donelson, and the two leaders, Robertson and Donelson, named the fort in honor of Francis Nash, a Revolutionary War general, who died at the Battle of Germantown three years earlier. This remarkable fort, which has been entirely reconstructed, was built without a nail, with hinges, latches, and blinds fashioned from wood. The clapboard was held in place by the weight of parallel logs, held apart by "spacers." The black locust-wood structure consisted of a palisade, two blockhouses, cabins connected by "dog-trots," or breezeways, puncheon floors and handmade furniture. The reconstructed fort at 1st Avenue N. and Church Street is maintained by the City of Nashville.

Two other early forts in the vicinity were **FORT UNION,** at Spring Hill Cemetery, Nashville, built also in 1780, and **FORT DUNHAM,** west of Nashville. Fort Dunham is on the site where stands the Belle Meade Home, one of the most famous horse-breeding farms in America. John Harding built the fort in 1798.

FORT LOUDOUN, southwestern outpost of the English in Colonial America and the first important English-built structure in the Tennessee Valley, was erected in 1757 at the request of the Cherokee Indians three years after the start of the French and Indian War. The fort, built after the European military manner of the mid-eighteenth century, with a bastion at each corner, was located near the mouth of the Tellico River, five miles from the town of Chota, the Cherokee capital. It was named for John Campbell, Fourth Earl of Loudoun, who had just been made commander in chief of British forces in the United States.

Fort Loudoun had a short life. Although the Cherokee were allies of the British at the time of its erection, and asked for protection against French aggression, in 1759 they were influenced by the French to turn on their allies. In 1760, following an incident in which several Indians were killed, the Cherokee laid siege to the fort. The garrison, forced to kill and eat their dogs and horses, surrendered after five months, on August 9, 1760. Chief Oconastota of the Cherokee promised that the white men could march out and make their way to Fort Prince George in South Carolina without molestation. But that night the Indians attacked the camp and killed 4 officers, 23 privates, and 3 women. The others were made prisoners, but later were ransomed. The Cherokee occupied the fort a short time and then burned it.

Today, under the auspices of the Fort Loudoun Association, the fort has partially been restored.

FORT VIRGINIA, built on the north bank of the Little Tennessee River about a mile from Chota, was never garrisoned. It was abandoned when Fort Loudoun was completed on the opposite side of the river.

FORT ASSUMPTION stood on the site of Memphis, the center of the most disputed area in the early settlement of the territory. This historic corner at Auction Avenue and North Front Street is today occupied by the Memphis Dog Pound. Fort Assumption was built by Jean Baptiste le Moyne de Bienville in 1739 on what was then the Lower Chickasaw Bluff, as a base of operations against the Chickasaw Indians. The garrison consisted of some 1,200 men, while double that number of Indians and Negroes are said to have been quartered there.

In 1795 Don Manuel Gayoso de Lemos, a Spaniard, erected **FORT SAN FERNANDO DE LAS BARRANCAS** on the ruins of Fort Assumption. The fort was named for the Prince of the Austrias with the added Spanish word *barrancas,* which meant broken ground or hills cut by deep gullies. Two years later the United States Government insisted that Gayoso's fort represented an invasion, and sent Captain Isaac Guion so to notify the Spaniards. By the time Captain Guion arrived, the Spaniards had removed their garrison and re-established it across the Mississippi River.

Captain Guion built a new fort on the site and named it **FORT ADAMS,** after the then President, John Adams. In 1803 Captain Zebulon M. Pike, who three years later was to discover and name Pikes Peak, arrived under orders of General James Wilkinson. Finding a suitable location two miles down the bluff, Pike built **FORT PICKERING,** named for the Secretary of State under Washington. Fort Adams was renamed **FORT PIKE.**

FORT WATAUGA, on the Watauga River near Elizabethton in eastern Tennessee, had an important role in the early history of the state. It was built in 1772 by settlers from Virginia and North Carolina as a protection against Indians. In the same year the Transylvania Treaty with the Cherokee was negotiated at this fort, whereby the Indians agreed to sell the company the land between the Ohio River and the watershed of the Cumberland River. These settlers had met during the spring of 1772 at Elizabethton and formed the Watauga Association, the first compact of its kind west of the Allegheny Mountains. Several years later, during the Cherokee siege of Fort Watauga, Mrs. William Bean, mother of the first white child born in Tennessee, was captured and ordered burned. Nancy Ward, a Cherokee woman known as the "Beloved Woman," saved her life. It was from here that settlers in 1780 moved westward to build Fort Nashborough. Nancy Ward's grave is near Benton. And at Benton, too, is a contemporary fort known simply as **OLD FORT TENNESSEE BLOCKHOUSE.** Although built 12 miles from Benton, the structure has been moved to Benton. It is constructed of hewn pine logs; the upper story has 32 loopholes and the lower 28.

FORT ROBINSON had been built in 1761 near the fording place on the Holston River at what is today Kingsport. Here, as in other parts of eastern Tennessee, the settlers were plagued by Indian troubles. Later, at the beginning of the Revolution, FORT PATRICK HENRY was established on the same site. It was then an outpost of white civilization beyond the mountains. After the battle with the Cherokee in Kingsport in 1776, the Treaty of the Long Island of Holston was made with the Cherokee.

FORT CRAIG, around which the town of Maryville grew, was built by John Craig in 1785. It was a stout little structure enclosed by a stockade covering two acres. Indians were on the warpath once more; though they attacked, they failed to take the fort. Sam Houston as a youth lived here for a time with his widowed mother.

OLD STONE BLOCKHOUSE, at New Providence near the Red River bridge, was built by Colonel Valentine Sevier in 1788. Constructed with massive walls of local limestone, it repulsed an Indian attack on November 11, 1794. During the Civil War the Confederates named it FORT DEFIANCE. FORT BLOUNT, on the east bank of the Cumberland River near Gainsboro, was built as a protection against Indians in 1788. It was named for William Blount, territorial governor.

WHITE'S FORT was built in 1786, at what was later to be termed Knoxville, by Captain James White, a Revolutionary soldier. At the time this was in the State of Franklin, of which General John Sevier was governor. The State of Franklin was short-lived, as North Carolina claimed it and Sevier was arrested for treason. The territory was ceded to the Government in 1789 and became a part of the State of Tennessee. The site of the old fort is near the present Hotel Farragut.

FORT SOUTH WESTPORT was established on the north bank of the Tennessee River in 1792 by John Sevier (who had been freed of his charges of treason) on orders of Governor William Blount. Troops were stationed here to prevent raids by the Cherokee. ISH'S FORT, not far from the present Maryville, was where General Sevier with 300 militiamen defeated 1,000 Indians on their way to attack Knoxville. GILLESPIE'S FORT, near Knoxville, was not so fortunate. Indians captured and burned it after killing 30 men, women, and children. It was afterward known as Burnt Station.

FORT PRUDHOMME, near Henning, was built in 1682 by Robert Sieur de la Salle, on the First Chickasaw bluff near Memphis, and named for his armorer, Pierre Prudhomme. It was not far from here that at the beginning of the Civil War **FORT PILLOW** was erected near the mouth of Coles Creek and the Mississippi River. It was garrisoned by Negro soldiers and Tennessee Unionists who were called "self-made Yankees." On the morning of April 13, 1864, General Nathan Bedford Forrest of the Confederate cavalry captured the fort and massacred the garrison. A congressional committee called what was to become known as the Massacre of Fort Pillow an atrocity. General William Tecumseh Sherman was ordered to investigate, but never did. This fort, originally erected by the Confederates, was named for General Gideon J. Pillow.

FORT DONELSON, a Confederate fortification and now a National Military Park, was built at the start of the Civil War 70 miles down the Cumberland River from Nashville. Named for Colonel John Donelson, who came to Tennessee in 1780, it covered 97 acres with earthworks, rifle pits, and water batteries. General U. S. Grant's capture of this fort on February 16, 1862, was one of the critical events of the war. It gave the conflict a new impetus in the North by permitting Federal troops to occupy a base in Tennes-

see, and it brought discouragement to the South. As the result of the capture of the fort, General Grant was established in the confidence of President Lincoln and was later named to command the campaign in Virginia that ended the war. General Simon B. Buckner, who succeeded General Gideon J. Pillow in command, surrendered 13,500 men, 3,000 horses, and 20,000 muskets.

FORT HENRY, on the east bank of the Tennessee River, twelve miles from Fort Donelson on the Cumberland, was built at the start of the Civil War. Forts Henry and Donelson guarded the two rivers. General Grant captured Fort Henry on February 6, 1862, ten days before he took Fort Donelson.

FORT JOHNSON was the name given Nashville's State Capitol in 1862 when Federal troops surrounded it with a stockade and made it their headquarters. In the same year, Union General James S. Negley erected **FORT NEGLEY** in Nashville. This old fort of stone and iron was restored in 1937 on the site at Chestnut Street and Ridley Boulevard. Its guns opened the Battle of Nashville in December, 1864, when General Thomas Hood unsuccessfully sought to wrest the city from the Federals. During the Reconstruction period the fort was used as a meeting place for the Ku Klux Klan.

FORT GRANGER, at Franklin, was the name given to extensive Union earthworks on a hill. It was named for the commander, General Gordon Granger, who had 8,500 men and 24 pieces of artillery. Here, on November 30, 1864, was fought one of the bloodiest battles of the war. The Confederates lost 6 generals, and in 55 minutes 8,500 men fell.

REDOUBT BRANNAN was built by Union troops in 1863 to protect Murfreesboro against Confederate invasion. These earthworks are well preserved.

The remains of at least two ancient Indian forts are in the state. One is called **OLD STONE FORT,** and is near Manchester at the foot of the Cumberland Plateau near Duck River. The walls are twenty feet thick. Another is the **INDIAN FORTRESS** on a cliff between the Cumberland and Harpeth rivers near Sydney Bluff, north of Nashville.

MISSISSIPPI

Admitted to the Union in 1817 as the twentieth state.

General James Wilkinson, general-in-chief of the United States Army, needed a commanding officer at **FORT ADAMS** on the Mississippi River at what was known as Loftus Heights. He ordered Lieutenant Colonel Thomas Butler, an experienced Revolutionary officer, to take the post.

But with the order to go from New Orleans to Fort Adams was another requirement. Colonel Butler was ordered to cut off his queue. Butler refused, and so began a controversy that raged for several years and ended only in Butler's death and a bizarre act of revenge on the general-in-chief after Butler was placed in his coffin. . . .

It was in 1801 that General Wilkinson issued a general order at Pittsburgh directing that everyone in the army cut his hair short. Officers had been wearing their hair long, braided in a queue in the back with a black rosette at the end. Wilkinson, who cropped his own queue, considered that especially in a southern climate the queue was "a filthy and insalubrious ornament that was inconvenient, expensive and unnecessary."

Much grumbling occurred among the old Revolutionary officers. They used flour and tallow on their hair and braided their queues on slender sticks of wood. Colonel Butler was the last holdout.

"I will not give up my queue!" he stated flatly.

Wilkinson, out of consideration for Butler's age and health and previous war record, was tolerant for a time, but finally he could not put up with Butler's arrogance. Wilkinson had him tried before a court-martial. The court ordered Butler to cut his queue and report to Fort Adams. Still Butler held on to his cherished braid of hair. Wilkinson became furious. He ordered another court-martial, and this one sentenced Butler to a suspension from the army for a year without pay.

But the sentence came too late. Thirteen days earlier, Butler had died of yellow fever. His last act was to instruct his doctor to have a hole cut through his coffin and his queue pulled through so it could be seen by all—and especially by General Wilkinson.

Wilkinson had to get another commander for his fort. He had built Fort Adams in 1798–1799 on a site recommended by Major Isaac Guion, of the 3rd Infantry (the one stationed today at Washington, D.C., as the ceremonial regiment). The fort was named for President John Adams. It had strong earthworks, a magazine, and barracks. Today it is a small farming center of that name, sixty miles below Natchez.

FORT ROSALIE (later called **FORT PANMURE**) was established on the site of present-day Natchez by Governor Bienville in 1716, and named in honor of the Duchess of Pontchartrain. Built on a bluff, it was an irregular pentagon with a bastion fashioned from thick planks, and surrounded by a ditch, or moat. The friendly Natchez Indians supplied the timber and labor. But in 1729 these Indians attacked the fort, killed 237 persons, and captured 227 soldiers and settlers. They left the fort in ruins.

In 1763, by a treaty with France, West Florida, including Mississippi Territory south of the 31st parallel, became an English province. The next year the King extended the boundaries north to the mouth of the Yazoo, including Mississippi settlements. It was not until 1778 that the British rebuilt and garrisoned Fort Rosalie and promptly renamed it Fort Panmure, after the Baron of Panmure. The Spanish next occupied this fort in 1779 when the British surrendered all forts in West Florida, but two years later the people of Natchez rebelled and captured the fort. Three months after this, Spanish troops once more took Fort Panmure. Following treaties with the United States, Spain finally relinquished this territory, and in 1798 the Spanish garrison evacuated Fort Panmure. General Wilkinson arrived to take charge of the forts in this territory.

Today, under the old name of Fort Rosalie, the site of this historic fort is directly in the rear of Rosalie, a square red-brick house built by Peter Little in the early 1800's at the foot of South Broadway in Natchez. The house was taken over as Union headquarters in 1863 and later occupied for a few days by General Ulysses Grant and his family.

FORT DEARBORN was built in 1803 to protect Washington, the capital of Mississippi Territory. Plans were furnished by Secretary of War Henry Dearborn and the fort was named for him. It also was known as **FORT WASHINGTON** and **CANTONMENT WASHINGTON.** It was here that regiments assembled for the Creek War in 1813, and British prisoners were held here for a time following the Battle of New Orleans. All traces of this fort have disappeared.

FORT NOGALES, on Fort Hill in the Vicksburg National Military Park, was built in 1791–1798 as a Spanish stronghold. It was located one and one-half miles below the mouth of the Yazoo River on a high bluff, with twelve cannon facing the Mississippi River and four howitzers in blockhouses in the rear. The Spanish evacuated this fort in 1798 and American troops renamed it **FORT McHENRY,** after the Secretary of War. They abandoned it in a year or so.

Also on Fort Hill in the Vicksburg National Military Park was **FORT MOUNT VIGIE,** as a part of the Spanish military post of Nogales and built in 1791–1798. Four hundred yards to the right and left were two small blockhouses, named respectively **FORT GAYOSO** and **FORT IGNATIUS.**

FORT ST. PETER was built by French missionaries on the Yazoo River where the so-called delta ends, thirty miles from Rolling Fork. In 1729 the Yazoo Indians joined with other hostile tribes and massacred the garrison. During the siege of 1863 this stronghold was called **FORT SNYDER.** A monument south of the bridge spanning the Yazoo River today marks the site of this fort.

FORT DE MAUREPAS, erected in 1699 by Pierre Le Moyne, Sieur d'Iberville, near Biloxi, was the seat of government in French Louisiana until the seat was moved to Fort Louis de la Mobile, Alabama, in 1704. Around this fort began the first settlement in Mississippi. It was strongly built of square logs two to three feet thick, one placed upon the other, with cannon embrasures and musket portholes. A ditch surrounded the fort. Today the site of this fort is on a private estate near Ocean Springs.

OLD SPANISH FORT, at Pascagoula, was built in 1718 when King Louis XIV of France gave the Duchess de Chaumont, one of his favorites, the title to Pascagoula Bay. After the French and Indian War the English were in possession until the Spanish took the territory in 1779. This fort became known simply as Old Spanish Fort. A strongly built structure with walls of oyster shells, moss and mortar that are fifteen to thirty inches thick, its ruins are to be seen today in a pecan grove.

PATTON'S FORT, at Old Winchester, near the Chickasawhay River, was built in 1813 during the Creek Indian War. Ditches of the old stockade still are visible.

FORT MASSACHUSETTS, built on the western tip of Ship Island, a low sandy bar lying between the Gulf of Mexico and Mississippi Sound off Biloxi, was built by the Government just prior to the Civil War. In May, 1861, Union forces partially destroyed the fort to keep it from being occupied by the Confederates. However, the Confederates did occupy the fort for three months, but set fire to it in September. General Benjamin Butler moved in with seven thousand men, and named it Fort Massachusetts for his home state. The unfinished and partially destroyed fort was used as a prison for Confederate soldiers. In 1875 the garrison was withdrawn, and in 1935 the Gulfport American Legion purchased the fort and grounds.

FORT PEMBERTON, a Civil War fort near Greenwood, was built across a narrow neck of land separating the Yazoo and Tallahatchie rivers. Manned by Confederates, it helped delay the fall of Vicksburg. It was not until two months after the war was over that the garrison learned of the fact. The site today is marked by one of the fort's cannon.

FORT ROBINETT was a Civil War stronghold in the town of Corinth. Called a fort, but actually consisting of entrenchments, it was the scene of considerable fighting in October, 1862. The site of the fort is in Confederate Park, maintained by the Corinth Chapter of the Daughters of the Confederacy.

The Midwest States

MICHIGAN

WISCONSIN

ILLINOIS

INDIANA

FT. WILKINS

FT. DE REPENTIGNY
FT. BRADY
FT. DRUMMOND

FT. LA POINTE

FT. MICHILIMACKINAC

FT. GEORGE
FT. MICHILIMACKINAC
FT. MICHILIMACKINAC

FT. LA BAYE
FT. HOWARD

• FT. ST. ANTOINE

WISCONSIN

MICHIGAN

Lake Michigan

FT. SAGINAW •

FT. WINNEBAGO •

FT. ST. JOSEPH •
FT. SINCLAIR •

• FT. SHELBY   • FT. ATKINSON

FT. PONTCHARTRAIN
FT. LERNOULT
FT. WAYNE

FT. DEARBORN
FT. ST. JOSEPH
FT. CHECAGOU

FT. SHERIDAN •

• FT. MIAMI

• FT. ST. JOSEPH

FT. DIXON
T. LOUIS DU ROCHER
ARMSTRONG

FT. PAYNE •

FT. BEANE •

FT. MIAMI
FT. WAYNE

• FT. WILBOURN

INDIANA

• FT. CLARK
FT. CREVE COEUR •
• FT. DOOLITTLE

• FT. OUIATENON

• FT. BENJAMIN HARRISON

ILLINOIS

• FT. HARRISON

• FT. TURMAN
FT. AZATLAN

• JOHN HILL'S FT. • FT. SACKVILLE
• FT. CHILTON
• FT. BRANCH
• FT. DE CHARTRES
• FT. KASKASKIA

SCALE OF MILES

0   50   100   150   200

FT. MASSAC •

165

MICHIGAN

Admitted to the Union in 1837 as the twenty-sixth state.

On the morning of the birthday of King George III, June 4, 1763, the forest and cleared space around **FORT MICHILIMACKINAC** were filled with Indians. They showed a great friendliness for the English, and invited the garrison to watch a game of ball, known as *baggattaway*. It was a gay and exciting scene. Then one of the players, Chief Matchikuis of the Ottawa, caught the ball in his racquet and sent it in a lofty curve over the pickets of the fort. This was the signal for the warriors to rush toward the fort, and in their hands appeared knives and tomahawks that had been concealed on their persons. A bloody massacre ensued. Of the garrison, 21 were killed and 17 captured. This had all been a part of the great Pontiac Conspiracy, by which the powerful Ottawa chief sought to drive the English from former French-held territory in the Northwest. Pontiac did not succeed, and a year later the English were back in Fort Michilimackinac, also called **FORT MACKINAC** and pronounced "Mackinaw."

In 1780–1781 the British moved their garrison at "Old Mackinaw" to Mackinac Island, when they became alarmed by the success of George Rogers Clark in Illinois. After the Revolutionary War they refused to leave Mackinac Island, and remained there until 1796. At the beginning of the War of 1812, they recaptured the island and enlarged the fort, building another fort 325 feet above the waters of the strait, and 168 feet above Fort Mackinac. This they called **FORT GEORGE** in honor of George III. Later the Americans recaptured the island and changed the name of the latter fort to **FORT HOLMES,** in honor of Major Andrew Holmes, who was killed in a futile attempt to recapture the island on August 4, 1814.

Fort Holmes was reconstructed in 1936 by the Works Progress Administration, in accordance with the original design of logs with earth embankments ten feet thick in places. The eastern entrance is flanked by a storehouse and cook shanty, both sunk deep in the

The Griffon *approaching Fort De Buade, 1679*

ground, with only a few feet of log structure showing above ground. Within the U-shaped enclosure is a two-story blockhouse.

The older fort on Mackinac Island, built of local limestone, cemented in place with lime, is as sturdy as when it was erected in 1780. On the massive ramparts are hand-hewn cedar pickets and iron spikes that are exact copies of the originals.

The first **FORT MICHILIMACKINAC** was at St. Ignace, across the Strait from Mackinaw City. It had originally been known as **FORT DE BUADE,** having been built to protect Father Marquette's mission to those parts. It soon became known as Fort Michilimackinac, and was there when La Salle visited St. Ignace in the *Griffon* in 1679. In 1701, Commander Antoine de la Mothe Cadillac moved the garrison to Detroit. On the hill back of Marquette Park in St. Ignace are visible outlines of the ancient earthworks. The fort has been partially restored by Federal funds.

After removal of the garrison from St. Ignace, the second Fort Michilimackinac was built in 1715 on the present site of Mackinaw City. It was abandoned in 1760 by the French after the capitulation of Canada, and the British took over in the following year. Nearly twenty years later the British built the third **FORT MICHILI- MACKINAC** on Mackinac Island, as already shown.

FORT MIAMI was erected on the site of present-day St. Joseph, around 1679, by René Robert Cavelier, Sieur de la Salle. This fort was destroyed, but in 1700 a Jesuit mission and a second fort were built there. For more than half a century the French flag flew over the settlement until the British conquered Canada. In 1763 Chief Pontiac captured the fort and destroyed it.

FORT ST. JOSEPH, at Port Huron, was the second fortified post established by the French fur traders in lower Michigan. It was built in 1686 by Daniel Duluth. The stockade was burned in 1688, and Duluth transferred the garrison of fifty to Fort Michilimackinac. In 1814 **FORT GRATIOT,** named for Captain Charles Gratiot, Chief Engineer for General William Henry Harrison, was built on the site of old Fort St. Joseph to cut off the communications of the Indians with Mackinac. Fort Gratiot was important in the movement of Federal troops during the Black Hawk War, and was occupied off and on until the Civil War. It was abandoned in 1879.

FORT ST. JOSEPH at Niles, the second fort of that name, was built by the French in 1697. This fort later was turned over to the British, and was captured by Pontiac during his uprising. Returned to the British in 1764, it was not garrisoned by them until the Revolution.

FORT PONTCHARTRAIN, a palisade fort about two hundred feet square, was built on the site of Detroit in 1701 when Cadillac, as the first commandant of the French territory, moved the garrison from Fort Michilimackinac. This fortified community was named in honor of the French Minister of Marine, and became an important trading post. In 1760 Major Robert Rogers, of "Rogers' Rangers," received the surrender of Detroit here following the capitulation of Canada. Pontiac besieged it in 1763, and after fifteen months of weary but stubborn resistance the garrison was relieved.

FORT LERNOULT was built at Detroit in 1778, farther up the river from the old stockade, and got its name from its commander, Major Richard Lernoult. He had taken the place of Lieutenant Governor Henry (The Hair-Buyer) Hamilton when the latter went to Vincennes, Indiana. It was called **FORT DETROIT** when General William Hull disgracefully surrendered it to the British on August 16, 1812. General William Henry Harrison recaptured it a little more than a year later and renamed it **FORT SHELBY** in honor of Kentucky's Governor Isaac Shelby, who accompanied Harrison in his victorious campaign. In 1826 the fort was given to the City of Detroit, and in the spring of 1827 the embankments were taken away, the ground leveled, and streets continued over its site. At the Fort Street entrance of the Federal Building in Detroit is a plaque marking the site of old Fort Shelby.

FORT WAYNE, a United States military post, was established in Detroit in 1842 on the Detroit River. It was named for General Mad Anthony Wayne. Built on a bluff overlooking the bend in the river, it occupied sixty-three acres. Michigan troops were mobilized here during the Civil War. The fort was never attacked. It has been restored by the WPA.

FORT DE REPENTIGNY was built in 1751 at Sault Ste. Marie, or "The Soo," by Louis de Gardeur, Sieur de Repentigny, to protect France's fur trade. However, in the following year the British captured the fort and in the same year it was destroyed by fire. The British continued to cling to this territory even after the War of 1812, but in 1823 Lewis Cass, as governor of Michigan, took possession and ordered General Hugh Brady to build **FORT BRADY** at what is South Street and Ryan Avenue today. This brought to an end British rule in The Soo. In 1890 the fort was reconstructed on orders of General Philip Sheridan.

FORT SINCLAIR was built on the site of St. Clair, by Patrick Sinclair, a British officer, in 1765. Sinclair was in charge of transportation of supplies from Detroit to Michilimackinac. The fort was abandoned twenty years later.

FORT DRUMMOND, on Drummond Island, was named for Lieutenant General Sir Gordon Drummond, commander of the lake district for the British. It was built in 1815 after the British lost Mackinac Island under the Treaty of Ghent following the War of 1812. The British never had title to this island, but the United States did not become aware of it until 1922, when the Government assumed control. Ruins of Fort Drummond, called the "Gibraltar of the Great Lakes," stands on the island's southwestern promontory.

British general officer, 1812

FORT SAGINAW, on the west side of the Saginaw River, was built under orders of Governor Lewis Cass when he made a treaty with the Chippewa Indians in 1819. The fort was not garrisoned until 1822, and was abandoned in 1823. Its site is where the Hotel Fordney stands today in Saginaw.

FORT WILKINS was an Army post on Lake Fanny Hooe established in 1844. In 1921 it was bought by Houghton and Keweenaw counties and given to the state for recreational purposes. Today it is Fort Wilkins State Park, and the old fort has been restored.

WISCONSIN

Admitted to the Union as the thirtieth state in 1848.

Two blockhouses had been completed and a third was under construction. The fort at Prairie du Chien, where the Wisconsin River emptied into the Mississippi, had been named **FORT SHELBY** after the governor of Kentucky, Isaac Shelby. The Regular Army troops leaned on their axes and adzes, and said, "Let the British and Indians come!" And come they did on the afternoon of July 17, 1814.

There were 1,500 of the enemy and only 60 American soldiers under Lieutenant Perkins. Colonel McKay, the British commander, sent a demand of surrender to the fort. Lieutenant Perkins refused, and the British and their allies opened fire on this remote outpost in the War of 1812. The fight lasted until the morning of July 20th, when Lieutenant Perkins surrendered on condition that he and his men be given safe conduct down the Mississippi to St. Louis. This was granted. The fort was promptly occupied and named **FORT McKAY,** after the British colonel. The British blew it up at the end of the war.

Fort Shelby had been built after Governor William Clark of the Missouri Territory had visited the place and decided to fortify it to ensure American possession of Prairie du Chien. In 1816, partly because of the demands of John Jacob Astor, the fur trader, a new fort, **FORT CRAWFORD,** named in honor of William H. Crawford,

Secretary of War, was built here. In 1829 the fort was abandoned because of high water, and another was built one mile southeast. The site of this second fort today is occupied by St. Mary's College. The site of the original Fort Shelby is occupied by Villa Louis, a mansion built in 1843 by Hercules L. Dousman, agent of Astor. This is now Dousman Park. An earlier fort was believed to have been built in 1683 at Prairie du Chien by Nicholas Perrot, who had been commandant of the Green Bay district.

At the time Astor requested the building of Fort Crawford, he also asked for a fort at Green Bay, so as to have protection at the two ends of the Fox and Wisconsin rivers waterway. Because Astor's requests had weight with the Government, as he had subscribed millions of dollars to help finance the War of 1812, **FORT HOWARD** was built in 1816 to help protect his fur trade. It was named in honor of General Benjamin Howard. Captain John O'Fallon, a grandson of George Rogers Clark, was a member of the force that built and garrisoned the fort. General Zachary Taylor assumed command in 1817, but in 1818, when Wisconsin became a part of Michigan Territory, military rule ceased here. The fort site is now marked by a white flagpole in Green Bay.

Nicholas Perrot, who had been French commandant of the Wisconsin area for the French, a fur trader who began trade with the Sioux and other tribes, and who worked lead mines in southwestern Wisconsin, built **FORT LA BAYE** at Green Bay in 1684. In 1717 this fort was rebuilt and called **FORT ST. FRANCIS.** In 1761, after the conquest of Canada, Lieutenant James Gorrell occupied the town, rebuilt the old French fort, and named it **FORT EDWARD AUGUSTUS** after the Duke of Kent. The fort was abandoned during the Pontiac Uprising.

Nicholas Perrot, after building Fort La Baye, a year later erected a trading post and stockade in 1685, near what is today Centerville. In 1731 Linctot, a French officer, built a fort on the site and maintained it for five years. This area has now been set aside as Perrot State Park.

Perrot in 1686 erected **FORT ST. ANTOINE** on the shore of Lake Pepin in the name of Louis XIV. Here, three years later, he

held an elaborate ceremony at which he declared that all lands drained by the upper Mississippi River were the possessions of the French Empire.

FORT LA POINTE, on Madelina Island, one of the Apostle Islands in Lake Superior, was built at the present town of La Pointe by the French in 1718. This was the second fort built on the island, the first having been erected by Le Sueur in 1693, but abandoned five years later. The garrison of the second fort was withdrawn in 1759 during the French and Indian War.

FORT WINNEBAGO, east of Portage, was built in 1828 under supervision of Lieutenant Jefferson Davis, later President of the Confederate States of America, to protect white settlers of the region. A rough log building, which was the Surgeon's Quarters, still stands just across the canal from the restored Kinzie Indian Agency House. It was here, a year before the fort was built, that Chief Red Bird of the Winnebago surrendered after an Indian uprising. Red Bird received his name because he wore two stuffed red birds on his shoulders as epaulettes.

FORT ATKINSON, on the site of the present town of Fort Atkinson, was built in 1832 when General Henry Atkinson paused in the pursuit of Chief Black Hawk to erect a stockade with two blockhouses at the confluence of the Rock and Bark rivers.

ILLINOIS

Admitted to the Union in 1818 as the twenty-first state.

On the morning of Saturday, August 15, 1812, Captain Nathan Heald, following orders of General William Hull to evacuate **FORT DEARBORN,** marched out his garrison. With the soldiers went officers, families, and a few settlers. Although an experienced officer,

Captain Heald had misjudged the temper of the supposedly friendly Indians. His party had gone but a short distance down the beach of Lake Michigan on the way to Fort Wayne when the Indians fell upon the men, women, and children, killing all but a small number. One historian has said: "Thus, due to the timidity of General Hull and the bullheadedness of Captain Heald Chicago is indebted to the only military drama in its history."

Fort Dearborn

In the November 7, 1812, issue of *Niles' Weekly Register*, which printed Captain Heald's letter about what was to become known as the "Fort Dearborn Massacre," there is on the same page an account of American prisoners at Quebec. Among those listed, oddly enough, is John Whistler, 17th Infantry, of Detroit. Captain John Whistler, grandfather of the famous American painter, was made prisoner when Hull surrendered Detroit. It was Captain Whistler who, in 1803, built Fort Dearborn on the site of present-day Chicago. It was a crude structure of logs fifteen feet high, enclosing a space large enough to contain a small parade ground, officers' quarters, troop barracks, guardhouse, powder magazines, and two blockhouses, and stood on an eminence on the south side of the Chicago River, between the Wabash Avenue Bridge and the Michigan Avenue Bridge of today.

In the early days the French built **FORT ST. JOSEPH** where Chicago's "Loop" is today. And on a map of 1683 is marked "**FORT CHECAGOU**," which was said to have been abandoned after the French and Indian War. Neither fort was in existence when Fort Dearborn, named for Secretary of War Henry Dearborn, was built.

Following the massacre, the Indians burned Fort Dearborn, and it was not rebuilt until 1816. It fell into disuse after the Black Hawk War and was abandoned in 1837. It was torn down except for a small building in 1857, and this last vestige of Fort Dearborn was destroyed by the Chicago Fire in 1871.

A reproduction of the fort today stands near Lake Michigan at Twenty-sixth Street, nearly three miles south of the original site.

FORT CREVE CŒUR, just below Peoria on the Illinois River, was the second French fort built in the West. It was erected in 1680 after Robert Cavelier de la Salle ascended the Illinois River and made friends with the Peoria Indians. *Creve Cœur,* or "broken heart," was supposed to have commemorated a fort by that name captured by the French in the Netherlands. During La Salle's absence his garrison mutinied and plundered the fort, and raiding Illinois Indians burned the settlement. This area of fourteen acres on the left bank of the river is now a state park, with a granite monument marking the possible site of the old fort.

FORT ST. LOUIS DU ROCHER was built on the summit of Starved Rock on the Illinois River in 1682 by La Salle and Henri de Tonti after the destruction of Fort Creve Cœur. This fort, planned as key to the vast empire of forts and commerce conceived by La Salle, was maintained by De Tonti fifteen years after La Salle's death in 1687. French traders later occupied it until 1721, when it was captured and burned by Indians.

FORT DE CHARTRES, in what is now Fort Chartres State Park, is on the Mississippi River seventeen miles north of Kaskaskia. In its day it was the most formidable of all the French strongholds in the Mississippi Valley. It was built in 1720 by Pierre Duque, Sieur de Broisbriant, and named for the Duc de Chartres, son of the French regent. A new foundation with walls eighteen feet high, enclosing four acres, was built in 1753. Ten years later the French turned the fort over to the British, but in 1772 the British abandoned it because the Mississippi River was washing away the foundations. Today the old fort has been partially restored.

FORT KASKASKIA, in Fort Kaskaskia State Park, a fifty-seven-acre tract, was erected in 1733 and rebuilt three years later with the aid of a special grant from the French Crown. The British took over this fort in 1763 after the conquest of Canada, and renamed it FORT GAGE, after Major-General Thomas Gage, who that year became commander in chief of British forces in America. At the start of his Northwest campaign, George Rogers Clark captured the fort on July 4, 1778. It was renamed FORT CLARK, but its original name later was restored.

FORT MASSAC, in what is now Fort Massac State Park on the Ohio River, was built by the French in 1759 and first named FORT ASCENSION. Later it was rechristened FORT MASSIAC in honor of the then French Minister of Marine. After the conquest of Canada, the Cherokee Indians destroyed the fort. Washington ordered General (Mad) Anthony Wayne to rebuild it, and he called it Fort Massac, which many believed was short for "Massacre," but was the American corruption of *Massiac*. This fort was in ruins in 1778 when George Rogers Clark passed it on his way to capture Kaskaskia. The outside walls originally measured 135 feet each, with bastions at each angle. The walls were palisaded with earth between the wood. Scarcely recognizable bastions and ditches remain on the site of the old fort. A statue of George Rogers Clark by Leon Harnant stands in the center of the ruins.

Several small forts were erected in Illinois during the War of 1812. One was at St. Jacob, east of St. Louis, and was known as FORT CHILTON. Another, FORT CLARK, also named for George Rogers Clark, was at Peoria, at Liberty and Water streets. JOHN HILL'S FORT was built in Carlyle, six blocks south of the present courthouse. As late as 1833 people were digging around the area of the fort, trying to find the body of a young man who had been killed and buried in the vicinity. His mother was supposed to have sewed $5,000 in his clothing.

FORT WILBOURN, erected during the Black Hawk War on the south side of the Illinois River across from Peru, was the mustering place of the Illinois volunteers. Here on June 16, 1832, Abraham Lincoln enlisted as a private in Jacob N. Early's Company. Lincoln was chosen captain of a company, but his company did not see service. Leonard Crunelle's statue showing him as a captain stands in a park in Dixon, the site of **FORT DIXON. FORT DOOLITTLE** at Pekin was a schoolhouse that was fortified during the Black Hawk War. **FORT PAYNE,** built at Naperville in 1832, during the same war, is now the site of Fort Hill Campus of North Central College.

FORT SHERIDAN, an Army post of 725 acres on the wooded bluffs of Lake Michigan, north of Chicago, was used first as a camp in the Spanish-American War and is now headquarters of the 5th Army Corps. It was named for General Philip Sheridan.

FORT ARMSTRONG, on Rock Island across from Davenport, Iowa, was built in 1816. This area had been a battleground in the War of 1812, and there was considerable activity there during the Black Hawk War. Formerly it had been a trading center for the American Fur Company. Today the United States Arsenal and Armory are located there. A reconstructed blockhouse near the end of Government Bridge over the Mississippi marks the site of the fort.

INDIANA

Admitted to the Union in 1816 as the nineteenth state.

At exactly ten o'clock Thursday morning, February 25, 1779, **FORT SACKVILLE** was formally surrendered to the Americans. The red cross of St. George was lowered on the flagstaff, and as the drummer boy rolled his drum, George Rogers Clark, with his men and the townspeople, watched with pride as the Stars and Stripes were run up. A great cheer arose from Frenchmen and Americans alike.

After an incredible journey in midwinter from Kaskaskia to Vincennes, Clark had broken British power in the Northwest by his capture of Fort Sackville. Lieutenant Governor Henry Hamilton, known as "The Hair-Buyer" because it was said he purchased the scalps of colonists from the Indians, was made a prisoner.

The fort at Vincennes had been built around 1713 by Jean Sacqueville, a French fur trader and soldier of the Detroit Fur Company, some years before the settlement was named for Francis Morgane, Sieur de Vincennes. The English called it "Sackville" when they acquired it under the Treaty of Paris in 1763. After George Rogers Clark captured it, he renamed it **FORT PATRICK HENRY,** in honor of the governor of Virginia.

Today on the site of the old fort is the George Rogers Clark Memorial, erected by the Federal Government in 1931–1932 at a cost of $1,500,000, and dedicated by President Franklin Delano Roosevelt.

FORT OUIATENON, four miles below the site of the present-day Lafayette, is thought to have been built a few years after Fort Sackville, and is believed to have been, with the latter fort, one of a chain of fortifications envisioned years before by La Salle to protect the interests of the French fur trade. The fort, built at what was then called Wea Town (Ouiatenon), a settlement of Wea (Ouia) Indians, was garrisoned by the French until the end of the French and Indian War. During Pontiac's war the British garrison was captured. Fort Ouiatenon became primarily an Indian meeting place, and in June, 1791, during the Indian Uprising, General Charles Scott destroyed not only this place but upper Ouiatenon, or Kethtippecanuck (Tippecanoe), which later was known as Prophet's Town. It was here that Tecumseh's brother, the Prophet, had his headquarters.

In 1930 a blockhouse was erected on the site of the old fort, on the hill overlooking the Wabash River.

FORT MIAMI, at Fort Wayne, was the third of the French forts to fit in with the earlier plans of La Salle. It was built in 1722 as a "new fort" on the site of an earlier one on the east bank of St. Marys River. This fort was burned by Indians in 1748, then rebuilt on the east bank of the St. Joseph River. The French were forced to give it up after the conquest of Canada in 1763. It was then garrisoned by the British, only to be temporarily lost to followers of Chief Pontiac. According to legend, the British commandant, Ensign Robert Holmes, was lured from the stockade by his Indian sweetheart. He was slain and his head displayed to the garrison by the Indians. The garrison surrendered.

The British later recaptured the fort but finally discontinued the garrison. The site of the fort at what was then Miami Town is today indicated by a marker at Delaware Street and St. Joseph Boulevard on the east bank of the St. Joseph River.

FORT WAYNE, on the site of Fort Wayne, was built by Anthony (Mad Anthony) Wayne in 1794 across the St. Marys River from Miami Town and the ruins of old Fort Miami. Fort Wayne, which stood on the top of a hill overlooking the river, was in the form of a square with a blockhouse at two opposite corners. The important Treaty of Fort Wayne was ratified here September 30, 1809, by chiefs of the Miami, Wea, and Delaware tribes. William Henry Harrison, governor of Indiana Territory, bought, for $10,000 and a small annuity, 3,000,000 acres between the Wabash and White rivers. The northern boundary of this tract was the famous "Ten o'Clock Line," so called because the Indians insisted this line be determined by the shadow cast from the stick in the ground at 10:00 A.M. on the day of signing. The line ran roughly from the mouth of Raccoon Creek in the Wabash southeast to a point near Vallonia in Jackson County. However, the treaty was broken when the War of 1812 started and the Indians under Tecumseh tried unsuccessfully to capture Fort Wayne. Eventually the city was named for the fort, the site of which is designated by a marker at the northwest corner of Clay and Berry streets.

FORT HARRISON, on the highlands of Terre Haute overlooking the Wabash River, was built in 1811 by General William Henry Harrison during his campaign in 1811 against the Prophet, brother of Tecumseh. Harrison at the Battle of Tippecanoe destroyed Prophet's Town, a rendezvous for Indians who were being incited against the United States by the Prophet and Tecumseh. The Indians under Tecumseh a year later attacked both Fort Wayne and Fort Harrison. The latter fort, ably defended by Captain Zachary Taylor, was partially burned, but the Indians were eventually beaten off when the garrison was relieved by Kentucky troops. For his defense of the fort Captain Taylor was brevetted a major, the first time this privilege had been conferred on an officer of the United States Army. A brevet rank was one higher than that for which pay was received, and was a military honor. It is interesting to note that Harrison who built this fort and Taylor who defended it both later became Presidents of the United States.

A country club now stands on the site of this fort. The fort was 150 feet square with a two-story blockhouse at each corner. The second story of each blockhouse projected so the sides of the fort could be protected by rifle fire. Between the blockhouses were barracks, and on the east side of the fort was a gate.

FORT TURMAN, or **TIERMAN,** at Sullivan, was an outpost where General Harrison issued regimental orders on his northward march to the Battle of Tippecanoe. **FORT BRANCH,** near Princeton, also was built in 1811. The stockade stood a half mile west of a present-day five-foot limestone monument. Nearby off Highway State 64 is the town of Fort Branch.

FORT BEANE, on whose site is Goshen, was a refuge of white settlers in the early Indian troubles. The place of the old fort is marked by a stone tablet just south of the Goshen High School.

FORT AZATLAN, near Merom in Sullivan County on the Wabash River, is believed to be defense works of the Mound Builders. It consists of an irregular three-sided enclosure with a circumference estimated at 2,450 feet. Inside are to be found 5 mounds and some 45 pits that are believed to be foundation sites of buildings.

FORT BENJAMIN HARRISON, at Indianapolis, was established in 1903 as a United States Army Post. It has a reservation of 2,030 acres.

The North Central States

NORTH DAKOTA

MINNESOTA

NEBRASKA

SOUTH DAKOTA

IOWA

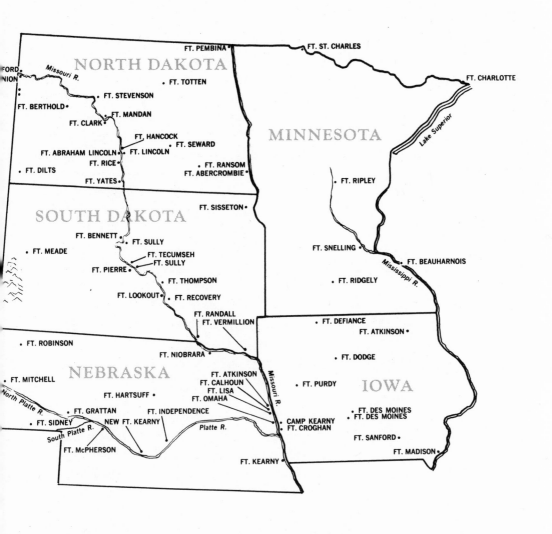

NORTH DAKOTA

FORD.
NION.

Missouri R.

FT. PEMBINA •

• FT. ST. CHARLES

FT. CHARLOTTE

• FT. TOTTEN

• FT. STEVENSON

FT. BERTHOLD •

• FT. MANDAN

FT. CLARK •

FT. HANCOCK

FT. ABRAHAM LINCOLN •• • FT. SEWARD
• FT. LINCOLN

FT. RICE •

• FT. DILTS

FT. YATES •

FT. RANSOM •
FT. ABERCROMBIE •

MINNESOTA

Lake Superior

SOUTH DAKOTA

FT. SISSETON •

FT. RIPLEY

FT. BENNETT •
• FT. SULLY

• FT. MEADE

FT. TECUMSEH
FT. SULLY

FT. PIERRE •

• FT. THOMPSON

FT. LOOKOUT • • FT. RECOVERY

FT. RANDALL
FT. VERMILLION

FT. SNELLING •

FT. BEAUHARNOIS

Mississippi R.

• FT. RIDGELY

• FT. ROBINSON

FT. NIOBRARA •

• FT. DEFIANCE

FT. ATKINSON •

• FT. DODGE

NEBRASKA

FT. ATKINSON
FT. CALHOUN
FT. LISA
FT. OMAHA

Missouri R.

• FT. PURDY

IOWA

• FT. MITCHELL

FT. HARTSUFF •

• FT. SIDNEY

North Platte R.

FT. GRATTAN

FT. INDEPENDENCE

NEW FT. KEARNY

South Platte R.

FT. McPHERSON

Platte R.

CAMP KEARNY
FT. CROGHAN

• FT. DES MOINES
FT. DES MOINES

FT. SANFORD •

FT. KEARNY •

FT. MADISON •

SCALE OF MILES

0   50   100   150   200

185

NORTH DAKOTA

Admitted to the Union in 1889 as the thirty-ninth state.

The band played "The Girl I Left Behind Me," wives and sweethearts waved good-bye, and the men of the 7th United States Cavalry marched out of Fort Abraham Lincoln, guidons fluttering in the breeze, General George Armstrong Custer at their head. This was on the morning of May 17, 1876. General Custer, known to the Indians as "Yellow Hair," because of his long wavy locks, was going to teach the Sioux a lesson. There came days of anxious waiting at the fort. Then, at midnight, July 5, the steamer *Far West* docked with the wounded men from the command of Major Marcus A. Reno, who had been cut off in the battle at Little Big Horn on June 28. Upon inquiries as to what had happened to Custer and his men, Captain Grant Marsh of the steamer sadly shook his head. He said: "A Crow Indian came on board, and when I asked him about Custer he kneeled down and drew a group of dots on the deck. He then made the signal for white horse-soldiers. Around the dots he drew a circle of dots and made the sign for Sioux. With a swipe of his hand he wiped out the center dots." This was the first news of the annihilation of Custer's command of 267 men by the Sioux under Sitting Bull.

FORT ABRAHAM LINCOLN had been built on the west bank of the Missouri River below Bismarck in 1872 mainly for the protection of surveyors and construction workers on the Northern Pacific Railroad. It took in a smaller fort named **FORT McKEEN** for Colonel Henry Boyd McKeen, killed in the Civil War, and built the same year. The site for Fort McKeen had been selected where the Mandan Indians had founded their fortified town, known as Slant Village, two hundred years before.

Shortly after the building of Fort McKeen on the heights, the name was changed to Fort Abraham Lincoln, which was constructed on the banks below nearer the mouth of the Heart River. The fort was no longer of use after the completion of the railroad in 1883, but was not abandoned until 1891. Today the ruins are to be found in the state park. Blockhouses of Fort McKeen have been restored, as well as several Mandan earth lodges.

FORT ABERCROMBIE was built in 1857 as the first permanent military post in North Dakota. It was on the Red River thirty-two miles south of Fargo and the town of Abercrombie grew up around it. This fort was termed the "Gateway to the Dakotas," for settlers passing through on the way to the plains of the Northwest. The fort, named for Lieutenant Colonel John J. Abercrombie, was besieged for five weeks during the Sioux uprising in Minnesota in 1862. The fort had no stockade at the time of the initial attack by Indians, but when reinforcements arrived from Fort Snelling in Minnesota a heavy oak-log stockade with three blockhouses was built, enclosing ten acres. The fort was abandoned in 1877. The blockhouses and part of the stockade have been rebuilt. The site is owned by the State Historical Society.

Fort Abercrombie

FORT RICE, south of Mandan, on the west bank of the Missouri River, was established by General Alfred H. Sully on his Indian expedition in 1864. It was built of cottonwood logs, adobe lined. For many years it was one of the most important posts on the upper Missouri, enabling military authorities to keep hostile Indians in check and protecting river transportation. Four years after it was built, it was the scene of a peace conference with the Sioux that

Cavalryman, 1875

eventually led to the Fort Laramie Treaty—a treaty that was violated in 1875 by the Indian Bureau and War Department and resulted in Custer's tragic battle. In 1877 this fort was succeeded by Fort Yates down the river. The site of Fort Rice today is maintained by the State Historical Society, and two of the blockhouses have been restored.

FORT YATES, on the site of the present town of Fort Yates, was completed in 1878 to succeed Fort Rice, a few miles up the Missouri River. It was named for Captain George Yates of the 7th Cavalry, who was killed at the Battle of Little Big Horn. Fort Yates was headquarters of the Standing Rock Indian Agency. It was here on December 15, 1890, that Sitting Bull, who had led the attack against Custer and was then chief exponent of the "Ghost Dance" religion, was killed by Indian police when he was said to have resisted arrest. He was buried at Fort Yates. Later his bones were dug up by Gray Eagle and his band from Bullhead, South Dakota, and transferred to Mobridge, South Dakota, where they remain. Fort Yates was abandoned in 1895 when **FORT LINCOLN** was authorized about two miles south of Bismarck. Fort Lincoln was not garrisoned, however, until 1903, and was not a fort in the strict sense of the word. It is not to be confused with Fort Abraham Lincoln.

FORT UNION, built at the mouth of the Yellowstone River in 1829 by John Jacob Astor's American Fur Company, was for almost forty years one of the most important posts in the Northwest. It has a thrilling history. It was here that the first steamboat to navigate the Missouri, the *Yellowstone,* made a trip in 1832. This ten-acre area has been designated by the National Park Service as a National Historic Landmark. The site, owned by the State Historical Society, preserves only the area of the sutler's cabin and some of the center of the fort itself.

General Alfred Sully, after a visit to the fort in the 1860's, recommended Government control of this and other trading posts because of drunkenness and trouble with the Indians.

Thus **FORT BUFORD,** named for General John Buford who distinguished himself at Gettysburg, was built in 1866 across the river from the mouth of the Yellowstone. It not only supplanted Fort Union, but materials from this fort were purchased by the Government and brought down to build Fort Buford. It was at Fort Buford that Sitting Bull and Gall surrendered in 1881 after their flight to Canada following the Custer battle. In 1895 the fort was abandoned. Today the State Historical Society has control of a portion of the old Fort Buford site, including the officers' quarters, powder house, and military cemetery.

FORT RANSOM, on the west bank of the Sheyenne River near the present town of Fort Ransom, was built in 1867 by General A. H. Terry and named for General Thomas Ransom, a Civil War officer. This fort was one of a chain of forts for the protection of immigrants crossing the plains. It was constructed of log buildings, surrounded by a palisade and two blockhouses. The fort was abandoned in 1872 when the Northern Pacific Railroad reached Jamestown. The site was acquired by the State Historical Society.

FORT SEWARD, near the city of Jamestown on the James River, was built in 1872 as the frontier moved westward. It not only took the place of Fort Ransom, but materials from the latter fort were used in its construction. The fort was first called **CAMP SYKES,** then **FORT CROSS,** and finally Fort Seward for Lincoln's Secretary of State, William H. Seward. The fort was abandoned in 1877, and in 1925 the site was donated by the Northern Pacific Railway as a state park.

FORT STEVENSON, at the mouth of Garrison Creek on the Missouri River, was built in 1864 after General Alfred H. Sully had selected the site. It was named for Brigadier General Thomas G. Stevenson. The fort was abandoned in 1883 and the military reservation was turned over to the Indian Department. For a short time the buildings were used as a school for Indian children of the Fort Berthold Agency.

FORT BERTHOLD itself had been a trading post of the American Fur Company, built in 1845 and named in honor of the founder, Bartholomew Berthold, a Tyrolese. General Sully had stationed troops here until Fort Stevenson was established.

FORT TOTTEN, on the south shore of Devils Lake, where the town and Indian reservation of the same name are now located, was established as an Indian post in 1867. It was named for Major General Joseph Gilbert Totten, former chief of the United States Army Engineer Corps, who had died three years earlier. This fort was built of logs that were later replaced by bricks made on the spot. As a result it is today in a fine state of preservation and is in a historic park established and operated by the North Dakota Historical Society.

FORT DILTS, a sod-wall fort built in 1864 by an immigrant party under Captain James L. Fisk, is preserved as a historic site by the State Historical Society. It was named for a scout of the expedition who was killed by the Sioux in their attack on the stronghold. The besieged party were saved by troops from Fort Rice. This spot is not far from the town of Rhame.

FORT MANDAN, fourteen miles west of the town of Washburn, on the north bank of the big bend in the Missouri, was built by Lewis and Clark in the winter of 1804–1805 when they paused here on their way to the Pacific. It was here that they were joined by Sacajawea, or the Bird Woman, a Shoshone captive of the Mandan

Indians. Warring Sioux destroyed the fort after Lewis and Clark's departure, and later, because of changes in the channel of the river, the site was inundated. However, a marker has been placed on the east side of the river at what is believed to be the site.

FORT CLARK, on the site of the present village of Fort Clark, was established in 1829 by the American Fur Company. It apparently was just across the river from the site of Fort Mandan, and was named for William Clark of the Lewis and Clark Expedition. The site of this fort, in its time second only to Fort Union, is owned by the State Historical Society.

FORT PEMBINA was established in the spring of 1870 at the confluence of the Red and Pembina rivers on the northern boundary of the state. General Winfield S. Hancock, in his annual report of November 1, 1870, said the fort was necessary because of "the existence of internal revolutionary disturbances in the 'Red River Settlement' of the British province of Manitoba" and as a protection against the hostile Sioux "driven from Minnesota and Dakota in the outbreak of 1862." The small fort served its purpose well in suppressing two attempts to raid Canada from American soil by the so-called Fenian Society, a political association of Irish and Irish-Americans organized for the overthrow of British authority in Ireland as well as in Canada. The fort stood on the site of the

Sioux

present-day town of Pembina. It was abandoned in 1895, and the fort and military reservation were sold at auction April 2, 1902.

CAMP HANCOCK, also known as **FORT HANCOCK,** was built in 1873 on the present site of Bismarck. One of the original log buildings still stands and is the oldest building in Bismarck. Since 1950 an exhibit of transportation has been held here, including an old-time locomotive of the Northern Pacific Railway.

MINNESOTA

Admitted to the Union in 1858 as the thirty-second state.

Men, women, and children from the surrounding country flocked into Fort Ridgely on Monday, August 18, 1862. Arms were passed out to those of the men who seemed capable of handling them. Only twenty-two soldiers of the fort were fit for active duty.

The refugees brought tales of murder and desolation. The Sioux were on the warpath. Little Crow, their leader, had gone to war, it was said, because the $71,000 annuity the Government owed the Indians had been delayed. The Indians claimed they were starving.

On the very day word of the uprising reached Fort Ridgely on the Minnesota River in Nicollet County, and the settlers began to swarm into the fort, five men arrived from Saint Paul with a heavy keg. This contained the $71,000 in gold.

The Indians, a thousand strong, attacked the fort two days later, on August 20. The next day it rained and all was quiet, but on August 22 the Indians again attacked and once more were repulsed. Little Crow withdrew his warriors, and they began a widespread massacre throughout the state. It was one of the bloodiest and most terrible in the annals of Indian warfare.

Had it been possible to inform Little Crow of the gold that was in the fort at the time of his attack, this might have saved the lives of a thousand white people, yet some historians claim that payment of the annuity would not have stopped him. The uprising was believed to have been fomented by Confederate agents, and the Indians, realizing that the state was being drained of young men for the Union Army, thus seized on the chance to settle old scores with the whites.

Arapaho

Three hundred Indians involved in this uprising were later sentenced to death, but President Lincoln commuted the sentences of all but thirty-eight, who were executed in a mass hanging at Mankato, the day after Christmas, 1862.

FORT RIDGELY was established in 1853, and named by Jefferson Davis, Secretary of War in 1854, to honor three Maryland Army officers who died in the Mexican War: Captains Randolph Ridgely and Thomas P. Ridgely, and Lieutenant Henderson Ridgely. The site of this old fort is now a State Park. The stone commissary building, which was the main refuge for some three hundred settlers, has been reconstructed.

FORT SNELLING, for more than three decades one of the most important military outposts in Indian country, was established in 1820 at the junction of the Minnesota and Mississippi rivers, seven miles from St. Paul and eight miles southeast of Minneapolis. While this spot was well known to early fur traders and explorers, in 1805 title to the land was said to have been obtained from the Sioux by Lieutenant Zebulon Pike for sixty gallons of whiskey. In 1819 Colonel Josiah Snelling began construction of **FORT ST. ANTHONY** at the present site on the bluffs overlooking the two rivers. In 1825 the name of the fort was changed to honor Colonel Snelling, builder and commanding officer.

Fort Snelling

While Fort Snelling never saw active service, it had an active existence as a distribution point for those military posts that were in conflict with the enemy during the various Indian wars. The fort was the headquarters of the campaign against the Sioux during their outbreak in 1862.

Today 590 acres of the original reservation of more than 2,000 acres are owned by the United States and administered by the Veterans Administration. This area contains the site of most of the fort, where stand 4 of the original 16 buildings. The fort structure as seen from the Mississippi River is an irregularly shaped bastion wall conforming in outline to the 300-foot high plateau of land upon which it is situated. The buildings standing are the quarters of the commanding officer, the officers' quarters, the hexagonal tower, and the round tower. The two towers are the earliest structures of pioneer days still there. Both are built of native limestone. In 1937 the round tower was converted into a museum of the Minnesota State Historical Society.

FORT RIPLEY, on the east bank of the Mississippi River where the town of Fort Ripley is today, was built in 1849–1850 and occupied until 1878. Established first under the name of **FORT GAINES** as a protection against Indians, it gave safety to settlers during the 1862 Sioux uprising. When the Chippewa Indians joined the Sioux, a Chippewa Indian named Bad Boy, who had refused to join his tribesmen, notified the fort of the approaching danger. Howitzers were placed in the blockhouses of the fort, but the Indians never attacked. Only the ruins of the powder magazine remain today. The site is now included in the 20,000 acres of the National Guard cantonment, Camp Ripley.

FORT BEAUHARNOIS, established as the first Christian mission on Minnesota soil in 1727 by Michel Guignas and Nicolas de Gonnor. This fort, which lasted only a few years, was not far from Frontenac Station on Sand Point, a spit of gravel jutting into Lake Pepin.

FORT CHARLOTTE on the Portage Trail, an overland passage of nine miles from Lake Superior to Pigeon River, was another eighteenth-century fort and trading post. **FORT ST. CHARLES,** on the southern shore of Lake of the Woods of the Northwest Angle Inlet, is another.

NEBRASKA

Admitted to the Union in 1867 as the thirty-seventh state.

It was bitter cold outside the barracks at Fort Robinson on the night of January 9, 1879. No one at the fort thought that the small band of northern Cheyenne Indians held prisoners there would try to escape. But the Indians, who had made their way from their hated reservation in Indian Territory, outmaneuvering and outfighting hundreds of American soldiers before they were captured and confined to the fort, were ready to die in an effort to regain their freedom. The Government had ordered them taken back to their reservation the next day.

So on this night, at a signal from their chief, Dull Knife, they began assembling their weapons. Instead of surrendering their arms when captured, they had taken the guns apart and concealed some under blankets, while children had worn bracelets and necklaces of hammers, firing pins, and other small gun parts. The parts were put together, and then the Cheyenne made their break for liberty.

At the first alarm the soldiers began to shoot them down—men, women, and children. Their bodies fell, staining the snow with blood. Some managed to get away but were rounded up and brought back. Only a few, including Chief Dull Knife, eluded the soldiers and escaped to make their way back to their old home in South Dakota. Thus ended one of the saddest sagas of the American Indian—the last fight of the Cheyenne for their birthright. It was their final hopeless struggle to roam the prairies and forests once more, instead of being confined on a reservation.

FORT ROBINSON had been built at the junction of the White River and Soldier Creek near the present town of Crawford in 1874. It was named for Lieutenant Levi H. Robinson, who had been killed by Indians near Fort Laramie that same year. Located in the heart of the Indian country near the Red Cloud Agency, it played an important part in the tragic drama of the Cheyenne and Sioux nations. For five years it was the scene of much excitement. The battles of Powder River, Tongue River, Slim Buttes, the Rosebud, Little Big Horn, Mackenzie's fight with the Cheyenne near Crazy Woman's Fork, and General Miles at Wolf Mountain all had their effect on Fort Robinson. It was here that Crazy Horse, the Oglala chief, surrendered and was bayoneted to death in April, 1877.

To the end of its active career as a military post, the fort continued to render important service. It was abandoned in 1947. The vast reservation, which covers some 21,404 acres in Dawes and Sioux counties, is owned by the Government and administered by the United States Department of Agriculture. The State Historical Society leases about 30 acres.

FORT ATKINSON, on the Missouri River sixteen miles above the present city of Omaha, was established in 1820 as the first military stronghold in Nebraska Territory. The town by the same name also was the first in the Territory. A temporary post known as Camp Missouri had been built near the site a year before. Soldiers under General Henry Atkinson moved more than a mile to the commanding top of Council Bluff and built Fort Atkinson. In 1825 the treaty of Fort Atkinson was signed here, whereby the Pawnee Indians acknowledged the supremacy of the Federal Government. The fort was abandoned in 1827. The town of Fort Calhoun was established nearby in 1854–1855, and the brick and stone of the ruins of old Fort Atkinson were used by settlers to build their homes.

FORT CALHOUN is opposite Council Bluffs on the Iowa side of the river. Some historians say that Lewis and Clark had a council with the Oto and Winnebago Indians on the Nebraska side in 1804. Others say this council was on the Iowa side.

FORT LISA, named for Spanish-born Manuel Lisa, called the "founder of old Nebraska," was built as headquarters for the Missouri Fur Company in 1812, some ten miles above Omaha. Lisa's wife spent the winter of 1819 in the fort, and was believed to have been the first white woman in Nebraska. The site of this fort is north of the northeast entrance of Hummel Park in Omaha.

FORT KEARNY, on the west bank of the Missouri River where Nebraska City now stands, was built in 1847 as a blockhouse and abandoned the next year. The fort was named for General Stephen Watts Kearny.

NEW FORT KEARNY was built in June, 1848, some 160 miles west of the old fort site, on the Platte River near the town of Kearney. This was done to afford more protection to emigrants moving along the Oregon Trail. Lieutenant Daniel P. Woodbury, with 175 men, used sun-dried adobe bricks in part of the construction of the new fort. Two corner blockhouses were built of heavy timber. The fort was manned during the Civil War and also during the building of the Union Pacific Railroad. It was abandoned in 1871 and is now Fort Kearny State Park covering 80 acres. The town and county are erroneously spelled "Kearney," and are so shown on maps and official records.

FORT McPHERSON, located on the south side of the Platte River just southeast of North Platte, was built to protect emigrants and stagecoaches on the Oregon Trail. The fort, erected in 1863 on the bluffs overlooking the narrowest part of the river and commanding the entire valley, was first named **FORT McKEAN** in honor of Major Thomas J. McKean, commanding officer of that territory. In 1864 it was called **FORT COTTONWOOD,** from Cottonwood Springs where it was located. In 1866 it became known as Fort McPherson, in honor of Major General James P. McPherson.

This fort was the center of community life for the surrounding country. The Grand Duke Alexis of Russia visited there in 1872, and Buffalo Bill Cody, with one hundred Indians, escorted him on a buffalo hunt. It was headquarters of Major Frank North and his famous Pawnee Scouts. These Indians, who stripped to their breechclouts during battle, at other times cut the seats out of the pants of their uniforms so they could ride better. Kit Carson and many other famous people came to this fort.

In 1873 the fort's burial ground became a national cemetery. Bodies were transferred there from the burial grounds of twenty western Army posts. Spotted Horse, noted Pawnee scout, and twenty-seven soldiers, who with Lieutenant John Grattan were killed near Fort Laramie by the Sioux, were buried here. The fort was abandoned in 1887. In the Lincoln County courthouse at North Platte are to be found many relics of this fort.

FORT GRATTAN, at the mouth of Ash Hollow on the North Platte River, was a fort built of sod in 1855. It was named in honor of the above-mentioned Lieutenant Grattan, killed by the Sioux near Fort Laramie when he tried to get back a Mormon's cow. This fort was abandoned the same year.

FORT MITCHELL was established on the Oregon Trail on the North Platte River, at what is today Mitchell, as an outpost of Fort Laramie, Wyoming. This was originally **CAMP SHUMAN** named for a Captain Shuman, but was later named for General Robert Mitchell, commander of the district.

Fort Mitchell

FORT INDEPENDENCE was built, in what is Grand Island on the Oregon Trail, by William Stolley in 1864. Stolley raised a home-made American flag above his stronghold, which was a log structure 24 feet to a side, with 25 loopholes, and heavily banked with sod as a protection against Indians' flaming arrows. Some of the timbers of the old fort have been used to build structures in the present-day Stolley State Park.

FORT SIDNEY, near the town of Sidney, was built in 1867 for protection of the construction workers of the Union Pacific Rail-road. It was named for Sidney Dillon, New York solicitor for the railroad. It was at first a subpost of Fort Sedgwick in Colorado, but was made an independent post in 1870. This fort was maintained until the Indian wars were at an end in 1894.

FORT OMAHA was built in 1868 at what is now Thirtieth Street between Fort Street and Laurel Avenue in Omaha. It was called **SHERMAN BARRACKS** in honor of Lieutenant General William Tecumseh Sherman, but soon afterward it was named **OMAHA BARRACKS** and finally Fort Omaha.

FORT HARTSUFF was built on the north side of the Loup River, seventy-six miles from Grand Island, in 1874, to protect settlers from the Sioux Indians. It was abandoned in 1881. **FORT NIOBRARA** was built on the south bank of the Niobrara River in 1880, not far from Valentine. It is today in the Niobrara Game Preserve.

SOUTH DAKOTA

Admitted to the Union in 1889 as the fortieth state.

In the fall of 1817 a French fur trader, Joseph La Framboise, came overland from Prairie du Chien in Wisconsin Territory and stopped at the mouth of the Bad River on the Missouri River. Because this looked like a good place for a fort and trading post, he and his men erected one from driftwood. Thus began the first permanent white settlement within the present border of the State of South Dakota, across from the site of the present city of Pierre.

Some say this fort was called **FORT LA FRAMBOISE,** and others said it was **FORT TETON,** as the Bad River also was called the Teton River. But five years later, when Joseph Renville's Columbia Fur Company rebuilt the fort, it was named **FORT TECUMSEH** for the great Shawnee who was killed in the War of 1812. In 1831 the first steamboat on the upper Missouri, the *Yellowstone,* ascended the river to Fort Tecumseh, and the following year Pierre Choteau, Jr., who was to acquire John Jacob Astor's western interests of the America Fur Company, built **FORT PIERRE CHOTEAU,** which became known in time as **FORT PIERRE,** and thus gave its name to the city.

Fort Pierre

In 1855 the Government bought the fort, and General William S. Harney moved in 1,200 troops. In the following year he met with many troublesome Sioux here and made what was known as the

Harney Treaty. In 1865 a treaty was made at this fort that settled the War of the Outbreak, or the aftermath of the Sioux Uprising in Minnesota in 1862. The Sioux had continued to give trouble after being removed to Dakota Territory.

Today all that is left of Fort Pierre is the name of the town of Fort Pierre, across the Missouri River from Pierre.

FORT RECOVERY, on American Island in the Missouri River at Chamberlain, was among the numerous combination fort and trading posts in South Dakota. It is believed to have been built on the site of **FORT AUX CEDRAS** (or **CÈDRES**), which had been established in 1809. Fort Recovery was built after the earlier fort had been destroyed by fire.

FORT VERMILLION, on the Missouri at the mouth of the Vermillion River where the town of Vermillion now stands, was built by the American Fur Company in 1835. In 1843 John James Audubon, the American naturalist, visited this fort on his travels in search of new material.

FORT RANDALL, on the south side of the Missouri River across the Fort Randall Dam from Pickstown, was built in 1856 by General William S. Harney, after selecting the site a year earlier. He had led an expedition into Sioux Territory for purposes of seeking a treaty, which he made shortly afterward at Fort Pierre. Fort Randall was named for Colonel Daniel Randall, Army paymaster. Sitting Bull was confined at this fort for two years after his surrender in Canada, where he had fled following the Battle of the Little Big Horn. In 1884 the Government abandoned the fort, and auctioned all the buildings. Only a yellow stone church, built by men of the First Infantry, remained. This was spared during the construction of the Fort Randall Dam, which backed up the waters of Lake Andes, and was restored in 1950 from original plans.

FORT SULLY, named for Brigadier General Alfred H. Sully, had two sites. The first Fort Sully, which actually was only a headquarters for troops stationed in that section, was built in 1863 near Pierre during Indian disturbances of the Civil War. The second fort was erected about thirty miles north of Pierre, in 1866. During the Ghost Dance troubles of 1890, it was the center of military activities. Fiorello (Little Flower) H. La Guardia, mayor of New York City from 1934 to 1945, lived at this fort as a young man, when his father was bandmaster. The fort was abandoned in 1894, and today a monument marks the site on the north side of the bend in the Missouri River.

FORT SISSETON, on the elevated tablelands known as Coteau des Prairies, and partly surrounded by the Kettle Lakes, was built in 1864, following the removal of the Sioux to South Dakota after the uprising in Minnesota. It was first named **FORT WADSWORTH** in honor of General James Wadsworth who died in the Battle of the Wilderness. But in 1876, when a treaty was made establishing the Sisseton Indian reservation, the fort was renamed for the tribe living there.

In the 1880's this fort became the social center of life in that section of the country. It was abandoned in 1888. The reservation is maintained by the South Dakota Game, Fish, and Parks Department. The restoration of the old fort was begun in the 1930's by the National Park Service, Marshall County, and the WPA.

FORT MEADE, near Sturgis, was built in 1878 by General Phil Sherman and named for George B. Meade, commander of the Union forces at the Battle of Gettysburg. This important post, which was a cavalry post for more than sixty-five years, now accommodates the Fort Meade Veterans Hospital. Some of the original buildings still stand on the 13,127-acre reservation. It was here that Comanche, the mount of General Custer and the only creature to survive the Custer battle at the Little Big Horn, lived for ten years. Comanche died at Fort Riley, Kansas, and was given military honors.

Among other military forts along the Missouri built during the Indian troubles were **FORT BENNETT, FORT LOOKOUT,** and **FORT THOMPSON,** now administrative headquarters for the Indians of the Crow Creek Agency.

IOWA

Admitted to the Union in 1846 as the twenty-ninth state.

At exactly midnight on October 11, 1845, Captain James Allen, commander of Fort Des Moines, brought his right hand down smartly and gave the order, *"Fire!"* The cannon of the fort boomed. There was a loud roar from the crowd of people nearby, and the race began. The homesteaders whipped up their teams and speeded toward land sites, where they burned Indian tepees and homes and staked out claims. The Sac and Fox Indians had relinquished their rights to this territory, and it had been thrown open to settlers.

Captain Allen had built **FORT DES MOINES** in May, 1843, at the fork of the Des Moines and Raccoon rivers. He had proposed to call it Fort Raccoon, but the War Department considered this "shocking," and ordered that it be named Fort Des Moines after the river. Troops occupied the fort until 1846, but the name of the settlement continued to be called Fort Des Moines. However, the word "fort" was dropped from the name in 1857 when the city became capital of the state.

The site of old Fort Des Moines is marked by a granite monument, surrounded by warehouses and factories, at West Riverbank and Elm Street.

In 1901 a second **FORT DES MOINES** was built just outside the city. Two years later it was dedicated as a cavalry post. It is located at Army Post Road and S.W. Ninth Street.

The first fort to be named Fort Des Moines was on the Mississippi River, a few miles above the mouth of the Des Moines River. This was established in 1834 at what is today Montrose, when Iowa was a part of the Territory of Michigan. The fort was abandoned in 1837, and today a bronze plate on a small granite rock marks the spot.

FORT MADISON, on the site of the town of Fort Madison, was the first fortification built in Iowa. Named for President James Madison, it was built as a Government trading post in 1808. But Indians

205

continually threatened the fort, as they considered it a violation of their treaty with the United States. In August, 1813, during the War of 1812, the Sauk, with young Black Hawk among them, attacked the fort, but were fought off. They then decided to starve out those in the fort. On the night of September 3, the occupants of the fort made their escape by crawling along a trench down to the river where boats were waiting. They left one man behind to set fire to the fort. The town later grew up around the remaining chimney.

CAMP KEARNY, a blockhouse, was built near the present site of Council Bluffs in 1837, to protect Potawatomi Indians who had been removed to that area. The fort was named for Colonel Stephen Watts Kearny, United States Dragoons, who had selected this site along with others, including that for Fort Des Moines, after John Dougherty, Indian agent at Fort Leavenworth, Kansas, had recommended to the War Department a chain of military posts to protect Indians as "untutored children."

Father Pierre Jean de Smet

Father Pierre Jean de Smet, the notable missionary to the Indians of the Great Plains and Rocky Mountains, arrived here in 1838 and had a mission to the Potawatomi Indians in the blockhouse for three years. Troops had remained in this blockhouse only about four months. The site is marked today by a large boulder and a bronze tablet at East Broadway and Union Street.

FORT CROGHAN was built in 1842 on what is now the site of Council Bluffs. This site, too, had been selected by Colonel Kearny. The fort was named for Major George Croghan, hero of the War of 1812.

FORT SANFORD was built on the Des Moines River, between present-day Ottumwa and Cliffland, in 1842 by the American Fur Company. However, as the location proved too close to that of the Choteau Company, which had a fort on the south side of the river, the fur company relinquished it on orders from Washington, and a military post was established. Captain James Allen, with a company of Dragoons, formally opened the fort on May 20, 1843, and named it in honor of Major Sanford, who had originally built it.

However, as early as 1835 Colonel Stephen W. Kearny had studied and recommended this place as a site for one of the chain of forts to protect Indians of the territory.

FORT ATKINSON, now on the site of the town by that name in Winneshiek County, was established in 1840. One of the notable things about this fort was that it was built of limestone quarried nearby, while earlier forts in the west were of logs in the blockhouse style.

The site for this fort had been recommended by Colonel Stephen W. Kearny in exploring the section some five years before the American Fur Company made application to build a fort and trading post. When taken over by the military, the fort was named for General Henry Atkinson.

FORT DODGE, on the site of the present town of Fort Dodge, was built by the Federal Government in 1850 and then called **FORT CLARKE,** after the commander of the 6th Infantry, Brevet Major Newman S. Clarke. A year later the name was changed to Fort Dodge for Henry Dodge, United States Senator from Wisconsin, who had fought in the Black Hawk War. The fort was abandoned in 1853 after roving bands of Indians had been subdued. The site of the old fort is marked with a five-foot boulder bearing a bronze tablet on the northwest corner of First Avenue and North Fourth Street, and the Wahkonsa School occupies the site of the old barracks.

FORT PURDY, at Denison, was built during the so-called Spirit Lake Massacre in 1857 when a renegade band of Sioux roved the country, killing forty-two white people. The fort was erected by John Purdy.

FORT DEFIANCE, on the site of present-day Estherville, was built after the Sioux outbreak in Minnesota in 1862. It was occupied a short time by soldiers, but after the Indian troubles the fort was abandoned. Today the Fort Defiance State Historical Preserve of 186 acres contains the site of the old fort. A blockhouse has been reconstructed in the state park.

The South Central States

ARKANSAS

MISSOURI

OKLAHOMA

LOUISIANA

KANSAS

TEXAS

FT. LE
• FT. RIL

• FT. WALLACE   • FT. HAYS

                              • FT. HARKER
                          FT. ZARAH

FT. ATKINSON   KANSAS
    FT. MANN
                          • FT. LARNED

        FT. DODGE

• FT. NICHOLAS   • SEWELL'S STOCKAD
                  • CAMP SUPPLY

    • BENT'S FT.   • FT. CANTONMENT
    • ADOBE WALLS
                          OKLAHOMA

                      • FT. RENO

                  • FT. COBB
                          • CAMP MA
                  • FT. SILL
                          • FT. A
                  FT. WASHITA •

FT. ST. LOUIS DE CARLORETTE •

                              FT. RICHARDSON
FT. PHANTOM HILL •   FT. BELKNAP

        FT. GRIFFIN •

• FT. BLISS   TEXAS

                                      Brazos R.

    FT. STOCKTON •   • FT. LANCASTER   • FT. CONCHO

    • FT. DAVIS   • FT. McKAVETT   • FT. MASON
                  Pecos R.
                                          • KENNEY

                              • FT. SAM HOUSTON
                              • THE ALAMO

                          • FT. CLARK

                          • FT. DUNCAN
                                          FT. ST. LOUIS •

SCALE OF MILES

0   50   100   150   200

                          • FT. McINTOSH
                          • OLD STONE FT.

212

                          • FT. RINGGOLD
                                      • FT. BROW

FT. BUFFALO
FT. CLARK
WOOD'S FT.
FT. HOWARD
FT. LOOKOUT
FT. KOUNTZ

FT. D'ORLEANS
COOPER'S FT.
FT. ZUMWALT
FT.
CLEMSON

FT. BELLEFONTAINE
WHITE'S FT.
DANIEL M. BOONE'S FT.

FT. OSAGE
FT. HANNAH COLE

JEFFERSON BARRACKS
HOWELL'S FT.
POND'S FT.
FT. SAN CARLOS
FT. SAN JUAN DEL MISURI

COTE SANS
DESSEIN

Missouri R.

TH

NG
T
Y
R

FT. CARONDELET

FT. LEONARD WOOD
FT. WYMAN
FT. DAVIDSON
FT. D
FT. A
FT. B
FT. C

MISSOURI

WAYNE
SPUNKY
FT. GIBSON
FT. GIBSON

ARKANSAS

FT. ESPERANZA

FT. COFFEE
EDWARDS
HOLMES

FT. SMITH

Arkansas R.

FT. LOGAN H. ROOTS

CULLOCH
FT. TOWSON
PRESTON

ARKANSAS POST

Mississippi R.

FT. SELDEN
FT. SAINT-JEAN BAPTISTE
PRESIDIO DE NUESTRA SENORA DEL PILLAR DE LOS ADAIS

FT. BEAUREGARD

FT. JESUP
OLD STONE FT.

RKER
FT. HOUSTON

FT. DE RUSSEY

LOUISIANA

FT. McCOMB
FT. PIKE

FT. ST. FERDINAND
FT. BOURGOGNE
SPANISH FT.
FT. ST. JEAN
JACKSON BARRACKS

FT. LIVINGSTON

FT. SAN CARLOS
FT. BOURBON
FT. ST. PHILIP

FT. IBERVILLE

FT. JACKSON

213

ARKANSAS

Admitted to the Union in 1836 as the twenty-fifth state.

Henri Joutel, with five haggard Frenchmen, staggered out of the wilderness into an open space.

"We discovered a great cross and at a small distance from it a house built after the French fashion. We knelt down . . . to give thanks to the Divine Goodness for having conducted us so happily."

Thus wrote Joutel, historian of the La Salle expedition. The scene he described was in the summer of 1687 and the place was **ARKANSAS POST** on the Arkansas River.

The Divine Goodness had in fact conducted Joutel and his companions happily.

A few years earlier La Salle had paused at the mouth of the Arkansas River in his descent of the Mississippi. And then, in going on to seek to discover the mouth of the Mississippi to the sea, he had become lost. He landed in Texas and later was murdered. Joutel and his companions, as survivors of the party, completed the circuit by coming back to Arkansas by land.

Arkansas Post, actually a fort with crude fortifications, and one of the oldest white settlements in Arkansas, had been built by men under La Salle's lieutenant, Henri de Tonti, known as "The Man with the Iron Hand." Tonti had found the Quapaw Indians, called by the French *Acansa* (which later became "Arkansas"), friendly. So he named the place **POSTE AUX ACANSAS.**

In 1763 France ceded to Spain all of Louisiana west of the Mississippi River, and Arkansas Post passed to the Spaniards, who promptly named it **FORT CHARLES III.** It was described in 1770 by Philip Pittman, a British captain, as a stockade fort, polygonal in shape and mounting a 3-pounder in the flanks and faces of each bastion, and situated two hundred yards from the water. The fort was garrisoned by a captain, lieutenant, and thirty soldiers.

The fort in early days saw little action, although in 1783 it was unsuccessfully attacked by Chickasaw Indians. In 1800 Louisiana went back to the French, and in 1803 Napoleon sold it to the United States. The following years Arkansas Post, as it again became known, was taken over by United States troops. In time it became the seat of government, but in 1819 Little Rock was made capital of the Territory.

During the Civil War this post became **FORT HINDMAN,** named for Brigadier General Thomas C. Hindman, chief leader of the Confederate troops in Arkansas. On January 11, 1863, 25,000 troops under General John A. McClernand stormed and took the fort, capturing 5,000 Confederate soldiers. Fort Hindman was blown up.

This historic spot is now a state park, embracing sixty-two acres. A lake covers the old Confederate trenches, and all that remains of the ancient fort is a well that was probably dug by a Spanish garrison.

FORT ESPERANZA, on the west bank of the Mississippi River opposite Memphis, was built in 1797 by the Spaniards. They had erected Fort San Fernando de Las Barrancas on the site of present-day Memphis two years earlier, but because of pressure by the United States moved across the river into Arkansas. The settlement around the fort later was called Hope Encampment, as *esperanza* is the Spanish word for "hope." Out of this name grew the name Hopefield. Hopefield was burned during the Civil War, and what remained of the town and fort was swept away by the Mississippi River.

FORT SMITH, which gave its name to the city of Fort Smith, was established in 1817 to maintain peace between the Osage and Cherokee Indians, as well as for protection against white and red outlaws. The first fort, a log structure, was built at the junction of the Arkansas and Poteau rivers on a spot called Belle Pointe by the early French. The fort was named for General Thomas A. Smith, departmental commander. Two blockhouses and rows of cabins for soldiers were erected in the form of a square fronting the river. In 1824 most of the troops were moved to the mouth of the Verdigris River, where they built Fort Gibson, now in Oklahoma.

The original Fort Smith fell into decay, and in 1838 the Government purchased 296 acres and began erection of a new fort of

Infantryman, 1835

stone. Zachary Taylor took command in 1841. As emigrants began moving westward, Fort Smith became an important point, as it marked the beginning of the Fort Smith–Santa Fe route. Thus, military protection was afforded the emigrants, and when at one time the troops were withdrawn in the hope of halting the westward flow of Arkansans, such indignation was expressed that the Government brought back the soldiers. General Matthew Arbuckle was ordered to the fort in 1851. The fort changed hands several times during the Civil War. Troops were kept there until 1871, when the land was turned over to the Department of the Interior.

During one period the garrison building was converted into a courtroom and jail. In 1875 Judge Isaac C. Parker was appointed to head the Federal court, which had jurisdiction over 74,000 persons not only in Arkansas but also in Indian Territory. Judge Parker gained a nation-wide reputation as the "Hanging Judge." In all, he sentenced 151 men to the gallows, and of this number 83 were hanged.

The commissary building of the second fort, made of stone and located to the rear of the Frisco Railroad Station, is now a museum. The courtroom of Judge Parker has been restored. The site belongs to the city of Fort Smith.

FORT LOGAN H. ROOTS, on the Arkansas River opposite Little Rock, built in 1893 and garrisoned until World War I, is now utilized by the United States Veterans Administration Facility.

MISSOURI

Admitted to the Union in 1821 as the twenty-fourth state.

When Mildred Cooper was helped astride her horse, her father asked if there was anything she wanted.

"Only a spur," she replied. A spur was fastened to her shoe. The gates of Cooper's Fort were thrown open. Mildred sank the spur into her horse's flank, and out of the fort they sped. The Indians in the woods were taken by surprise, but soon there were whoops and shots, and those inside Cooper's Fort had little hope that Mildred had got safely through.

Mildred, the daughter of Captain Braxton Cooper, had volunteered to ride to Fort Hempstead, some six miles distant, for help. Soon after she left, the Indians renewed their attack. Powder and lead were becoming scarce in the fort. The situation seemed hopeless, but soon Mildred reappeared at the head of the rescue party. The Indians, caught between two fires, hastily withdrew.

COOPER'S FORT, at the site of present-day Petersburg on the Missouri River, was the largest and most important of the so-called Boon's Lick forts during the War of 1812. Colonel Benjamin A. Cooper, for whom Cooper's Fort was named, had been warned at the outbreak of the war by Governor Benjamin Howard to move with other settlers nearer St. Louis. To this he had replied: "We have maid our Hoams here & all we hav is here & it wud ruen us to Leave now. We are all good Americans, not a Tory or one of his Pups among us & we hav 2 hundred Men and Boys that will Fight to the last and we have 100 Women & Girls whut will tak there places wh. makes a good force. So we can Defend this Settlement wh. with Gods help we will do. So if we had a fiew barls of Powder and 2 hundred Lead is all we ask."

DANIEL M. BOONE'S FORT, named for the son of the great Daniel Boone who had come to Missouri from Kentucky, was one of the strongholds protecting St. Charles on the Missouri during this war. This fort was in what was called Darst's Bottom. Other

218

forts considered outposts of St. Charles were **WHITE'S FORT,** **HOWELL'S FORT,** and **POND'S FORT,** all named for settlers who had built them. **FORT KOUNTZ,** west of St. Charles on Boon's Lick Trail, was built by John and Nicholas Kountz during the war. **FORT LOOKOUT** was a blockhouse one and a half miles below St. Charles at Portage des Sioux.

FORT ZUMWALT, west of St. Charles, was built as a cabin in 1798 by Jacob Zumwalt and enlarged into a fort during the War of 1812. It was here in 1817, according to local tradition, that Captain Nathan Heald and his wife moved. Heald, who had been taken prisoner after evacuating Fort Dearborn in Illinois, had escaped. The life of his wife had been spared, and she had been given her liberty when the clerk of John McKinzie gave her Indian captor a mule and two bottles of whiskey. It was said that in 1831 this Indian visited the Healds in their Missouri home. This is now Fort Zumwalt State Park, and a remaining stone chimney and ruined log rooms are said to have belonged to the old fort.

FORT HANNAH COLE had been built by the Widow Cole, first settler of Boonville. She and her nine children erected the house and then helped reconstruct it into a fort. **FORT HOWARD,** at the confluence of the Cuivre (Copper) and Mississippi rivers, was named for Benjamin Howard, governor of Missouri Territory. It was near here that the famous Battle of the Sinkhole was fought on May 24, 1814. Indians had killed three of a party of five soldiers and then, when pursued, had sought refuge in a sinkhole. Captain Peter Craig, in command, was killed, along with several others of his company of Rangers. Black Hawk was at this battle, and later wrote about it.

One of the most notable defenses of a fort came in April, 1815, at **COTE SANS DESSEIN** (Hill Without Design) on the Missouri at the mouth of the Osage River. Here three men and two women, including Baptiste Louis Roi and his wife, fought off an attack by a large force of Sauk and Fox Indians. The chief hazard was the use of fire arrows by the Indians that ignited the blockhouse roof on a half dozen occasions. The drinking water was used to put out the fire, then their milk supply, and finally, in desperation, the con-

tents of a "Vessel familiar in all bed chambers." The baffled Indians gave a final whoop, and disappeared.

Other War of 1812 forts included **FORT BUFFALO** on the Mississippi near the town of Louisiana; **FORT CLEMSON,** on Loutre Island where the Loutre River joins the Missouri; **FORT CLARK** near the site of Troy, named for the builder and first settler, Christopher Clark; **WOOD'S FORT** at Troy whose site is marked at Main and State streets in that town.

FORT SAN CARLOS, whose site was near the present Old Courthouse in St. Louis, was one of the historic strongholds of that city, which was at various periods under domination of French, Spanish, English, and finally Americans. The fort, erected by the Spanish in 1778, was attacked two years later when General Sir Frederick Haldimand was ordered by England to reduce all Spanish and American forts on the upper Mississippi. On May 26, 1780, 1,200 troops and Indians stormed the fort and city but were repulsed by 50 soldiers and 280 townsmen, aided by a small reinforcement from St. Genevieve.

George Rogers Clark, who had driven the British out of Illinois and the Old Northwest, crossed the river at this time and rallied the garrison during the attack.

The battle was commemorated by a song that began:

> "When the enemy first appeared,
> To arms we ran, no one afeared:
> Townsmen, traders, grave and gay,
> Bravely to battle and win the day."

In Old Courthouse, on the north interior of the dome, is a fresco of "Indians attacking the Village of St. Louis, 1780." Outside, on the south façade, is a bronze plaque commemorating the nearby site of Fort San Carlos. Land for an earlier courthouse here was given by John Baptiste Charles Lucas and René Auguste Chouteau and his wife.

FORT BELLEFONTAINE, the first military post within the limits of the Louisiana Purchase, was established by order of General James Wilkinson in 1805 at a point on the bank of the Missouri River about fourteen miles above St. Louis. Prior to this, the spot had been the site of a Spanish military post over a third of a century earlier. Hardly had the fort been built when Zebulon Montgomery Pike set out from there to locate the source of the Mississippi River, and in the following year, while on an Indian mission, he discovered Pikes Peak. In 1809, when St. Louis was incorporated as a city, Fort Bellefontaine became headquarters of the Department of Upper Louisiana. In 1827 the garrison was removed to the present site of Jefferson Barracks, on the other side of the city overlooking the Mississippi River.

JEFFERSON BARRACKS, named in honor of Thomas Jefferson, was established on the Mississippi River on the opposite side of the town of St. Louis from Fort Bellefontaine, to supplant this latter fort. The site for Jefferson Barracks was selected in 1826 and consisted of 1,702 wooded acres. This post served as a distribution point for troops and munitions, and many notable names are associated with it. Lieutenant Jefferson Davis, later President of the Confederate States of America, came there in 1828 after his graduation from

West Point. Following the Black Hawk War, he brought Chief Black Hawk of the Sauk there. Colonel Robert E. Lee was in command of the post in 1855, and Lieutenant Ulysses S. Grant was stationed there in 1843. Today the section has been set aside as Jefferson Barracks Historical Park.

FORT CARONDELET was built in Vernon County in 1784 by Pierre Chouteau, the fur trader. It was later named for Baron Francisco Luis Hector de Carondelet, Spanish governor of Louisiana and West Florida in 1791–1794, who had become convinced that Americans would invade Louisiana. Relations between the United States and Spain were sorely taxed at the time.

FORT D'ORLÉANS was established in 1723 on the Missouri River just west of the mouth of the Grand River, in present Carroll County, by Étienne de Bourgmond to keep out the Spanish and seek to obtain military control of the river. However, the fort was abandoned five years later.

FORT SAN JUAN DEL MISURI, a small log fortification, was built by the Spanish at the end of the eighteenth century near the Missouri River near Dutzow. Later a village composed of Creoles and Anglo-Americans grew around the fort, and in 1804 this was known as La Charette (The Cart). The site of town and fort was eventually washed away by high waters.

FORT OSAGE, on the Missouri River 330 miles above its mouth, was built under the direction of William Clark, of the Lewis and Clark Expedition, in 1808 near the town of Sibley in Jackson County. Also known as **FORT CLARK,** it was both a military and a trading post. After blockhouses had been erected, Clark, then governor of Missouri, made a treaty with the Osage Indians which provided that in return for all of Missouri east of a line running from Fire Prairie to the Arkansas Line, the Government would guarantee the Indians protection. Many Osage lived near the fort. After the War of 1812, the post moved to Arrow Rock near Boonville, but a trading post remained. This was closed in 1822, and the fort became a military storehouse until it was superseded by Fort Leavenworth, Kansas, in 1827. In recent years Fort Osage has been reconstructed in accord with original plans.

FORT D was one of four strongholds erected by Union troops in Cape Girardeau on the Mississippi River during March, 1861. This unique fort consisted of earthworks and a moat surrounding a small parade ground, which has been preserved as a public park. Fort D was one of the major defenses of the town when General John S. Marmaduke attacked it on April 17, 1861. The battle ended in Marmaduke's retreat to Jackson. Between periods of duty the soldiers bowled with 32-pound cannon balls on an alley on the parade ground. The three other forts in Cape Girardeau were **FORT A, FORT B,** and **FORT C.**

FORT DAVIDSON was erected by Federal troops during the Civil War to protect Pilot Knob and the Iron Mountain mineral deposits. The fort was attacked in September by Confederate General Sterling Price with from 12,000 to 20,000 men, with the intention of moving on to take St. Louis. But Union General Thomas Ewing, with 1,000 men, gave Price such a stiff fight that the first attack was repulsed with a loss of 1,200 Confederate soldiers. Ewing then spiked the fort's cannon, and fled, leaving two soldiers to blow up the magazine. By pursuing Ewing, Price gave St. Louis sufficient time to fortify itself.

FORT LEONARD WOOD was one of the forts erected by Federal troops to protect the town of Rolla. Another was **FORT WYMAN.** There were 20,000 troops stationed in this 400-foot-square fort, whose outside log walls were slanted to cause Minié rifle balls to glance off and upward.

OKLAHOMA

Admitted to the Union in 1907 as the forty-sixth state.

One evening in the fall of 1862 a young Caddo Indian boy ran into the camp of his tribe at Fort Cobb and told a terrifying story. He had seen two Tonkawa Indians shoot and kill another Caddo youth who was hunting deer. Watching from a bush cover, he had seen the Tonkawa dismember the dead youth's body and then call to their women to cook the meat for supper.

A group of Caddo went to the place and there found what was left of the body of the boy. This was proof to them that what they had believed for years was true. The Tonkawa were cannibals. The Kiowa called these Indians *Kia-hi-piago,* or "Eaters of Human Beings," and the Comanche termed them *Neuma-takers,* which meant the same thing.

When the Caddo party reported back to their camp, the word spread like prairie fire. Runners carried the message to the Osage, Shawnee, Delaware, and other tribes, some of them in Kansas. It was agreed that the Tonkawa tribe must be wiped from the face of the earth.

On the night of October 23, 1862, the allied tribes made a concerted attack on the fort, the Wichita Agency, and the Tonkawa village. The agency buildings and fort were fired, and the bodies of white men killed were thrown into the flames. The attackers pursued the Tonkawa and almost exterminated the tribe.

While blame for the attack and massacre was placed on the act of the Tonkawa, the major cause was much deeper. Tribes in the Indian Territory were then split over issues of the white man's Civil War. Fort Cobb was occupied by Confederate troops. The year before it had been under the command of Brigadier General Albert Pike, explorer and poet, who later was to lead a Cherokee Indian brigade in the Battle of Pea Ridge. Pike had sought to line the tribes up under the Confederate banner.

There had been rumors around Fort Cobb that Indians sympathetic to the Union cause, including the Shawnee, Osage, Delaware, and others, were going to wipe out the agency, fort, and the Tonkawa village. Oddly enough, the Tonkawa seemed then to favor the Union. The killing of the Caddo boy had sparked the outbreak.

FORT COBB had been established on the Washita River not far from the agency in 1859. It got its name from Cobb Creek nearby, and was built of pickets and adobe. Its main purpose was to restrain the Kiowa and Comanche from raiding across the Red River into Texas. But at the outbreak of the Civil War the Union garrison evacuated it and the Confederates moved in. After the Tonkawa massacre the fort was not reoccupied until General Philip H. Sheridan's campaign against the southern Plains tribes in 1868–1869. The fort was abandoned on the establishment of Fort Sill.

All evidence of the fort has disappeared, but the town of Fort Cobb remains. Nearby is the Tonkawa Valley, where the bones of the Tonkawa lay bleaching for many years.

FORT SILL, one of the most famous of western forts, was built in 1869 at the eastern edge of the Wichita Mountains. It was established on orders of General Philip H. Sheridan during his campaign to subdue the Plains tribes. Colonel Benjamin H. Grierson selected the site of the fort on Medicine Bluff Creek and first named it Camp Wichita. Sheridan later renamed the post Fort Sill in honor of his former West Point classmate, Brigadier General Joshua W. Sill, who was killed at the Battle of Stone River, Tennessee, in 1862.

For more than thirty years Fort Sill was a cavalry post. General George A. Custer was there with his 7th Cavalry for a time. Beginning in 1870, it became a testing ground for President Grant's so-called Peace Policy, by which the conquest of the Indians, especially the Kiowa and Comanche, was to be through kindness rather than by force. However, these tribes continued to raid into Texas, and by 1874 this policy proved a failure and Fort Sill was the base of operations in the bloody Red River War. Careers of such renowned Kiowa chiefs as Satanta, Satank, and Big Tree were connected with the fort. The three were arrested and sent to Texas for trial. Satank was killed on the way. The others were sentenced to be hanged, but were paroled. Later Satanta, after three raids, surrendered, and killed himself by diving through a window.

The famed Comanche chief Quanah Parker surrendered here, and after living a peaceful life on the reservation nearby died and was buried on Cache Creek, but in 1956, when the United States Army decided to enlarge the firing range, the bodies of Quanah and his white mother, Cynthia Ann Parker, were removed to the military cemetery. The body of Geronimo, who died a prisoner at Fort Sill in 1909, also was removed to the military cemetery.

Fort Sill buzzed with activity in 1901 when the surrounding land was thrown open to white occupation. In 1909 work was begun on a new post, and two years later the Artillery School of Fire was established there. By 1930 Fort Sill had become the permanent location of the Field Artillery School. The appearance of the fort has hardly changed over the years. Today most of the structures, built of native limestone, still stand.

FORT GIBSON, known as one of the strongest links in a chain of fortifications stretching from the northern to the southern borders of the United States, was first recommended as a site for a fort in 1806 by Lieutenant James B. Wilkinson, second in command of the Zebulon M. Pike expedition. But it was not until 1824 that Colonel Matthew Arbuckle built the fort on the Grand (Verdigris) River near the present town of Fort Gibson as a transportation and communication link between Fort Smith, Arkansas, and Fort Leavenworth, Kansas.

However, as the Cherokee Indians were coming into this section after being removed by the Government from their native lands east of the Mississippi, Fort Gibson assumed a new character. Here the bewildered Indians were received, cared for, and located, as well as afforded protection from the resentful Plains Indians. Chickasaw, Choctaw, Creek, and Seminole Indians followed, and a federation known as the Five Civilized Tribes was formed, with 84,507 Indians advancing along the "white man's road." While more civilized than their Plains neighbors, they split into both Union and Confederate factions when the Civil War began and they were forced to free their slaves. Fort Gibson was held by troops from both North and South during this turbulent era.

Three important military expeditions to the Plains originated at this fort. It also was the center of trade and travel. Keelboats and,

Keelboat passing Fort Gibson

later, river steamers loaded and unloaded here, and as the Texas Road, linking American settlements in Texas and the Mississippi Valley, passed here it became a stopping place for freighters, traders, and immigrants.

The fort was abandoned in 1890 and the reservation turned over to the Department of the Interior. In 1936 a log stockade and a number of outlying buildings were reconstructed on the site. On a ridge overlooking the reconstructed site is what is known as the second **FORT GIBSON,** a group of stone buildings built during the Civil War.

FORT HOLMES, actually a subpost of Fort Gibson, was established in 1834 by Lieutenant Theophilus Hunter Holmes, Dragoon officer, on the south bank of the Little River near its confluence with the South Canadian River. Holmes had been sent from Fort Gibson to make a treaty with the Plains Indians. The post, having served its purpose, was abandoned, and soon a firm of traders, Edwards and Shelton, established **FORT EDWARDS** directly across the river. Jesse Chisholm, half-breed Cherokee, a guide and scout for whom the well-known Chisholm Trail was named, married Edwards's daughter and lived for a time at the post. The site is not far from Holdenville and was originally on the busy California Trail.

Other subposts of Fort Gibson were Forts Arbuckle, Washita, Wayne, and Coffee. **FORT ARBUCKLE** was built in 1851 on Wild Horse Creek, near Davis, under supervision of Captain Randolph B. Marcy. It was named for General Matthew Arbuckle, who commanded in the Indian country for years. The purpose of this fort was to protect immigrant Chickasaw from raids by Plains Indians and to provide assistance to California-bound travelers. One of the log buildings of this old fort is now occupied as a private residence, and the old quartermaster building is now a barn.

FORT WASHITA, the first of this series of subforts, was established in 1842 at the mouth of the Washita River by General Zachary Taylor. One of its purposes was to protect immigrant Choctaw and Chickasaw from the wild tribes. Confederates occupied the post in 1861. The old limestone buildings are in fairly good shape, and preservation and restoration work is being done by the Oklahoma Historical Society.

FORT WAYNE, at Spavinaw Creek near the Arkansas line, dates back to 1832 when Captain Nathan Boone, son of Daniel Boone, conducted some of his early Indian Territory boundary surveys. By 1842 its importance as a military post had ended and the garrison was withdrawn. Four years later it became the meeting place for disgruntled Cherokee Indians whom Stand Watie gathered around him and proposed to lead against John Ross, chief of the Cherokee Nation. In 1861 Stand Watie again used the fort as a recruiting station for Confederate Army Indian troops. He led two regiments of Cherokee at the Battle of Pea Ridge and in other actions. He later surrendered at Fort Towson. Hardly a trace of old Fort Wayne is to be seen today.

FORT COFFEE, a final subpost of Fort Gibson, stood near the Arkansas line on the Arkansas River not far from Fort Smith, Arkansas. It was near the Butterfield Overland Mail Route.

FORT TOWSON, in Choctaw County, near the present town of Fort Towson, was erected in the same year as Fort Gibson, 1824, in anticipation of the settlement in Indian Territory of the Five Civilized Tribes. It served mainly to protect the Choctaw from raiding Plains Indians and marauding outlaws along the Red River. At one time it was used as the Choctaw Indian Agency, but during the Civil War it was taken over by the Confederates. It was here in June, 1865, two months after the closing of the war, that General Stand Watie, the Cherokee, surrendered. Some hewn-log and stone buildings, overgrown by vegetation, remain on the site.

FORT RENO, established in 1874 on the North Fork of the Canadian River about two miles from the Darlington Indian Agency, was first known as the **CAMP NEAR THE CHEYENNE AGENCY.** It had been built during the Cheyenne uprising when the Indian agent had been forced to appeal to Fort Sill and Fort Leavenworth for help. The Fort Sill troops did not reach the agency, but met the hostiles at Anadarko, while the Fort Leavenworth troops did arrive, and established the fort. Finally, a year later, the Indians were subdued. In 1876 the fort became a permanent post and was named Fort Reno in honor of Union General Jesse L. Reno, who had been killed in the Battle of Antietam.

One of the most dramatic events of the fort's existence came in 1878 when Chief Dull Knife led his small band of northern Cheyenne from the agency in a final and heartbreaking effort to reach their native lands in the valley of the Rosebud River. This remarkable dash for freedom ended tragically at Fort Robinson, Nebraska.

Following this, the garrison, besides supervising the 1,500 Indians of the agency, were employed in expelling so-called "Boomers," who sought to settle the Indian territory. In 1889 troops were kept busy guarding the boundary of the new land finally opened for white settlement. Military supervision was necessary to keep "Sooners" from jumping the line ahead of the starting gun. The garrison was withdrawn in 1908, but it became a remount station

that year. In 1948 the installation was declared surplus, and transferred to the Department of Agriculture. The Old Military Trail
between forts Reno and Cantonment was one of the West's most
important thoroughfares.

FORT CANTONMENT, established in the spring of 1879, near
Canton, sixty miles due northwest of Fort Reno and connected
with this fort by the famous Old Military Road, also served the subagency of the Cheyenne and Arapaho Indians. The garrison's main
duty was to suppress the hostile feeling between the northern and
southern Cheyenne. After all dissatisfied northern Cheyenne returned to their original homes, necessity for the fort was at an end.
It was abandoned in 1882.

CAMP (FORT) SUPPLY, at the point where Wolf and Beaver
creeks join to form the Canadian River, came into existence as a
supply center and base of operations in 1868 for General Philip H.
Sheridan's campaign against the Plains Indians. It also was a haven
for cattle drivers, as the famed Western Trail ran close by it.

It was from here that Lieutenant Colonel George A. Custer left
to surprise the Cheyenne camp of Black Kettle along the Washita
River on November 27, 1868, massacring men, women, and children.
Camp Supply, erected as a temporary installation, was officially
designated Fort Supply in General Orders Number 9, Headquarters

Division of Missouri, on December 30, 1878, and given permanent status. The old name persisted, but today the town of Fort Supply occupies the site. Troops were withdrawn in 1894 and the following year, the fort was turned over to the Department of the Interior. It became the Western State Hospital in 1903. The fort originally was constructed of heavy timber, with blockhouses, and was surrounded by a stockade ten feet high. Among the old buildings still standing is the "Custer House."

FORT McCULLOCH, on the south bank of the Blue River north of Durant, was built in 1862 by General Albert Pike, who organized a Confederate Army force of Cherokee Indians, and was named for Brigadier Ben McCulloch, commander of Confederate forces in the Indian Territory. It was here that Pike resigned his command after a series of military intrigues.

FORT NICHOLAS was built by Kit Carson in 1865 on orders of the War Department. Carson was directed to erect the fort in New Mexico, but chose a high spot on the banks of Carrizzo Creek, some four miles east of the New Mexico–Oklahoma border and west of Boise City. Farmers have gradually hauled away the rocks of the old fort's walls.

SEWELL'S STOCKADE, on the old stage route from Kansas to Fort Sill, as well as near the Osage Black Dog War Trail, was mainly for protection against so-called Osage "Mourning Parties." These were Indians on the lookout for scalps to bury with dead warriors, thus assuring them entry into the Happy Hunting Grounds. The stockade was near the present town of Jefferson, formerly Pond Creek Station.

FORT SPUNKY, near Catoosa, was a fortified farmhouse that served as a station for the Star Mail Route. The crumbling stone chimney and framework are all that remain.

CAMP MASON, at the present town of Lexington, was one of the first military camps and trading posts established so far west in Indian territory. In the late summer of 1835, a great council between the Five Civilized Tribes and Plains Indians was held here, and terms of peace were agreed upon that lasted until the Civil War. The Chouteaus also had a fur trading post here.

LOUISIANA

Admitted to the Union in 1812 as the eighteenth state.

On Sunday, September 23, 1810, amid cheers from the Patriots, the Lone Star Flag was raised over **FORT SAN CARLOS** at Baton Rouge, and the Republic of West Florida was proclaimed. Led by Reuben and Samuel Kemper, English and American settlers, unhappy and discontented with the rule of the Spanish, had assembled at Francisville and marched on the town and fort. In the battle the Spanish governor was killed.

The flag, similar to that which the Texas revolutionaries would later adopt, did not float long over the fort, however, and the new republic was short-lived. On October 27, President Madison issued a proclamation by which he declared West Florida to be a possession of the United States. After the Louisiana Purchase, seven years earlier, Spain had refused to concede that this territory was a part of Louisiana.

The French had built the first fort at Baton Rouge and established a military post to subdue the Indian tribes. But in 1763 this territory was included in that ceded to Great Britain. Spain moved in and took the fort and town in 1779, and by 1781 the whole of West Florida was ruled by that country. They strengthened the fort by building a stockade.

After the United States soldiers took possession in 1810, they found many pieces of cannon, several hundred stands of muskets, and other valuable military stores that had been seized by the Patriots. By 1825 the so-called Pentagon Buildings and an arsenal had been completed on the site of the former Spanish fort. The United States occupied the fort until 1861, when the Confederates captured it. But the following year it was back in Union hands, after the fall of New Orleans. Discontinuance of the post was ordered in 1879, and on June 6 of that year the garrison withdrew, and for the first time in 160 years Baton Rouge ceased to be a military post. The buildings and grounds were turned over to the Department of the Interior in 1884 and two years later lent to the State of Louisiana. In 1902 Congress gave the grounds to the state for the use of Louisiana State University. The Pentagon Buildings were used as dormitories for girls until the university moved to its new location at the southern part of the city. Today the buildings still stand, and the university has converted them into apartment houses. On Building "D" is a marble slab that carries the legend: "On this site stood the Spanish fort captured by the Republic of West Florida, September 23, 1810."

FORT IBERVILLE, at what is today the small town of Phoenix, some thirty-eight miles down from New Orleans on the left bank of the Mississippi River, was built in 1700 as Louisiana's first fort. Here Pierre Lemoyne, Sieur d'Iberville, French explorer, decided to establish the French claim to the Mississippi River. He ordered his brother, Sieur de Bienville, to erect this fortification after learning how De Bienville had met an English expedition at what was called Détour des Anglais (English Turn) and turned them back by giving false information about the river. D'Iberville described the structure as "a square house, twenty-eight feet on each face, with two stories and with *mâchicoulis* [a projecting parapet or turret], with four cannon [4-pound] and two eighteen-pound cannon and a moat twelve feet across."

The fort was believed to have been garrisoned until 1711, then abandoned after the founding of New Orleans. The exact site was in doubt until 1930 when a ridge of the old fort was identified, and lines of the moat traced. The measurements checked with old plans, and a four-pound cannon ball was dug up in a canal nearby.

FORT SAINT-JEAN BAPTISTE was built in 1714 by Antoine Juchereau de Saint-Denis, to protect the French in the Red River Country from the Spanish. This fort was at the head of navigation where Natchitoches is now located. Ruins of the fort are to be seen in the American Cemetery, and an oak tree said to have been planted by Saint-Denis still stands.

PRESIDIO DE NUESTRA SEÑORA DEL PILLAR DE LOS ADAIS, near present Robeline, was built in 1721 to protect Spanish territory from the French. The Presidio was the capital of the

Province of Texas until 1773, and was called "Los Adais" from the inhabiting tribe of Indians, the Adai. In 1806 the United States took over the fort, and the Spanish retired beyond the Sabine River. Today this ground is a historic park, and in 1933 the Daughters of the American Colonists placed a bronze tablet and erected a flagpole here.

SPANISH FORT, on the west bank of Bayou St. John, was erected in the eighteenth century as the first fort in the immediate area of New Orleans. In the beginning it was called **FORT ST. JOHN,** and was no more than a redoubt. The Spanish later enlarged it and rebuilt it of brick. During the War of 1812, when the British unsuccessfully tried to take New Orleans, General Andrew Jackson garrisoned the fort. In later years Spanish Fort became a resort. Today only the foundations of the old fort remain.

FORT ST. JEAN, another early fort in New Orleans, stood at what is North Rampart and Barracks streets until 1803. Rampart Street obtained its name from the ramparts, which extended from Fort St. Jean to **FORT BOURGOGNE** at Iberville Street. **FORT ST. FERDINAND** stood in Beauregard Square. It was erected during the Spanish occupation, but in 1803 this and other old forts in the city were demolished as a part of the campaign to stamp out yellow fever, thought to have been caused by the stagnant water of the moats and other filthy conditions of the ruins of the old forts at the corners of the city's ramparts.

FORT ST. PHILIP and **FORT JACKSON** were two historic fortifications at Plaquemine Bend near the mouth of the Mississippi. Fort St. Philip, which stood on the north bank of the bend, was erected in 1795 during the administration of Spanish Governor Carondelet. During the British attack on New Orleans in 1814–1815 General Andrew Jackson strengthened the fort and garrisoned it with 366 men. They made a heroic stand against five British vessels that hurled more than 1,000 shells at the fort during a 9-day attack. The British finally withdrew without capturing the fort, leaving two Americans dead and seven wounded. Fort Jackson was built in 1815 on the other side of the river, and later a unit was added by the Confederates in 1861.

These two forts, both strong fortifications, guarded the entrance to New Orleans, and were the leading defenses of the Confederates. Although the best of military experts said it was impossible for wooden craft to oppose defenses of such strength and pass under the forts' guns, on the morning of April 18, 1862, Admiral Farragut brought a fleet of 24 wooden gunboats and 19 mortar schooners within striking distance of the forts, disguising the masts with willow boughs. For four days and nights a hail of bombs and shells were rained on the forts. On the fifth day Farragut ran past the forts with 17 war vessels, and despite Confederate gunboats and rams, he succeeded in subduing the enemy. On April 28 the forts surrendered. Farragut thus gained a bloodless victory at New Orleans, some 60 miles upriver.

Fort Jackson was abandoned in 1920 and a levee built through the fort, destroying most of it. Fort St. Philip was garrisoned until 1871, after which the property was sold at public auction. Later, when it was determined that it was being used to hide smuggled liquor, the Government confiscated it. Today it is overgrown with trees, weeds, and grass. About a mile above the site of Fort Jackson stood an ancient French fortress known as **FORT BOURBON.** But all trace of it has disappeared.

FORT PIKE, on Lake Pontchartrain at the outlet of the Rigolets, northeast of New Orleans, was built in 1793 under Governor Carondelet. It was then known as **FORT PETITES COQUILLES** (Little Shells), from the name of the island on which it stood. In 1814 General Andrew Jackson began reconstruction of the fort when the British sought to capture New Orleans. In 1827 it was renamed Fort Pike for General Zebulon M. Pike, who had been killed in Canada in 1813. Confederates took possession of the fort in 1861, but evacuated it the following year when New Orleans was captured by the Union. The fort was abandoned in 1865 but reconstructed in 1935, and is now a part of the Louisiana Purchase Memorial Park. The massive brick ramparts with old gun emplacements and the semicircle moat give an Old World feudal atmosphere to the structure.

FORT McCOMB, not far from Fort Pike and also a part of the

Louisiana Purchase Memorial Park, is on the site of a smaller fortification called **FORT CHEF MENTEUR** (Chief Liar, the name given a Choctaw chief who was a notorious liar) and garrisoned with free Negroes by General Jackson in 1814–1815. It was later called **FORT WOOD** and finally Fort McComb after the War Department in 1820–1828 spent $360,000 in rebuilding it of brick. It was occupied by both Confederates and Federals during the Civil War, but was abandoned when the barracks were destroyed by fire. With massive outer walls, the interior is honeycombed with passages and dungeon-like chambers.

FORT LIVINGSTON, on the southern point of Grande Terre Island, directly across Barataria Pass from Grand Isle, home of Jean Lafitte's piratical Baratarians, was built in 1835–1861. United States soldiers had first occupied the place when Lafitte withdrew from Grand Isle. The fort was named for Edward Livingston, Andrew Jackson's Secretary of State. The Confederates took possession shortly after it was completed, but evacuated it on the seizure of New Orleans by the Federals. After the war the fort was no longer garrisoned and following a hurricane in 1893 it was completely abandoned. Ruins of the high brick walls and a few rusted cannon are all that remain.

FORT SELDEN, near Grand Ecore, was established in 1820 by Lieutenant Zachary Taylor, and named in honor of Joseph Selden, a major in the Regular Army during the War of 1812. The fort served as headquarters of the Western Department of the United States Army, stationed there to protect the western boundary of Louisiana. In 1822 the Department was moved to Fort Jesup.

FORT JESUP, established in 1822 first as **CANTONMENT JESUP** by Colonel Zachary Taylor on the Sabine River, became in that same year headquarters of the Western Department of the United States Army. It also was important as the focal point of the American expansionist movement in the Southwest, and was often termed "The Cradle of the Mexican War." Located twenty-four miles from Natchitoches, it was named for Thomas Sidney Jesup, then quartermaster general of the Army, and one of the outstanding heroes of the War of 1812. The fort was situated on the San Antonio Trace, the old El Camino Real (Royal Road). During the Texas Revolution, troops were dispatched from the fort into Texas, supposedly to enforce the neutrality laws, but when President Jackson received protests that they actually were aiding the Texans in their fight with Mexico he ordered them back. In 1844 Zachary Taylor, then a brigadier general, became commander of the fort

with instructions to prepare for trouble, as Texas probably would vote for annexation with the United States on July 4, 1845. When this came about as predicted, General Taylor marched with troops into Texas and engaged in two sharp battles with the Mexicans. Following the victorious war, as the border of the United States then was moved to the Rio Grande, Fort Jesup's importance was at an end. This old fort has now been restored under supervision of the Louisiana State Parks and Recreation Commission.

FORT BEAUREGARD, located at Harrisonburg on the Ouachita River, was one of four forts built by Confederates in 1863 within two miles below the town and one mile above. These defenses were to prevent Federal gunboats from ascending the river. On May 10, 1863, four Union gunboats did come up the river, demanded surrender of Fort Beauregard, and, after firing some 150 shots, retired. On September 4 of that year the commander withdrew his garrison after partly destroying this fort and the others. The Union forces took over and completed the destruction. Fort Beauregard was named for General P. G. T. Beauregard, Confederate States of America.

FORT DE RUSSEY, between Marksville and the Red River, was built during the Civil War by Colonel Louis de Russey. This place was held both by Confederates and Federals during the war, but the site is now a peaceful picnic grounds.

JACKSON BARRACKS, facing Delery Street and the Mississippi River and extending to the St. Bernard Parish Line in New Orleans, was built on orders of President Andrew Jackson as a garrisoned military post for the defense of the city. It was designed in part after pioneer forts, with high surrounding walls and four towers (blockhouses) with rifle slots and cannon embrasures. Still standing, this fort maintains fourteen units of Louisiana National Guardsmen.

KANSAS

Admitted to the Union in 1861 as the thirty-fourth state.

The Kiowa Indians under their chief, Satanta, or White Bear, pitched their tepees near Fort Larned in the late summer of 1864 and soon were celebrating with a scalp dance. They had just returned from a successful raid near Menard, Texas, where they had killed and scalped several white persons and kidnaped Mrs. Dorothy Field.

The soldiers at the fort watched the dance with fascination and uneasiness. They knew that in the excitement of the dance, during which the Indians waved the scalps stretched on willow hoops, almost anything could happen. Soon several Indians led by Satank, or Sitting Bear, a fierce-looking chief with a long curled mustache, approached the gate of the fort. The sentry ordered them to halt. Satank at once fired two arrows into the sentry's body, killing him.

A general alarm was sounded, and the soldiers rushed out. But the Indians leaped upon their horses, and, in riding away, stampeded the cavalry mounts so the troopers could not follow them. Later Satanta sent back a sarcastic message in which he said he hoped the Army would provide better horses next time, as those his band had stolen were not much good.

This hostile act on the part of the Kiowa, and the reports of other disturbances, caused the authorities to consider that a general uprising was in progress, despite recent treaties and the fact that the year before a delegation of Comanche, Kiowa, Arapaho, Cheyenne, and Apache chiefs had been conducted from Fort Larned on a peace-making trip to Washington, D.C., to see Abraham Lincoln, the Great White Father.

FORT LARNED had been established at the confluence of Pawnee Creek and the Arkansas River in 1859, mainly to protect travelers on the Santa Fe Trail from Indian attacks. It was first known as the **CAMP ON PAWNEE FORK**, and later was called **CAMP ALERT**, but in 1860 it was renamed in honor of Army Pay-

240

master General Larned. The Kiowa called it "The Soldier Place on Dark-Timber River." By 1870, when the railroads pushed westward and the Santa Fe Trail was less used, new problems arose. In 1878 troops from Fort Larned were forced to pacify the Wichita and Osage Indians who resented the railroad's invasion of their hunting grounds. The garrison later was moved to Fort Dodge, and Fort Larned was officially abandoned in 1882. Today the fort is preserved by the Fort Larned Historical Society, and every original building facing the 400-foot-square parade ground has been reconstructed. The site is not far from the town of Larned.

FORT DODGE, located on the north bank of the Arkansas River on the old Santa Fe Trail, was founded upon the site of an old campground for wagon trains bound for Santa Fe, New Mexico. While a military camp was established here as early as 1864 by Major General Grenville M. Dodge, the fort itself was not built until the following year. General Dodge named it for his uncle, Colonel Henry L. Dodge. The fort itself was a base for operations against the hostile Arapaho and Cheyenne; and besides General Dodge, such notable military figures as George A. Custer, Philip H. Sheridan, and Nelson A. Miles were stationed here. As Dodge City grew up around the fort, it became a shipping point for buffalo hides, the end of the trail for cattle drives, and one of the wildest and most sinful towns on the western frontier. Its Boot Hill Cemetery became world famous.

The fort was discontinued as a military post, and the garrison was withdrawn in 1882. The reservation was relinquished by the Government three years later. Site of the old fort military reservation is marked by a tablet set in the pavement in front of the main entrance to the Lora Locke Hotel. Two of the adobe barracks built in 1864 still stand, and now, veneered with stone, are a state soldiers' home.

FORT LEAVENWORTH, whose name occurs so often in connection with Indian warfare in the West, was established on the Missouri River, near the mouth of the Little Platte River, in 1827, primarily to protect caravans on the Santa Fe Trail. Colonel Henry Leavenworth, commanding a detachment of the 3rd United States

Infantry, first designated the place **CANTONMENT LEAVEN-WORTH.** As the post proved extremely unhealthy, a large part of the command being ill from malarial fever, it was evacuated in 1829, but reoccupied a year later. It has been in continuous military occupation ever since. In 1832 the War Department gave it the name of Fort Leavenworth. As well as superseding Fort Osage, in Missouri, as a Government storehouse, it became the outpost of the white man's civilization, and base for many exploring expeditions to the West. During the Mexican War it was the outfitting point for troops and, later, for California gold seekers. The town of Fort Leavenworth was the first capital of the Territory of Kansas, which was set up in 1854. During the Civil War the fort was twice threatened by Confederates. Because of its large reservation, it has been the site of many other activities than those of the post itself. Before the establishment of the Territory, it usually was the site of an Indian agency or subagency. It was also the site for military service schools. Although the oldest military post west of the Missouri River, its buildings today are well preserved. There is a museum in which is exhibited, among other interesting things, the carriage in which Lincoln rode from Troy, Kansas, to Leavenworth in December, 1859.

FORT SCOTT, at what is now the town of Fort Scott, was built in 1842 because of the need for a post on the Military Road between Fort Leavenworth and Fort Gibson, Oklahoma. It was named in honor of General Winfield Scott. It was here that the First United States Dragoons, authorized in 1833 by the Government, proved more effective against fighting Indians than the Infantry. Dragoons were heavily armed men who could operate either from horseback or on foot. A twelve-foot-high stockade surrounded the buildings with three blockhouses, which were given their own names—**FORT HENNING, FORT INSLEY,** and **FORT BLAIR.** In 1855 the Government auctioned off the fort buildings, but the post became of military importance in the Civil War when a large quantity of supplies was stored there. It was again occupied by troops in 1870–1873 to stop whites settling on Cherokee lands in the Indian Territory. On the site, mainly owned by the city of Fort

Scott, the parade ground and several original buildings have been preserved.

FORT RILEY, an Army post on the United States Military Reservation of 19,447 acres on the Kansas River near Junction City, was established in 1852 as **CAMP CENTER** to protect caravans along the Santa Fe Trail. The name Camp Center was given the post because at that time this was near the geographical center of the United States. The fort was built in the following year and renamed for Major General Bennet C. Riley of Buffalo, New York, and in 1855 Congress appropriated funds to convert it into a cavalry post. Here in 1866 was formed the 7th Cavalry under Lieutenant Colonel George A. Custer, which he would lead to disaster at the Battle of Little Big Horn in 1876.

In 1891 Fort Riley became the home of the newly established School of Application for Cavalry and Light Artillery, which eventually became known as the Cavalry School. The post, with most of the original buildings still standing, is active and is the site of the United States Army Hospital and Army General School. Today, Fort Riley maintains a permanent garrison for the training of field artillery and other units.

FORT HARKER was established in 1864 on the north bank of the Smoky Hill River to protect caravans on the Santa Fe Trail, which crossed the river nearby. This post first was named **FORT ELLSWORTH** after Lieutenant Allen Ellsworth, but when this officer lost his commission the fort lost its name. Renamed for General Charles G. Harker, who was killed at the Battle of Kennesaw Mountain, it became one of the most important operating and distributing points west of the Mississippi River. Major General Winfield Scott Hancock employed such picturesque figures as Wild Bill Hickok, Jack Harvey, and Tom Atkins as express riders and scouts. The fort was moved in 1867 to about one mile east of the original site.

Henry M. Stanley, who gained fame by finding Dr. Livingston in Africa, visited this fort as a correspondent for a St. Louis newspaper that year, and said it looked "in its present naked state like a great wart on the surface of the plain." Kanopolis sprang up on the site of the fort and was a wild and woolly cowtown in the trail-driving era. The Old General Headquarters is now a two-story apartment building; two sandstone cottages that were formerly officers' quarters are used as dwellings. Even the Old Guardhouse has been converted into apartments. The fort was abandoned as a military post in 1873.

FORT ZARAH was established in 1864 north of the Arkansas River and not far from the present town of Great Bend as one of the links in the chain of forts that guarded the Santa Fe Trail.

Fort Zarah

General Samuel R. Curtis, who built the small fort, named it in honor of his son H. Zarah Curtis, who was killed by Quantrill's men the year before. President Andrew Johnson made this a military reservation of 3,700 acres in 1869, but the lessening of Indian trouble and light traffic caused the closing of the fort the following year. The fort itself disappeared, stone by stone, but part of the area is now Fort Zarah State Park.

FORT HAYS, on the Smoky Hill Trail to Denver, near the present town of Hays, was established in 1865 to protect employees of the Kansas Pacific Railroad Company from Indian attacks. It was first named **FORT FLETCHER,** but in the following year was renamed in honor of Brigadier General Alexander Hays, killed in the Battle of the Wilderness. The original site of Fort Hays was abandoned in June, 1867, because of a disastrous flood, and the fort was moved fifteen miles west on Big Creek, near the crossing of the Union Pacific Railroad. The fort was relinquished in 1889, and today the site has been leveled and used as a golf course. The original blockhouse and guardhouse remain, the former housing the Old Fort Hays Museum. Hays City, founded in 1867 as an outgrowth of the fort, soon became the gathering place for scouts, cattlemen, soldiers, and desperadoes. James Butler (Wild Bill) Hickok became United States marshal the following year.

FORT WALLACE, the last frontier post in Kansas and westernmost of the so-called Smoky Hill Trail forts, was established in 1865 as **CAMP POND CREEK,** near the present town of Wallace, to protect settlers and cattlemen from Indians. The following year it was renamed Fort Wallace in honor of General W. H. L. Wallace, a Mexican War veteran who also served in the Kansas Indian wars. This fort saw much Indian fighting. In 1867, while Colonel George A. Custer was in command, several hundred Cheyenne under Chief Roman Nose attacked the fort itself but were driven off. The following year a company from the fort went to the rescue of a small band of soldiers on Beecher's Island on the Arikaree River, who had held out for nine days against 1,000 Indians under Roman Nose. A strange incident happened during the fighting. An arrow driven into the skull of an Army scout could not be removed; and when comrades gave up, a bullet struck the arrow and knocked it out. The Indians were driven off and 46 men were rescued, one half of whom were wounded. The fort buildings have long ago disappeared, and the site of the fort is marked by a lone hackberry tree.

FORT ATKINSON was built on the Arkansas River in 1851 near the present Dodge City, as a far-flung outpost in hostile Indian country. It was not far from a small, crude log structure, called **FORT MANN,** on the Santa Fe Trail. Although it had a short existence, the important Fort Atkinson Treaty with the Comanche, Kiowa, and Apache was negotiated here in 1853, shortly before the closing of the post. By this pact the Indians agreed to remain at peace and allow the Government to establish roads and military posts in their territory. An Army officer described some of the actions of Shaved Head, principal chief of the Comanches and one of the signers of the treaty: "He assumes an air of gravity and solemnity of features I have never seen equalled by more civilized performers, and taking you by the right hand gives three shakes as slow and deliberate as the time to a funeral dirge, pressing your hand with a firm grip, and looking steadily into your eye; releasing your hand, he passes his arm through yours at the elbow, and thus facing in opposite directions he presses your arm firmly to his side; then the left arms perform the same measured function; and during the whole of his leave-taking he repeats, 'bueno, mucho bueno (good, very good)' with a grave accent." Fort Atkinson, first called **FORT SUMNER,** was renamed for General Henry Atkinson.

TEXAS

Admitted to the Union in 1845 as the twenty-eighth state.

"Got him!" exclaimed Bat Masterson, lowering his 50-caliber Sharps buffalo gun. He turned to Billy Dixon, Army scout and plainsman.

"How many did you get, Billy?" he asked.

" 'Bout eight," replied Billy.

"That's about what I figure I got," said Bat.

It was during the fight at **ADOBE WALLS** on the Canadian River in the Texas Panhandle. On June 27, 1874, Quanah Parker, chief of the Comanche, with seven hundred Comanche, Cheyenne, and Kiowa, had swept down on the adobe fort of the buffalo hunters in what was to be the last desperate effort of the Indians to rid the

Plains of the white men who were killing off the buffalo by the thousands. William Barclay Masterson, then a young man who was later to become famous throughout the West as the marshal of Dodge City and a gun fighter of note, was employed as a killer of buffalo because of his superior marksmanship. In addition to him and Billy Dixon there were twenty-six other men and one woman in the three adobe-walled structures that formed the buffalo hunters' fortification.

Adobe Walls

The Indians had been inspired to attack this stronghold because of the claims of a Comanche medicine man, Isatai. Isatai boasted he could ascend to heaven and talk with the Father of the Indians behind the sun. He could control the elements—wind, rain, thunder, lightning, and drought. Furthermore, his medicine was so powerful that it would cause the bullets of the white man to bounce off an Indian without hurting him. He could produce from his stomach a wagonload of cartridges.

But Isatai's medicine proved no good, and after three days in which the Indians repeatedly tried to take Adobe Walls they finally gave up. Quanah later remarked, "No use Indians fight adobe." It was estimated that more than a hundred Indians were killed, while only three white men died. After this, the hostile tribes were rounded up one by one by soldiers and placed on reservations. Adobe Walls, owing to this gallant stand by hardened buffalo hunters, which was compared by many to the bravery displayed by a small band at the Alamo, is now a Texas State Memorial. The site is owned by the Panhandle Plains Historical Society.

A mile and a half up the Canadian River from the site of this Adobe Walls were the ruins of the old **ADOBE WALLS,** sometimes called **BENT'S FORT,** as it was built by William Bent. It was here that Colonel Christopher (Kit) Carson, at the head of 321 California and New Mexico volunteers, on November 10, 1864, after attacking a troublesome Indian camp of 150 lodges, soon found himself battling 1,000 warriors. He managed to fight his way out, and the battle was a draw.

THE ALAMO, a fort in San Antonio de Bexar (old name for San Antonio), which fell to the Mexicans six months after Texas had declared its independence from Mexico in 1835, inspired the battle cry "Remember the Alamo!" which became a victory chant until the war was won. Colonel William Barret Travis had 187 men within the Alamo walls when Antonio López de Santa Anna and 4,000 Mexicans demanded its surrender on February 23, 1835. Travis replied with a cannon shot, and the Mexicans hoisted the red flag, signifying "no quarter." Travis managed to get a message through to Sam Houston asking for aid. But no aid ever came. Day by day the little garrison held out, some of the men dying from wounds and others from sickness. Before the fort fell, Santa Anna saw 1,000 of his men killed by the Texas sharpshooters. When he finally entered the fort on March 6, he found Travis dead at his post. Colonel James Bowie, sick on his cot, had killed five Mexicans with his rifle and famous Bowie knife before he was killed. Only David Crockett and five others still were alive. Santa Anna killed Crockett with a sword thrust, and the others were slain by the Mexican troops.

Not a man survived this gallant fight. Today on the spot where the Alamo stands is a monument with the inspiring inscription, "Thermopylae had its messenger of defeat, the Alamo had none." The low gray chapel (for the Alamo originally was a mission) and the crumbling ivy-colored walls around the courtyard northwest of the chapel are all that remain today in San Antonio's Alamo Plaza.

The establishment of the Alamo, as well as of other Franciscan missions in Texas, came about after La Salle had been shipwrecked in Matagorda Bay. La Salle had been seeking the mouth of the Mississippi River from the sea. He and his men built **FORT ST. LOUIS** on Garcitas Creek, where the ruins today are to be found on a ranch nineteen miles southeast of Victoria. The Spanish became alarmed by the presence of the French, and welcomed a proposal of Franciscan monks of a spiritual conquest of the territory by the establishment of missions. On May 1, the Mission San Antonio de Valero (the present Alamo) was founded and soon became a mission-fort.

FORT ST. LOUIS DE CARLORETTE, known today as **OLD SPANISH FORT,** seventeen miles from Nocona, was built in 1719 by Bernard de la Harpe, a French trader. This was near the principal village of the Caddo Indians, and when the French abandoned the fort several years later the Caddo used it in defeating an army led by Colonel Diego Ortiz Parrilla in 1750. But twelve years later the Spanish occupied it when the Louisiana Territory was ceded to them by France. Thus, while built by the French, it was thought of as a Spanish stronghold. Parrilla had described the fort as a high oval-shaped structure surrounded by a ditch and log stockade. Ruins of the old fort were discovered in 1859, and corresponded to Parrilla's description.

OLD STONE FORT is a name applied to two fortifications in

East Texas. One, at Nacogdoches, known as the birthplace of the Texas Republic, was erected of stone in 1779 by Captain Antonio Gil Ybarbo, a Spanish *ranchero*. The fort had a succession of occupants. It was garrisoned by Spanish, by filibusters, Mexicans, and Texans, and finally by Confederate soldiers. A reproduction of the historic structure, built entirely of stone from the original fort, now stands on the campus of the Stephen F. Austin State College.

The other **OLD STONE FORT** was built at San Ygnacio in 1835 to protect townspeople from Indian raids. The walls, 8 feet high and 2½ feet thick, still are in excellent condition. This fort has one unique feature. A sundial with hours carved in the stone both inside and outside is just over the entrance. For six months of the year the time is read on the face of the dial on the outside, and for the remaining six months on the inside.

FORT PARKER, or **PARKER'S FORT,** was built under the direction of Elder John Parker, pioneer settler on a site between what is today Mexia and Groesbeck. It was here that Parker's granddaughter, Cynthia Ann Parker, just nine years old, was taken captive by the Comanche on May 19, 1836. She was one of five captives taken after the Indians had killed several of the inhabitants. Cynthia Ann later became the wife of a Comanche chief and was the mother of Quanah Parker, famous chief of the Comanche. It was not until 1860 that a band of Texas Rangers, with soldiers and armed citizens, recaptured her. She mourned her "people," the Comanche, and died in the "captivity" of the whites. There is a reproduction of Fort Parker in Fort Parker State Park.

KENNEY'S FORT, two miles from present-day Round Rock on a bluff of Bushy Creek, was built in 1839. While it was a simple fort with a picket stockade eight feet high, it has its place in history as the starting point of the ill-fated Santa Fe Expedition, which President Jackson termed the "wild goose campaign against Santa Fe." The Texans left Kenney's Fort in June, 1841, in the hope of taking over Santa Fe by negotiation and opening a trade from Texas similar to that flowing across the Plains of Missouri. After an arduous journey the Texans straggled into Santa Fe, where the Mexicans promptly jailed them, finally sending them into the interior of Mexico, shooting one or two occasionally. The survivors gradually made their way back to Texas. Only the foundations of the cabins and a few cedar posts remain today of Kenney's Fort. The nearby town of Round Rock gained far more notoriety in later years when Sam Bass, the Texas bandit, was killed there.

FORT PRESTON, fifteen miles from Denison, on the Great Bend of the Red River, was established first as a trading post in the 1830's by Colonel Holland Coffee. In 1840 the new Texas Republic made this into Fort Preston. The fort became a meeting place for famous trappers and hunters, and Kit Carson, John Colter, "Old Misery" Beck, and other so-called "mountain men" visited here. Coffee's two-story log house, Glen Eden, remains in good condition.

FORT BROWN, a military post established at Brownsville in 1846 during the Mexican War, was first named **FORT TAYLOR,** after General Zachary Taylor, commander of the Army of the Rio Grande. After leaving Major Jacob Brown in command, Taylor engaged and routed a superior force of Mexicans, but on returning to the fort he found that Brown had been killed in its defense. He promptly ordered the name of the fort changed to Fort Brown.

While the garrison was up north fighting Indians during what was termed the "Reservation War," Juan N. Cortinas, leader of a revolt of Mexican landowners on the American side, who was called the "Red Robber of the Rio Grande," occupied Fort Brown. One Army officer wrote: "Thus was a city [Brownsville] of from two to three thousand inhabitants occupied by a band of armed bandits, a thing till now unheard of in the United States."

FORT RINGGOLD, near Rio Grande City, and named in honor of Brevet Major David Ringgold, who was killed at the Battle of Palo Alto, was established in 1848 but in 1859 saw much action because of the activities of Cortinas. It was about this time that Colonel Robert E. Lee was sent as the new commander of the Department of Texas, with specific orders to bring the Cortinas war to an end. This he succeeded in doing, but Cortinas lived to become a general in the Mexican Army. Fort Ringgold was active as late as World War I, but was declared surplus in 1944.

FORT McINTOSH, was built at Laredo in 1849 and was first named **CAMP CRAWFORD,** but the same year the name was changed to honor Colonel James S. McIntosh, who was killed in the Mexican War. The main occupation of the garrison was to prevent smuggling, but the fort was one of a line of defensive forts built after the Mexican War. Both Federal and Confederate forces occupied it during the Civil War. During the troubles with Pancho Villa in 1916–1917, northern troops were stationed here. It was not until 1945 that the more modern fort and 208-acre grounds were declared surplus by the Government.

FORT DUNCAN was established in 1849 at Eagle Pass on the Rio Grande to protect California "Forty-niners" who passed that way. It was then called **CAMP NEAR EAGLE PASS** or **CAMP ON THE RIO GRANDE.** The same year the name was changed to Fort Duncan to honor Colonel James Duncan, inspector general of the United States Army. This post became known as the "Grave of the Confederacy," as it was the last place the Confederate flag flew after the Civil War. It was on July 4, 1865, that Confederate General Joseph O. Shelby, with his unsurrendered division of Missouri Cavalry, struck the flag over the fort, crossed the Rio Grande, and tossed the weighted banner into the water. He followed this by throwing the plume from his campaign hat after the flag. Fort Duncan again was occupied by Federal troops and was not abandoned until 1883. The city of Eagle Pass announced plans for reconstruction of the fort some years ago.

FORT PHANTOM HILL, on the Clear Fork of the Brazos River twenty miles from Abilene, was established in 1851 on what was then the extreme western frontier. The building of this outpost was in accordance with the policy of locating an interior chain of forts in advance of white settlements stretching from Eagle Pass to Fort Preston on the Red River. Comanche and other Indian tribes protested the location of the fort, as it was in the heart of their winter hunting range. The fort was abandoned in 1854 and taken over by the Butterfield Stage Line as one of its rest and relay stations. Final abandonment came in 1880. Some stone chimneys and the walls of an arsenal stand today.

FORT MASON, at what is today the town of Mason, was built in 1851, and at one time there were as many as one hundred stone buildings on the military reservation. At the time the post was abandoned in 1861, it was headquarters of the 2nd Cavalry, commanded by Colonel Robert E. Lee. The fort was again occupied in 1866, but finally given up by the Government in 1869. The stone buildings gradually disappeared as the material was used in constructing houses in Mason. Only ruined foundations remain on Post Hill, south of the town.

FORT McKAVETT, built in 1852 at what is today the town of Fort McKavett, was first named CAMP McKAVETT in honor of Captain Henry McKavett, killed in the Battle of Monterrey in 1846. Finally abandoned in 1868, the buildings became residences as the town of Fort McKavett sprang up.

FORT CLARK, established as FORT RILEY in 1852, was considered by soldiers of the day as one of the most disagreeable posts in the country. "Service at Fort Clark is equivalent to honorable mention," the saying went. The fort was named for Major J. B. Clark, who was killed in the Mexican War. The post, with its reservation of 3,693 acres, dominates the town of Brackettville, settled mainly by families of Mexican and Seminole-Negro Indian origin. In the cemetery are 146 unmarked graves where bodies of soldiers found dead on the plains are buried. Colonel Ranald S. Mackenzie created an international incident in 1873 when, based at Fort Clark, he pursued Kickapoo and Lipan raiders into Mexico. For the next four years the fort figured prominently in the war against Chief Victorio's Apaches. The Army abandoned the post in 1949, and it is now a privately owned guest ranch.

FORT BELKNAP, on the east bank of the Brazos River about ten miles upstream from where the Clear Fork empties into it, was established in 1851 as a key link in the outer chain of forts protecting the Texas frontier from raiding northern Comanche and Kiowa Indians. The site had been recommended in 1849 by Captain Randolph B. Marcy, then blazing a road for California-bound Forty-niners. Lieutenant Colonel William G. Belknap, sent later by the War Department, concurred in the suggestion, and built the fort that bore his name. It was from Fort Belknap in 1852 that Captain

Marcy conducted his exploration of the upper Red River and some years later helped establish reservations for southern Comanche Indians and others near the fort. Settlers did not take kindly to the southern Comanche, although they, too, were enemies of the northern Comanche. The reservations later were abandoned. Confederates occupied the fort during the Civil War, and it was discontinued by the Government in 1867. The fort was finally abandoned in 1876. In later years the Fort Belknap Society, in cooperation with authorities of Young County, has restored the buildings of Fort Belknap, and the five-acre tract is a county park.

FORT DAVIS, in Jeff Davis County southeast of El Paso in the Davis Mountains, was built in 1854 to protect travel along the important road between San Antonio and El Paso. It was just west of the famed Comanche War Trail that led down into Mexico. The fort was named for Secretary of War Jefferson Davis, and when Confederates occupied it during the Civil War they saw no reason to change the name. Many of the old adobe buildings stand today just north of the town of Fort Davis, once known as Painted Coman-

Fort Davis

che Camp. One building has been made into a museum and now the four-hundred-acre reservation has been established by Congress as a National Historic Site.

FORT STOCKTON, near the town of Fort Stockton, was built east of Fort Davis in 1859 at Comanche Springs, right on the Comanche War Trail. This was a watering place for Indians on the way to raids into Mexico. Ruins of the old fort are to be seen today, and three units of officers' adobe quarters are used as private residences. **FORT LANCASTER,** east of Fort Stockton near Live Oak Creek, was on the Camino Real (Royal Road) or the San Antonio–El Paso route. It was established in 1854 as **CAMP LANCASTER,** and two years later became officially Fort Lancaster. Ruins of the fort are still in existence.

FORT SAM HOUSTON, first established in Bexar County as the **POST AT SAN ANTONIO** in 1845 during the War with Mexico, was abandoned to Texas State troops during the Civil War. It was re-established in 1865; and when a new site was occupied in 1879, the name was changed to Fort Sam Houston, in honor of the first President of the Republic of Texas. The reservation covers 470 acres. Sam Houston was honored earlier when **FORT HOUSTON** came into being as a military post of the Republic of Texas, located between Palestine and Buffalo, Texas.

FORT CONCHO, on the forks of the Concho River at the south edge of the City of San Angelo, was first occupied by United States troops, under the name of **CAMP HATCH,** in 1867. In 1868 it became known as **CAMP KELLEY** and in the same year was renamed Fort Concho. It was considered one of the most important posts of the period. It served as headquarters for such famous Indian fighters as Colonel Ranald S. Mackenzie, who dealt the final blow to the plains tribes at the Battle of Palo Duro Canyon, and Colonel Benjamin H. Grierson, who operated against Victorio and his band of Warm Springs Apaches. When the Indian troubles were at an end, the fort was abandoned in 1889. Many of the original buildings stand today, including the Fort Concho Museum, maintained by the Fort Concho Museum Board and the City Commissioners of San Angelo.

FORT RICHARDSON, one of the most elaborate of frontier posts, was built at Jacksboro in 1867. The mile-square area of the reservation contained some forty buildings constructed of native limestone. It was here in 1871 that the two Kiowa Indian chiefs, Santana and Big Tree, were held after being arrested for killing six members of an Army wagon train. They were sentenced to be hanged, but the Governor of Texas commuted this to life sentences, which they never served. This fort was abandoned in 1878, but today some of the buildings have been repaired as headquarters of the 131st Field Artillery, Texas National Guard. A forty-acre park surrounds the present area.

FORT GRIFFIN, on the Clear Fork of the Brazos River, was the base of many operations against hostile Indians. It was built in 1867 in what was termed real Indian country at that time. First called **CAMP WILSON,** its name was changed to Fort Griffin the next year. The town by the same name that sprung up around the fort became one of the most important supply depots and shipping points in the West. It was the center of the buffalo-hide business, and a stopping point on the old Western Cattle Trail. The last troops left the post in 1881. In 1936 a granite shaft was erected by the Texas Centennial Commission in the center of the parade ground, and the site is part of a Texas State Park.

FORT BLISS was established across the Rio Grande from El Paso del Norte in 1849, the year after the territory was ceded to the United States by the Treaty of Guadalupe Hidalgo. It was first called **POST OF EL PASO,** and was located in what is now downtown El Paso, first known as Magoffinsville and later as Franklin. In 1854 the fort was moved one and one-half miles above El Paso and renamed Fort Bliss in honor of Major William Wallace Smith Bliss, adjutant general of the Army who had died the year before. After two more moves, it was finally built on the northeast edge of the city in 1893. Today, where a replica of the second fort has been built, it is the United States Army Defense Center.

The Northwest States

WASHINGTON

OREGON

MONTANA

IDAHO

WYOMING

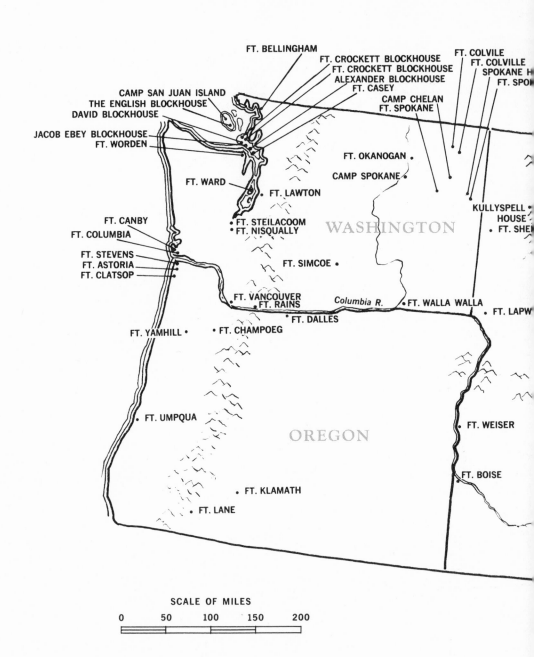

FT. BELLINGHAM

FT. CROCKETT BLOCKHOUSE
FT. CROCKETT BLOCKHOUSE
ALEXANDER BLOCKHOUSE
FT. CASEY

FT. COLVILE
FT. COLVILLE
SPOKANE H
FT. SPO

CAMP SAN JUAN ISLAND
THE ENGLISH BLOCKHOUSE
DAVID BLOCKHOUSE

CAMP CHELAN
FT. SPOKANE

JACOB EBEY BLOCKHOUSE
FT. WORDEN

FT. OKANOGAN

CAMP SPOKANE

FT. WARD

FT. LAWTON

KULLYSPELL
HOUSE
FT. SHE

FT. CANBY
FT. COLUMBIA

FT. STEILACOOM
FT. NISQUALLY

WASHINGTON

FT. STEVENS
FT. ASTORIA
FT. CLATSOP

FT. SIMCOE

FT. VANCOUVER
FT. RAINS

Columbia R.

FT. WALLA WALLA

FT. LAPW

FT. DALLES

FT. YAMHILL

FT. CHAMPOEG

FT. UMPQUA

OREGON

FT. WEISER

FT. BOISE

FT. KLAMATH

FT. LANE

SCALE OF MILES

0   50   100   150   200

258

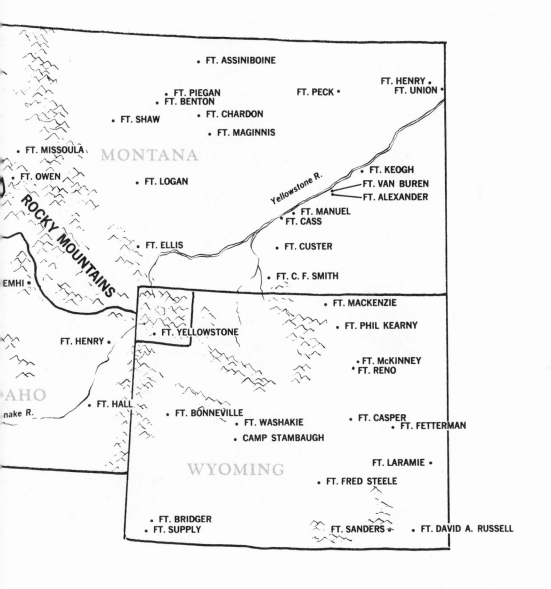

FT. ASSINIBOINE

FT. HENRY
FT. PECK
FT. UNION

FT. PIEGAN
FT. BENTON
FT. SHAW
FT. CHARDON
FT. MAGINNIS

FT. MISSOULA
MONTANA
FT. KEOGH
FT. OWEN
FT. LOGAN
Yellowstone R.
FT. VAN BUREN
FT. ALEXANDER

ROCKY MOUNTAINS
FT. MANUEL
FT. CASS

FT. ELLIS
FT. CUSTER

EMHI
FT. C. F. SMITH

FT. MACKENZIE

FT. YELLOWSTONE
FT. PHIL KEARNY

FT. HENRY
FT. McKINNEY
FT. RENO

AHO
FT. HALL
nake R.
FT. BONNEVILLE
FT. CASPER
FT. WASHAKIE
FT. FETTERMAN
CAMP STAMBAUGH

WYOMING
FT. LARAMIE

FT. FRED STEELE

FT. BRIDGER
FT. SUPPLY
FT. SANDERS
FT. DAVID A. RUSSELL

WASHINGTON

Admitted to the Union in 1889 as the forty-second state.

A pig belonging to Charles J. Griffin, manager of the Hudson's Bay Farm on San Juan Island, wandered over into the garden of Lyman A. Cutter, an American, on a bright summer day in 1859. Mr. Cutter promptly shot and killed the marauding porker and then, waving his gun, shouted that he would do the same to any Britishers who wanted to make something of the matter.

Tempers flared, and thus began the San Juan Boundary dispute, called by some the Northwest Boundary Dispute, and by others simply "The Pig War." British subjects and American citizens occupied the island as well as the San Juan Archipelago, consisting of some 172 islands in the straits between British Columbia and Washington Territory. As the international boundary line had not definitely been established in the treaty that settled the Oregon question in 1846, both countries claimed the islands and sought to impose taxes. No love was lost between Americans and British, and the killing of the pig brought the issue to a crisis.

Captain George E. Pickett, who would gain fame as a Confederate general in the Civil War by "Pickett's Charge" at Gettysburg, was then stationed with a company of the Ninth Infantry at Bellingham Bay. He was sent to establish a post on San Juan Island near Griffin Bay. The British meanwhile not only sent warships into the strait but also landed marines at the opposite end of the island on Garrison Bay. Pickett's fortification was called **CAMP PICKETT,** later **CAMP SAN JUAN ISLAND,** and was changed again to **CAMP FRED STEELE.** When it was discovered that this latter name conflicted with Fort Fred Steele, Wyoming, the name Camp San Juan Island became official.

The British fort had only the name of **THE ENGLISH BLOCK-HOUSE,** overlooking Garrison Bay. It was a typical frontier blockhouse with overhanging upper story and loopholes for rifles. What is left of it and two crumbling buildings still stand.

However, no bloodshed ensued during this heated dispute. Captain Pickett stood firm. General Winfield Scott intervened, and soon the British and Americans were feasting each other and became the best of friends. The question of the boundary line, however, dragged on until Germany's Emperor Wilhelm I arbitrated the matter and awarded the islands to the United States in 1872.

FORT BELLINGHAM, at the present city of Bellingham, eighteen miles from the Canadian border, had been erected as a blockhouse by settlers because of Indian unrest in 1855. The Government later sent troops here at the request of citizens, and it was here that Captain George E. Pickett was stationed at the time he was sent to San Juan Island during the Pig War. The town that grew up around the fort was called Whatcom, but later changed to Bellingham. The Captain George Pickett House, maintained by the Washington State Historical Society, still stands.

FORT NISQUALLY, about seventeen miles south of the present city of Tacoma, was built by the Hudson's Bay Company in 1833, and for many years it was the leading port of clearance for domestic and foreign trade on Puget Sound. Indians and traders gathered here to barter, and many ships anchored offshore, among them those of the Captain Charles Wilkes Expedition in 1841. In 1843 the fort, then owned by the Puget Sound Company, was moved two miles to the northeast, and the original spelling of the name Fort Nesqually was changed to the present Fort Nisqually, both from the Qually or Nisqually Indians. The Government purchased the fort and holdings in 1867. Today the reconstructed fort is at Tacoma in Point Defiance Park on the northern tip of the Tacoma Peninsula. Here are two of the original buildings, as well as the former Crockett Blockhouse, which stood on Whidbey Island.

FORT STEILACOOM, just north of the frontier village of Olympia, was the first United States Army post on Puget Sound to protect settlers from Indian attack. It had been established in 1849 after Snoqualmie Indians had attacked Nisqually Indians at Fort Nisqually. The fort was abandoned in 1868 after the Government had purchased Fort Nisqually.

FORT CROCKETT BLOCKHOUSE was one of two by the same

name that stood on Whidbey Island in Puget Sound. One built in 1855 was restored by the WPA in 1938. The other one was sold to Ezra Meeker, Oregon Territory pioneer, in 1909 as an entrance to his restaurant at the Alaska-Yukon-Pacific Exposition in Seattle. Later it was moved to Point Defiance Park at Tacoma. Another fortification, the **DAVID BLOCKHOUSE,** built in 1855, was restored by the Ladies of the Round Table, and a fourth, the **JACOB EBEY BLOCKHOUSE,** also built in 1855, was restored by Frank J. Platt, Jr., on his farm. At Coupeville is the **ALEXANDER BLOCKHOUSE,** built in 1855 by John Alexander, and restored by the American Legion.

FORT CASEY, on Whidbey Island at Admiralty Head overlooking Crockett Lake, and in the midst of these original and interesting blockhouses, was recommended as a fortification site to protect Puget Sound as early as 1851. It was not until 1866 that a military reservation was set aside, and the post was not officially occupied until 1899. It was declared surplus in 1950, but barracks and residences of the fort line a ridge overlooking Crockett Lake. The fort was named for Brigadier General Thomas L. Casey, Chief of Engineers.

Puget Sound became well guarded in later years. **FORT LAWTON,** a 640-acre military reservation on Magnolia Bluff at Seattle, was established in 1897 and a year later renamed for Major General Henry W. Lawton, who was killed in the Philippines. **FORT WORDEN,** at Port Towsend, named in honor of Admiral John L. Worden, who had commanded the *Monitor* against the *Merrimac* in the Civil War, became headquarters of the Coast Artillery District of Puget Sound in 1908. **FORT WARD,** on Bainbridge Island, established in 1910–1911 as a subpost of Fort Worden, was taken over by the Navy in 1938.

FORT OKANOGAN, established in 1811 by John J. Astor's agents of the Pacific Fur Company, near the confluence of the Okanogan and Columbia rivers, was the first permanent settlement within the bounds of the present state where the American flag was raised. As an American post, however, it had a short life. When news of the War of 1812 came, Astor sold his holdings to the British North

West Company, which soon was merged with the Hudson's Bay Company. In 1830 a new fort was built on the banks of the Columbia River, a mile away. The British began abandoning the fort after the Treaty of 1846, which gave the territory to the United States. Traces of the first fort, built of driftwood, were mostly swept away in the flood of 1894, although a stone tower marks the site. Nearby Fort Okanogan Historical Museum, built and maintained by the Washington State Parks Commission, interprets the history of this historic era.

FORT WALLA WALLA, built as FORT NEZ PERCÉ in 1817–1818 by Alexander Ross and Donald McKenzie of the North West Fur Company on the east side of the Columbia River not far from the present town of Wallula, was at one time considered the strongest and most complete fort west of the Rocky Mountains. It was an imposing fortification, 100 feet to each side, surrounded by an outer wall 20 feet high, with 4 cannon, 10 swivel guns, 60 stands of muskets and 20 boarding pikes, as well as a box of hand grenades. The fur traders took no chances, and Indians traded through a small window in the fort. The fort was abandoned by the British after the Oregon Treaty of 1846. Indians burned it, and when it was rebuilt of adobe it was called Fort Walla Walla. During its time it was a convenient stopping place between Fort Vancouver and points north and east of the Columbia. It became a military post in 1856 but was abandoned eleven years later. Today the site of this famous fort is covered by waters of the Columbia River backed up by the McNary Dam.

FORT VANCOUVER, built in 1824 by the Hudson's Bay Company on the Columbia River one hundred miles above its mouth, became the center of the company's activities in the Northwest. It was named by John McLoughlin, the fur company's representative who was known later as the "Father of Oregon," in honor of Captain George Vancouver who explored the Pacific Northwest coast in 1792. The fort was of the log stockade type with one blockhouse. Here McLoughlin entertained in style, seating at his table at times both friend and foe, a Highland piper standing behind his chair. He was an enterprising man, and furs from all stations were shipped from this point to England. He supervised almost two thousand acres of farmland, and among other things planted the Northwest's first orchards. Following the occupation of the Oregon Territory (of which Washington then was a part) by the United States, two companies of artillery occupied a location near the site of the fort. This was first named **COLUMBIA BARRACKS,** but on the same day was changed to Fort Vancouver. In 1879 the post was renamed **VANCOUVER BARRACKS,** which was not abandoned until 1946. The original site of old Fort Vancouver is embraced in the Pearson Army Airport, and the place where the stockade and buildings stood is marked out in concrete and asphalt. Visitor Center at the National Historic Site has an exhibit room that dramatizes the development of the Pacific Northwest.

SPOKANE HOUSE, built by the North West Fur Company below the falls at the junction of the Spokane and Little Spokane in 1810, soon became the headquarters of the company in the Columbia Territory. David Thompson, the noted English geographer-explorer, had built the fort when he moved there from Kullyspell House in Idaho. Two years after the opening of the stockaded Spokane House, John Clarke, a chief trader of John Jacob Astor's Pacific Fur Company, built **FORT SPOKANE** a short distance away. For a year the competitors traded side by side, but in 1813 Fort Spokane was purchased by the North West Company. In 1821 North West merged with the Hudson's Bay Company, and five years later all business was transferred to Fort Colville. The site of Spokane House is today indicated by a marker, not far from the City of Spokane. The United States established a **FORT SPOKANE** on the Spokane River near Lincoln. In August, 1879, **CAMP CHELAN** was established as a control point against Indians, but its site did not seem so advantageous as a point 160 miles away, opposite the Colville Indian Reservation near the juncture of the Spokane and Columbia rivers. So **CAMP SPOKANE** was established here in 1880, and the Camp Chelan troops were transferred there two years later. The post was officially designated as Fort Spokane. In 1899 the fort was turned over to the Department of the Interior and used as an Indian school.

FORT COLVILE was built in 1826 at Kettle Falls on the Columbia River, about one mile from the present town of Marcus, by the Hudson's Bay Company and named for Lord Colvile. It was here that headquarters of the fur company moved from Spokane House, as this point was more in line with the usual route of fur traders. The first gold rush in Washington Territory occurred near here in 1855. The fort served the company as late as 1871. Farther down the river, near the town of Colville (*sic*), the United States Army's FORT COLVILLE (*sic*) was built in 1859. It first was known as HARNEY'S DEPOT, in honor of General Henry S. Harney, who the year before had opened up the district north of Snake River to the whites. During the gold-rush days the nearby town of Colville saw much fighting and brawling, the soldiers from the fort doing their share. In 1861 soldiers raided the town's laundry, ran off the Chinese proprietor, and took all the wash. In the following year a lieutenant killed a civilian, but was never brought to trial because no one dared testify against him.

FORT SIMCOE, eight miles from White Swan on the Yakima Indian Reservation, was established in 1856 after a defeat of United States troops by the Yakima Indians. The site of the fort was on a small flat known by the Indians as Mool Mool, or Bubbling Springs. One of the unusual features of this fort was that four of the buildings, built in Maine, were knocked down and shipped around Cape Horn and up the Columbia River and over the hills by pack train to Fort Simcoe. It cost the Government $250,000. The main structure, formerly the house of Major Robert Selden Garnett, the commandant, still stands, and was at one time an Indian agency. Restoration of this fort was begun in 1953 under sponsorship of Federal, State, and the Yakima Nation governments. One of the original blockhouses still remains. The fort itself had a short life, as the garrison was sent to Fort Colville in 1859 and the fort abandoned.

FORT RAINS, near Bonneville, was built during the Yakima Indian War in 1856 by Major Gabriel Rains. The fort was besieged for two days until forces from The Dalles, Oregon, commanded by Colonel Edward J. Steptoe and Lieutenant Phil Sheridan, came to

the rescue. A blockhouse of timbers from the original fort has been restored by the Skamania County Historical Society.

FORT CANBY, originally known as **FORT CAPE DISAPPOINT-MENT,** was established in 1864, and overlooked the Columbia River entrance, after Congress, considering this place of major strategic importance, had appropriated money for permanent defenses. The fort was later named for Major General Edward Richard Canby, who had been killed by Modoc Indians. Cape Disappointment Lighthouse today stands on the former military reservation.

It was not until 1896 that **FORT COLUMBIA** was built on Chinook Point on the north bank of the Columbia River, as one of several fortifications at the river's mouth. Today this is a state park.

OREGON

Admitted to the Union in 1859 as the thirty-third state.

It was a wedding day at Fort Astoria. Duncan M'Dougal, representative of John Jacob Astor's Pacific Fur Company, and commander of the fort, was attired in his best. He was prepared to marry the daughter of Comcomly, the powerful one-eyed Chinook Indian chief.

"Here they come!" someone shouted.

Coming toward the fort was a procession of some three hundred Indian slaves of the Chinook chief. As they approached, they began laying beaver and other skins on the ground to make a path for the bridal party.

Comcomly soon appeared. Walking a pace behind him was his daughter, noted for possessing the flattest and most aristocratic head in this tribe, which considered the flattened skull a thing of beauty.

But more, she was attired in her wedding finery, which meant she was covered from head to foot with red clay and fish oil. As she drew nearer, the bridegroom got a good look at his mud-covered intended and then a whiff of the fish oil. Marriage with Comcomly's daughter would most certainly assure a peaceful relationship with the Chinook—but M'Dougal had not counted on the red clay and fish oil. . . .

He stepped forward and held up his hand. The wedding procession stopped. Comcomly frowned. M'Dougal began to speak in the Chinook jargon. To wed this beauteous daughter of the chief was the thing nearest his heart. He would become the son of the great chief. His sons would become leaders of men. . . . But there was one matter. In marriages among his people the bridegroom gave the bride her outfit. He had such an outfit prepared for his bride. But it could not be worn over red clay and fish oil. The bride must be scraped off and cleaned up.

Comcomly pondered. This man was powerful. Had he not on arrival stopped an attack by the Chinook when he threatened to uncork a bottle which he said would let loose the smallpox scourge? The Indians at once made peace with him, and he became known as the "Great Smallpox Chief." So now it would be as he wanted. The bride would be as he wished her. A witness reported: "By dint . . . of copious ablutions, she was freed of all adventitious tint and fragrance and entered into the nuptial state, the cleanest princess that ever had been known." Happiness reigned at Fort Astoria.

FORT ASTORIA, with picketed bulwarks at the mouth of the Columbia River on high land called Point George, was built in 1811. Its name was derived from that of John Jacob Astor. Trade flourished; but when the War of 1812 came, Astor sold the post to the British North West Company, which promptly renamed it **FORT GEORGE.** This company merged with the Hudson's Bay Company, and headquarters was moved to Fort Vancouver. But the thriving port of Astoria continued to grow. The site of the old fort at Fifteenth and Exchange streets is heavily outlined with paint on the sidewalks, and a marker stands on the northwest corner.

FORT CLATSOP was established in 1805 by William Clark and

Meriwether Lewis some eight miles southwest of the later Fort Astoria. This small stockade was set back three miles from the ocean on what was named the Lewis and Clark River, as Clark wanted relief from the repeated "rolling thunder" of the Pacific Ocean, which he called the Great Western Ocean. In his journal he said that he found it anything but *"Pasific."* Here the party passed the winter, and next spring set out to return to St. Louis. The fort, named for the friendly Clatsop Indians, has been reconstructed in Fort Clatsop National Memorial Park. Camp Clatsop, nearer the ocean, is used by the Oregon National Guard.

FORT CHAMPOEG (from the Indian *Champooick,* a name for an edible plant of that region) originally was built in 1811 as **FORT WALLACE** by William Wallace and J. C. Halsey, who came down from Fort Astoria to establish a post in the Willamette Valley for the Pacific Fur Company. The fort, of course, was named for Wallace. Following the sale of John J. Astor's holdings to the North West Fur Company, the post later was enlarged and renamed **FORT CHAMPOOICK.** Today the site of the fort is in the Champoeg Memorial State Park, the name having been derived from the original Champooick. This place represented the first settlement in the Willamette Valley, but the town of Champoeg suffered disaster from a fire in 1861, and it was virtually swept away by a flood of the Willamette River in 1892. In the park is a log cabin museum of Oregon historical data of that period.

FORT DALLES, 189 miles from the mouth of the Columbia River, was originally established by the United States Army as **CAMP DRUM.** Shortly afterward the name was changed to **FORT LEE,** from the commandant, Major H. A. G. Lee, but in 1853 it was renamed Fort Dalles. In 1847 Dr. Marcus Whitman had purchased the Methodist Mission there and established the Presbyterian Mission. His original mission was at Waiilatpu, Washington, and it was here in the same year that he and his wife and twelve other persons were massacred by the Cayuse Indians. What was to become Fort Dalles was established as a result of this uprising, with the additional task of protecting travel on the Oregon Trail. The Dalles had been an important meeting place of Indians from time immemorial. Lewis and Clark, pausing here in 1805, called it "the great mart of the country." French *voyageurs* named it because of the resemblance of the great rocks there to flagstone of French cities—*les dalles.* The fort was abandoned in 1867, but the town grew. It was called Fort Dalles, then Dalles City, but the post office labeled it The Dalles.

All that remains of Fort Dalles is the surgeon's quarters at Fifteenth and Garrison streets, which now houses the Old Fort Dalles Historical Society.

FORT KLAMATH, south of Crater Lake National Park, was established in 1863 to protect the emigrant route and the settlers in Klamath Valley from the hostile Modoc, Klamath, and Shasta Indians. In the fall of 1872 Captain James Jackson, with a troop of cavalry, was sent to arrest Captain Jack, chief of the Modoc, and place his band on a reservation. A fight ensued in which sixteen Indians were killed. This brought on the bloody Modoc War. Later, Captain Jack and three of his companions, after the surrender of the band, were tried and executed at Fort Klamath, which brought an end to southern Indian disturbances. This post was eventually abandoned in 1890 when the "caretaking detachment" left. All that remains today is a stone monument on a private ranch.

FORT LANE was established in 1853, between what is today Gold Hill and Medford, as military headquarters of the southwestern region of the Territory. It was named in honor of Joseph Lane, Oregon's first governor. It was a log and mud structure not far from Lower Table Rock. It was here that Lane had defeated the Indians in the same year the fort was erected. Lower Table Rock, considered a sacred place by the Indians, became the meeting place for the signing of the treaty of peace. The fort was turned over to the Department of the Interior in 1871, and today no trace is to be found in a private pasture where it once stood.

FORT YAMHILL, not far from Sheridan on the Grande Ronde Indian Reservation, was begun by Lieutenant William Hazen in 1855 and completed under Lieutenant Phil Sheridan. Its purpose was to protect settlers from Indians the Government was trying to confine on the reservation. It was a good-sized post with buildings of logs and rough sawed lumber. In his memoirs Sheridan tells how, after an Indian had filched his pistol in full view of the tribe, and others had killed a female witch doctor on the fort's parade ground, he rounded up sixteen Indians and made them help in finishing the buildings. The fort was finally closed down in 1866. In 1911 one of the remaining blockhouses was moved to the city park in Dayton, and on Sheridan Day, August 23, 1912, during the Grand Army of the Republic reunion, it was dedicated to Joel Palmer, founder of the city.

FORT UMPQUA was erected on the south side of the Umpqua River at Winchester Bay in 1856 at the close of the Rouge River Indian War, when the Spokane and allied Indian tribes continued to make trouble despite a treaty signed the year before. The fort had an unusual ending. In the summer of 1862 a paymaster arrived and found the entire garrison away on a hunting trip and no signs of any Indian disturbances. His report caused the closing of the fort. The old blockhouse and soldiers' quarters were moved to Gardiner, a few miles away, as memorials.

FORT STEVENS was constructed under supervision of the Army Engineer Corps in 1864, on the extremity of Point Adams at the mouth of the Columbia River. It was named in honor of Major General Isaac Ingalls Stevens, of the United States Volunteers. The original earthwork fort was rebuilt four years later. In 1901 Fort Stevens, along with Forts Columbia and Canby in Washington, were grouped to form the Artillery District of the Columbia, with Fort Stevens as headquarters. Twelve years later the name was changed to the Coast Defenses of the Columbia. Fort Stevens, with its reservation of 1,250 acres, saw service in World Wars I and II. In 1947 this installation was declared surplus, and in the following year the Civil Works Office of the Army Engineers occupied the site. It is not far from Astoria Municipal Airport.

MONTANA

Entered the Union in 1889 as the forty-first state.

Pocahontas shielded the head of Captain John Smith and looked appealingly at her father, Powhatan. Standing just above her and the white captive was the huge warrior with his great club raised to strike.

"Please, oh, please—" began the distraught princess.

Suddenly there was a great commotion in the hall. A Crow Indian scout rushed in and shouted that the Sioux were raiding the picket line. The commandant of Fort Custer signaled to the bugler. The sharp notes of "Boots and Saddles" sounded.

The actors, all Crow Indians taking part in the stirring drama *Captain John Smith,* rushed from the stage. The officers in full dress made for the door, buckling on their sabers. Chief Many Coups, who was garbed as Powhatan, dashed from the stage in full regalia and hurried to lead his Crow followers in pursuit. The officers' ladies huddled in a terrified group.

The play, staged by John Maguire, Irish minstrel and pioneer impresario, to relieve the boredom at Fort Custer, was at an end. With what horses were left, the Crow Indians and cavalrymen started in hot pursuit of the thieving Sioux. Although the Sioux had provided a surprise and interrupted a show, none were more surprised than they when they saw the colorful costumes of those chasing them. They cursed their medicine, and abandoned the stolen horses. But by the time soldiers and actors got back to the fort, it was too late to continue the play.

FORT CUSTER had been established on a bluff above the confluence of the Little and Big Horn rivers a year after General George A. Custer had been defeated by Sitting Bull's Indians and Custer's entire command wiped out. It was called the **BIG HORN POST** when it was first built by Lieutenant Colonel George P. Buell, but in that same year it was renamed to honor General Custer. There were no further Indian uprisings, and life was tame at Fort Custer.

274

But the fort was garrisoned until the spring of 1898. The buildings were then sold at auction and the materials used in building the thriving town of Hardin, two miles northeast of the fort site. Nothing remains today of the fort. The Daughters of the American Revolution have erected a marker on the site.

FORT KEOGH, also established as a result of the Custer battle, was built in 1876, by Brevet Major General Nelson A. Miles, on the south bank of the Yellowstone River at the mouth of the Tongue River. The post was first known as **CANTONMENT ON THE TONGUE RIVER** and as the **NEW POST ON THE YELLOW-STONE** and later as **TONGUE RIVER BARRACKS.** In 1877 a permanent fort was built a mile from the former site and named Fort Keogh, in honor of Captain Miles Keogh who was killed at the Battle of Little Big Horn. It was from this fort that General Miles finally forced surrender of Sioux and Cheyenne hostiles, and from here, too, he marched to engage Chief Joseph and his fleeing band of Nez Percé Indians in the decisive Battle of Bear Paw Mountain. The fort was garrisoned until 1908. Today the Range and Livestock Experiment Station of the United States Department of Agriculture occupies the site. Some original buildings of officers' row still are standing and are occupied by employees.

FORT C. F. SMITH, a companion post of Fort Kearny, Wyoming, was established on the Big Horn River about thirty miles south of present-day Hardin and two miles below the site of the Yellowstone Dam, in 1866, as Montana's first Army post. Named in honor of General Charles Ferguson Smith, a Union commander who led his division in the capture of Fort Donelson, it was built to protect travelers along the Bozeman Trail. This famous trail was established by John M. Bozeman, who led the first wagon train along this route two years earlier; it was a cutoff to the Montana gold fields from Fort Laramie on the Oregon Trail. From the very first, Fort C. F. Smith was besieged by Red Cloud's Sioux, and was abandoned in 1868 after several bloody encounters with these Indians, notably the so-called Hayfield Fight in which eleven soldiers and eight civilians fought off six hundred Sioux, sustaining only four losses. The Government abandoned the fort and stopped travel

along the trail to placate the Sioux. Chief Red Cloud then burned
Fort C. F. Smith.

FORT ELLIS, built near the present site of Bozeman in 1867,
played an important part for nineteen years in "taming" the frontier
in the Gallatin Valley. It was established primarily to protect Bozeman and the Bridger and Flathead passes. The fort, named for
Colonel Augustus Van Horn Ellis of the 124th New York Volunteers, participated in the Sioux wars of 1876–1881. The Washburn-
Langford expedition outfitted at this post in August, 1870, and its

reports of geysers, hot springs, terraces, paint pots, and other marvels led to the creation of Yellowstone National Park. The fort was abandoned in 1885 after the collapse of the Sioux. The site, where there are few remains of the old fort, is now occupied by the Fort Ellis Experiment Station of the Montana State University. A commemorative monument stands nearby on U.S. Highway 10.

FORT LOGAN, located in the Smith River Valley in 1869 to protect the miners of Diamond City from Indian raids, was first named **CAMP BAKER,** as a compliment to Major Eugene M. Baker, commanding Fort Ellis, of which Camp Baker was a subpost. In 1870 it was removed to another site ten miles to the south, and eight years later was renamed Fort Logan in honor of Captain William Logan, killed fighting Indians at Big Hole Pass in 1877. The post was abandoned in 1880. Traces are to be found today of most of the old buildings, and the blockhouse, still standing, was removed in 1962 to the center of the old parade ground. On its side is a plaque placed by the Daughters of the American Revolution. There is a small town named Fort Logan there, forty miles east of Helena.

FORT SHAW, established in 1867 west of Great Falls on the Sun River at the present small town of Fort Shaw, protected the Mullan Road and settlers of Sun River Valley from Blackfoot Indian raiders. It was first called **CAMP REYNOLDS,** but in the same year the name was changed to Fort Shaw to honor Colonel Robert G. Shaw, who lost his life in the assault on Fort Wagner in the Civil War.

Blackfoot

One of the buildings of this adobe-walled and shingled fort was 125 feet long. It was here that the first professional stage performance was given in Montana. General John Gibbon was commander of the post in 1876 when he led the 7th United States Infantry from there to join Generals Terry and Custer in the war on the Sioux. As Gibbon and Terry attempted an encircling movement, Custer and his command were annihilated at the Battle of Little Big Horn. This fort was closed in 1891 and used until 1910 as an Indian school. Some of the original buildings still stand as part of a county grade school.

FORT MISSOULA was established in 1877 at the already settled town of Missoula when citizens there asked protection at the time of Chief Joseph's attempt to lead his Nez Percé tribe into Canada. Another duty of the garrison was to restore the Mullan Road toward Coeur d'Alene, Idaho. It was at this post later that Lieutenant James A. Moss, who retired as a brigadier general, organized the "Infantry Bicycle Corps." Soldiers mounted on bicycles made several trips, one through Yellowstone Park, but the idea never caught on. After the Indian troubles were over, squatters crowded in and settled on the reservation. The post was discontinued in 1918 after serving as a mechanics school during World War I. It was regarrisoned in 1921, but in 1941 the Immigration Service was granted its use for five years. However, in 1944, during World War II, it was returned to the War Department, which held it two years and then declared the buildings surplus. The Officers' Club of logs and a stone powder house are all that remain.

FORT ASSINIBOINE, probably the largest military installation ever constructed in the state, was established in 1879 for the primary purpose of protecting citizens from the hostile incursions of the Sioux Indians under Sitting Bull, who had withdrawn across the International Boundary Line into Canada after the Battle of Little Big Horn. The fort was located near Havre, some thirty miles south of the border. During the building period, men who were familiar with brickmaking were enlisted, and the structures were built of brick and sand clay from Beaver Creek. In 1911 the fort was abandoned as a military post. Later, friends of Indians persuaded the

Indian Bureau, which had control of the land, to set aside 580,388 acres as homes for the wandering Chippewa and Cree tribes. In 1956, 451 Indians were settled here, and the name Rocky Boy Reservation was given the area. Most of the buildings on the actual fort site have disappeared. A building of the Northern Montana College is built of bricks from the fort structure and called Pershing Hall, as General John J. Pershing had served as young cavalry officer at the fort.

FORT MANUEL, Montana's first fort and trading post, was erected by Manuel Lisa, New Orleanian of Spanish descent, at the mouth of the Big Horn River on the Yellowstone River in 1807. Lisa first named his post **FORT RAMÓN,** for his son Ramón Lisa, but traders insisted on calling it **LISA'S FORT** or **FORT MANUEL.** In three years Lisa had three hundred trappers working for him.

FORT UNION, on the Missouri River near the mouth of the Yellowstone River, built as **FORT FLOYD** in 1828 by John Jacob Astor's agent Kenneth McKenzie, was to become the greatest concentration point of the western fur trade. Astor in 1808 had founded the American Fur Company, and in 1822 the St. Louis branch was organized with Pierre Chouteau, Bernard Orette, and others as partners. McKenzie was one of several agents of Canadian companies who came over to Astor in 1827 and was placed in charge of all upper Missouri trade. Fort Union became in its heyday the most famous post in that section. The steamboat *Yellowstone* reached here from St. Louis on June 17, 1832. Among the passengers was George Catlin, the artist. The following year Prince Maximilian of Wied-Neuwied arrived on the steamer *Assiniboine*. John James Audubon, famous naturalist; Father Pierre Jean De Smet, Jesuit missionary; and Jim Bridger, the scout, all visited the place. Fort Union, eleven miles from present-day Bainville, near the site of an earlier **FORT HENRY,** built in 1810 by Andrew Henry, was the spot where Lewis and Clark passed in pirogues in 1805. Its great log buildings were enclosed by a 20-foot-high stockade with two blockhouses. The fort was a lively trading post for Indians until during the last year of its existence the Sioux branded it "bad medicine" and kept other tribes from trading there. In 1868 the Government bought the fort and dismantled it and used the materials to build Fort Buford, North Dakota, eight miles down the river. **FORT VAN BUREN** was another fort built by McKenzie at the mouth of Rosebud Creek on the Yellowstone River. It was erected in 1835 but later burned, and Charles Larpenteur built another, which he called **FORT ALEXANDER** for Alexander Culbertson of the American Fur Company and former commander of Fort Union. McKenzie built **FORT CHARDON** at the mouth of the Judith River on the Missouri River, and **FORT CASS,** on the Yellowstone River, two miles below the Big Horn River.

FORT PIEGAN was built by the enterprising McKenzie close to the mouth of the Marias River and the Missouri River at present-day Loma in 1831. In the same year it was abandoned, and hostile Indians burned it, but, also in the same year, **FORT McKENZIE** replaced it. This latter fort also was burned by Indians in 1843.

FORT LEWIS was the next fort to be erected at the mouth of the Marias River. This was built in 1846 by McKenzie, but in 1850 Alexander Culbertson rebuilt the fort and named it Fort Benton, in honor of Senator Thomas H. Benton of Missouri.

FORT BENTON became one of the historic forts of the period. It was at the head of navigation on the Missouri River in 1859 when on July 2, 1858, the stern-wheeler *Chippewa* arrived there. A few hours later the *Key West* arrived. The year before, the famous Mullan Road to Walla Walla, the first wagon road over the northern Rockies, was started, and soon the fort became the supply point for the gold camps. Ox trains paused on their way to trading camps in Montana, Idaho, and up into Canada. Thousands of tenderfeet disembarked here and started toward the wilds to find fortunes or face failure. The so-called "Whoop-Up-Trail" from Fort Benton into Canada became notorious, and the Royal Northwest Mounted Police were forced to establish Fort McLeod in Canada on Old Man's River to stem the source of the illicit whisky trade with Indians. When Indian troubles worsened, the fort was taken over by the Government in 1869 and garrisoned by a company of infantry. The post was finally abandoned in 1881. It gave its name to the present town of Fort Benton. All that remains are some picturesque ruins with a historical museum.

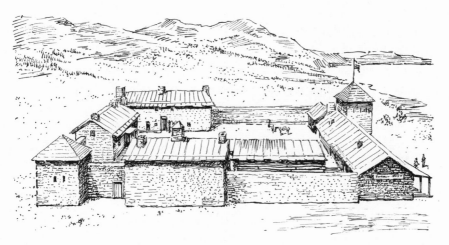

Fort Benton

FORT OWEN, in the Bitterroot Valley at present-day Stevensville, was erected on the site of St. Mary's Mission in 1850 after Major John Owen had purchased the mission buildings from Father Pierre Jean De Smet for $250. The mission itself had been established in 1841 at the request of the Salish Flathead Indians, a tribe that, curiously enough, never practiced the flattening of the head. In 1834 four chiefs had traveled to St. Louis to look for the white man's "Medicine Book," the Bible. They also wanted a Christian teacher. Three different missionaries were sent to them, but they were not satisfied until Father De Smet arrived. Father De Smet erected a chapel, a sawmill and a gristmill, the millstones of the latter having been first shipped from Antwerp, Belgium, to Fort Vancouver and then carried overland by ox train. When Major Owen purchased the mission, he added to it and, refusing to be diverted by the gold rushes and booms, remained at his fort and developed it into an important trade and travel center. Today Fort Owen (or St. Mary's Mission) has been restored and is a state historical monument.

FORT PECK, a fortified Indian agency and trading post, was built in 1869 by E. H. Durfee and Colonel Campbell K. Peck a few miles below the present-day Fort Peck damsite on the Missouri River. They did a thriving business, especially in hundred-pound sacks of flour, the Indians being not so interested in the contents of the sacks as in the lettering in red circles—"Durfee and Peck." They adopted the sacks as war dress by cutting holes for the arms and head. The Hunkpapa Sioux especially considered the bright red circles as "good medicine." The post was abandoned ten years after its establishment and later was swept away by high waters. Today there are the town of Fort Peck and the Fort Peck Dam, which cost millions and forms a lake with an estimated shoreline of 1,600 miles and a maximum depth of 240 feet.

FORT MAGINNIS, which gave its name to a town by that name, was built in the Judith Basin northeast of Lewistown in 1880. The fort, established to protect settlers and stockmen from Indian attacks, was named for Major Morton Maginnis, territorial delegate to Congress. Indians continued their raids, and finally, in 1890, the fort was abandoned. Ranchers and citizens of Lewistown later carried off the buildings, piece by piece.

IDAHO

Admitted to the Union in 1890 as the forty-third state.

It was a stormy session at Fort Lapwai on that Monday, May 7, 1877. General Oliver O. Howard already had held two councils with the discontented Nez Percé Indians, trying to persuade them to move on the Fort Lapwai Reservation, as provided in a previous treaty. Now at this third session, Too-hul-hul-sote, prophet, priest, and chief, arose and angrily said:

"The Great Spirit made the world as it is, and as he wanted it, and he made a part of it for us to live upon. I do not see where you get authority to say that we shall not live where he placed us—"

"Shut up!" ordered General Howard. "I don't want to hear any more such talk. The law says you shall go on the reservation to live, and I want you to do so, but you persist in disobeying the law [meaning the treaty]. If you do not move I will take the matter into my own hand and make you suffer for your disobedience."

Too-hul-hul-sote replied: "Who are you, that you ask us to talk, and then tell me I shan't talk? Are you the Great Spirit? Did you make the world? Did you make the sun? Did you make the river to run for us to drink? Did you make all these things, that you talk to us as though we were boys? If you did, then you have the right to talk to us as you do."

"You are an impudent fellow, and I will put you in the guard-house," said General Howard. He waved to a soldier and ordered him to arrest Too-hul-hul-sote. The Indian was marched off to the guardhouse.

The great Chief Joseph, who had remained silent, now arose and, drawing up his magnificent six-foot physique to its full height, said: "*I am going to talk now!* I don't care whether you arrest me or not." Turning toward his people he said: "The arrest of Too-hul-hul-sote was wrong, but we will not resent the insult. We were invited to this council to express our hearts, and we have done so."

Joseph agreed they would go on the reservation. General Howard

gave them but thirty days. After five days Too-hul-hul-sote was released. But he burned with indignation. A white man had killed his father. Other Indians had grievances, although the Nez Percé boasted they had never slain a white man. Joseph sought to placate them, but the young men insisted on war. One party swooped down on settlers on the Salmon River and killed five whites. When they rode into camp and displayed their trophies, another group joined them and they hurried back to the settlement and killed eight more white persons.

There was nothing to do now but to flee. Joseph decided to lead his band into Canada, and thus began one of the most skillful and masterly retreats in the annals of warfare. The Indians defeated soldiers at White Bird Canyon. They were dislodged on the Clearwater River southeast of Kamiah after a two-day battle, but continued their retreat over the Lolo Trail. It was not until September 29 that General Nelson A. Miles defeated Joseph at the Battle of Bear Paw Mountain, where the Indians were within a "sleep's march" of Canada and safety.

One of the agreements of surrender was that Joseph and his band be now placed on the Fort Lapwai Reservation, but instead they were sent to Fort Leavenworth, Kansas, and later to the Indian Territory. It was not until years later that they were allowed to go to the Colville Reservation in Washington.

FORT LAPWAI was established in 1862, but three years later troops were withdrawn. They were back in 1866, and when the Nez Percé War flared the garrison was increased. This post had an active part in this war as well as in the Bannock and Sheepeater Indians campaigns in 1878–1879. The post was discontinued in 1884 and made a subpost of Fort Walla Walla, Washington. It continued as an Indian agency, and today the former headquarters, or guardhouse where Too-hul-hul-sote was held, is the residence of an officer of the Nez Percé tribal council staff. A few other old buildings still stand south of the town of Lapwai.

FORT HALL, which was to become known as "The Gateway to the Oregon Country," was built on what was later the Oregon Trail about ten miles north of present-day Pocatello in 1834. It was named for one Henry Hall. Nathaniel J. Wyeth, heading the Columbia River Fishing and Trading Company of Boston, had entered that region the previous season and selected his site at the conjunction of the Snake and Portneuf rivers as a rendezvous for trappers and traders. Accompanying Wyeth on his second trip was Jason Lee, a Protestant minister, and on July 27, 1834, he held the first religious services in what was to become Idaho. He preached to a group of Indians "who sat on the ground like statues," not understanding a word he said, but kneeling and rising as the preacher did. Two years later the Hudson's Bay Company forced Wyeth to sell, and Wyeth's cottonwood stockade was covered with adobe, and the red flag of the company with its initials "H.B.C." (Hudson's Bay Company, or, as the trappers had it, "Here Before Christ") floated over the fort. It became a refuge in this area of Indians and sagebrush as the only inhabited place between Fort Bridger, Wyoming, and Fort Boise to the west. Indians, Spaniards, French Canadians, priests, doctors, and missionaries, as well as adventurers of all types, met here. Emigrant wagon trains emerging from the hot and lonely desert welcomed the sight of its cool white adobe walls. It took on the character of a wayside inn. Abandoned in 1855, it later was occupied by United States troops who were charged with protecting the emigrant trains until 1860. Floods washed away the fort in 1863. Troops were again on the scene in 1870 after President Grant set aside the Fort Hall Indian Reservation in 1869 for the Bannock, Shoshone, and other Indians of southern Idaho. The fort was finally abandoned in 1883, and in 1906, when Ezra Meeker retraced the Oregon Trail with ox team and dogs, he could not locate the site. But ten years later, rifle pits and the old well were found, and today a lava marker commemorates this historic spot.

FORT BOISE on the Snake River near the mouth of the Boise River, some fifty miles west of present-day Boise, was built in 1834 by the Hudson's Bay Company as a result of the establishment of Fort Hall to the east. The Hudson's Bay Company at that time monopolized the fur trade of the Northwest, and would brook no competition. Within two years it had acquired Fort Hall. The name of the fort was given by French traders first on the scene who cried "Les bois!" on seeing the numerous trees in this semiarid territory. John McLoughlin, the British overlord of the fur country, who built the fort, maintained it until 1846 when the boundary dispute between the United States and England was settled and it became United States Territory. The fort was abandoned in 1854 after a destructive freshet and an Indian outbreak in the vicinity. In 1863 the Government looked into the possibility of establishing a military post in the vicinity of old Fort Boise. But the site finally selected was just north of present-day downtown Boise, when a detachment of the 1st Oregon Cavalry encamped there and began construction of temporary barracks. Designated first as **CAMP BOISE,** its purpose was to protect emigrant trains against the Shoshone Indians of the Snake River. Soon the name was changed to Fort Boise, but in 1879 it became known as **BOISE BARRACKS.** In 1919 Boise Barracks was turned over to the Public Health Service, and twenty years later to the Veterans Administration. Part of the grounds today are maintained as a city park, and on the Veterans Hospital area are several stone buildings of the military period.

KULLYSPELL HOUSE, a fortified trading post of the British North West Company, was established in 1809 by David Thompson at the eastern end of Lake Pend Oreille, near the mouth of the Clark Fork River, as the first fort in what was to become the State of Idaho. Thompson and his men arrived at the lake searching for a canoe route to the Columbia River, and paused to trade for 125 furs with the Pend d'Oreille, or Kalispel, Indians. Thompson considered this a good place for a post, and built two houses of logs, one for trading goods and the other in which to store furs, as well as the third for his men. The last was named Kullyspell House, a corruption of the native Indian name, Kalispel, for Pend d'Oreille, as the first Europeans termed them because of their large shell earrings. While the post survived some years, Thompson himself moved on to Washington, where he founded Spokane House. It was not until 1923 that the exact site of Kullyspell House was located through the memory of an eighty-year-old blind Kalispel Indian, Klai-too, who had seen the stone chimneys as a boy. Citizens of Bonner County erected a monument there in 1929, commemorating not only the first house built on Idaho soil but also in honor of the builder, David Thompson.

FORT HENRY, on the Snake River near present-day St. Anthony, was built in 1810 when the Missouri Fur Company sent Major Henry to that section. However, he abandoned the fort the following year. It was not until 1927 that the location of the fort site was discovered when a rock was unearthed with the inscription "Al the cook, but nothing to cook," while two others bore the legends "Gov't Camp, 1811" and "Fort Henry 1811 by Captain Hunt." A monument now stands on the bank of the Snake River where U.S. 191 crosses a bridge at Rexburg.

FORT LEMHI was built by the Mormons near the present-day Lemhi in 1855. As characteristic of the Mormons in colonizing an area, the first structure they erected was a fort. They named this for Limhi, a character in the Book of Mormons, as indeed were named the forest there, the mountain range, valley, and river. This was historic ground. It was near the spot where Lewis and Clark camped atop the Continental Divide in a gap now called Lemhi Pass, twenty-five miles southeast of Salmon, and just across the river from where Sacajawea, the Shoshone "Bird Woman" who acted as guide, was born. The Mormons built a log stockade surrounding twenty-five cabins. They irrigated the land to some extent and sought to convert the Nez Percé Indians. However, three years later the Indians drove them out. Eventually the ruins were on a private ranch where only a portion of the original adobe-walled stockade and one of the irrigation ditches remained.

FORT SHERMAN, a military post selected by General William Tecumseh Sherman, was built in 1878 and abandoned in 1901, but gave its name to the present town of Sherman. FORT WEISER, at the confluence of the Snake and Weiser rivers, was built by a German trapper, Jacob Weiser. This fort gave its name to the town of Weiser.

WYOMING

Admitted to the Union in 1890 as the forty-fourth state.

French-born Captain Benjamin Louis Eulalie de Bonneville, a graduate of West Point and officer of the United States 7th Infantry, had been stationed in forts on the western frontier and had seen the huge sums of money made by fur traders. Then, in 1832, at thirty-seven years of age, he decided to make his own fortune. He obtained a leave from the Army and interested a group of wealthy men in New York in his plans. With 110 men he set out for the West.

In July of that year he crossed the South Pass of the Continental Divide with his wagon train. This place had been crossed before but never by wagon. Bonneville thought nothing of the feat, and continued on until he reached what was then the Green River Rendezvous, a place on the Green River in what is now Lincoln County near the town of Daniel. It was the custom in those days for the American Fur Company at certain times of the year to appoint this "rendezvous" for trade between trappers and Indians. The first day was devoted to "high jinks." There was much feasting, drinking, and gambling. The rough mountain men and savage Indian bucks intermingled, making merry. But on the next day everyone was sober and businesslike. Trade began. With business over, the place was soon deserted.

This spot appealed to the dashing, picturesque Bonneville. He would build a fort here, and trade, not just on certain days, but throughout the year.

The fort was built near the mouth of Horse Creek, and a writer who visited it said: "The fort presents a square enclosure, surrounded by post or pickets of a foot or more in diameter, firmly set in the ground close to each other, and about fifteen feet in length. At two of the corners, diagonally opposite each other, blockhouses of unhewn logs are so constructed and situated as to defend the square outside of the pickets and hinder the approach of the enemy

289

from any quarter. The prairie in the vicinity of the fort is covered with fine grass and the whole together seems well calculated for the security of both men and horses."

It was named **FORT BONNEVILLE,** but trappers looked on it with a jaundiced eye and called it Fort Nonsense and Bonneville's Folly. The Indians, as the trappers guessed, considered it an invasion of their territory. It was all right to rendezvous at certain periods, as such meetings represented nothing permanent. But to trade at an established fort! The menacing attitude of the Indians soon convinced Bonneville, and hardly had the fort been finished when he deserted it and went over to the headwaters of the Salmon River and established winter quarters.

By 1836 Bonneville was back in the Army. He considered his project a failure, but in time the contribution he had made in helping to open the Rocky Mountain country was recognized. While the fort disappeared to the last log, in 1916 the Oregon Trail Commission erected a marker on the site.

FORT LARAMIE, which was to become one of the most important and best-known forts of the West, was originally built by William Sublette and Robert Campbell, fur trappers, in 1834, on the west bank of the Laramie River two miles above its junction with the North Platte River. They called it **FORT WILLIAM** for William Sublette. The following year they sold out to a syndicate of trappers headed by Jim Bridger, and the year after this the trappers sold to the American Fur Company. The company rebuilt the fort and renamed it **FORT JOHN,** in honor of John B. Sarpy, one of its officers. In 1849 the fort was sold to the Government for $4,000 and was renamed Fort Laramie, from the river, which in turn derived its name from a French voyageur, Jacques La Ramée, who was killed near the stream by Arapaho Indians in 1820.

The fort was intended to protect travelers on the Oregon Trail and others entering the Territory. Two years after its establishment, a treaty was made with the Sioux, Cheyenne, Arapaho, Snake, and Crow tribes, whereby peace would reign and the Indians would receive $50,000 annually for certain lands. Despite sniping on both sides, the treaty appeared effective until the case of the Mormon

Fort Laramie

cow came up. A cow had strayed from a Mormon camp nearby, and a Miniconjou brave had taken the animal. This incident, reported to the fort, caused Lieutenant John Grattan to take a detail of men with two cannon to retrieve the cow. The consequences were that Grattan and thirty soldiers and the interpreter were killed, and a full-scale war was on.

The fort became of first importance in 1865, known as the "Bloody Year on the Plains" because of constant attacks by Indians on emigrant trains. The famous Fort Laramie Treaty was made in 1868; by it, white men were forbidden to go into the Powder River country. But greedy prospectors continued to make their way into the Black Hills, with the result that Indians continued raiding white settlements.

The Army erected new buildings, including a clubhouse, or officers' quarters, which became known far and wide as "Old Bedlam," costing between $60,000 and $85,000. The lumber had to be hauled overland from Fort Leavenworth. In 1852 the Reverend William Vaux, post chaplain, established a school at the fort long before the Territory was organized. The last military units at the fort left in 1890.

Today twenty-one of the old structures are preserved in the Fort Laramie National Historic Site. At the entrance of the old fort is a fourteen-foot concrete Oregon Trail Marker, erected in 1913. In 1927 the State bought the fort and gave it to the Federal Government.

FORT BRIDGER, second in importance to Fort Laramie, was built in 1842 by Jim Bridger, trapper and scout, and Louis Vásquez, on the site of the present town of Fort Bridger. It became a famous outfitting point for wagon trains on the Oregon Trail, and jokingly was called the "first tourist camp west of the Mississippi." In 1853 the Mormons purchased the fort, although Bridger later said he had "been robbed and threatened with death." The fort, reconstructed at a cost of $60,000, became the center of Mormon activity as they began to settle along the nearby Green River and its tributaries. But in 1857, when the trouble between Mormons and non-Mormons reached a crisis in the so-called "Utah War," the Mormons burned

Fort Bridger, as well as Fort Supply, which they had built twelve miles south. The United States Army now bought the fort and re-built it, and companies of Regular Army troops later protected sur-veyors and construction gangs of the Union Pacific Railroad. Besides being the second permanent settlement in Wyoming, it was here that the first oil well in Wyoming was drilled. The first schoolhouse was on fort grounds, and Wyoming's first newspaper was printed here. The fort originally consisted of two adjoining log houses with dirt roofs and a small picket yard of logs set in the ground to a height of about eight feet. Later, a stone wall encircled the fort. In 1855 it was rebuilt of boulders—100 feet square and 14 feet high. There were bastions on diagonal corners. The United States troops built their barracks and quarters of stone, logs, and lumber. They finally abandoned the fort in 1890. Today, in Bridger State Park, ·the buildings are being restored, and one barrack has been remod-eled as a museum.

FORT SUPPLY was built by the Mormons in 1853 after they had acquired Fort Bridger. This fort was in Black's Fork Valley at Wil-low Creek, twelve miles south of Fort Bridger. Its main purpose was to provide a base for relief trains in the colonization plans of the church. However, Fort Supply was burned by the Mormons in 1857 when General Albert Sidney Johnston's troops advanced west-ward in the Utah War. This fort was never rebuilt, and today a marker indicates its site.

FORT PHIL KEARNY, built in 1866 at the close of the "Bloody Year on the Plains," on Big Piney Fork of the Powder River some twenty-five miles south of present-day Sheridan, so angered the Sioux and allied tribes that they never ceased to keep it under siege during its two-year existence. Located on the Bozeman Trail, which led to the Montana gold fields, it was in the midst of the Indian hunting grounds. Colonel H. B. Carrington erected the fort and was its first commander. It was first named **FORT CARRINGTON,** but this was soon changed to Fort Philip (Phil) Kearny. Named for General Philip Kearny, the spelling somehow in the beginning became "Kearney," and many records carry it thus. It had a bloody existence. On December 21, 1866, Brevet Lieutenant Colonel William J. Fetterman set out with a column of 79 soldiers and 2 civilians to protect a wood train nearing the fort. He became diverted by some Indians, and chased them only to fall into an ambush. His entire command was wiped out. The so-called Fetterman Massacre took place on a ridge that became known as Massacre Hill. Following the massacre John ("Portugee") Phillips, trader and scout, made an incredible and historic ride of 236 miles in subzero weather through Indian-infested country to summon help from Fort Laramie. During 6 months the Indians made 51 hostile demonstrations in which 154 white men were slain near the fort. In 1867, in the so-called "Wagon Box Fight," 30 soldiers with new 1866 breech-loading rifles fought off some 800 Indians. Chief Red Cloud had lost his opportunity to destroy the fort in not following up his advantage after the Fetterman Massacre, but in 1868, when the fort was abandoned following the Fort Laramie Treaty, he pounced down on it and burned it. There is a monument on the site today as well as a portion of a stockade begun by the WPA.

FORT CASPER, originally called "Old Platte Bridge," was built about 1864 by volunteer soldiers who were a part of the Powder River Expedition under General Patrick E. Connor. It was named in honor of Second Lieutenant Caspar W. Collins who had lost his life at the bridge with four others when Indians attacked a wagon train he was escorting. A clerical error made it "Casper," and so the second largest city in Wyoming is also named Casper. The post was abandoned in 1867. The bridge and fort have been reconstructed.

FORT RENO, first known as FORT CONNOR, was founded in 1865 by General Connor, as a temporary base for his Powder River Expedition, on a mesa rising more than a hundred feet above Powder River. It was then garrisoned by a company of Indian Volunteers known as the Omaha Scouts. In the same year the name was changed to Fort Reno for Major General Jesse L. Reno. Located on the Bozeman Trail, it was one of the line of forts guarding that trail, including Fort Phil Kearny. It was a log stockade with blockhouses, built over a spring. The post was abandoned in 1868 following the Laramie Treaty. Mounds of earth trace the outlines of the stockade and blockhouses, and a small granite monument marks the site.

FORT McKINNEY was established in 1876 on the north bank of the Powder River, three miles above the site of old Fort Reno. It was then named **CANTONMENT RENO.** The following year the post was moved fifty miles north to Buffalo on Clear Creek, and renamed Fort McKinney, in honor of Lieutenant John A. McKinney of the 4th Cavalry. Later, General Philip H. Sheridan, thinking of possible future wars with conquered Indians, recommended that this be made a permanent post. The Government gave $40,000 to complete construction. This was the headquarters of one of the Army's most famous scouts, Frank Grouard. Born in the Paumoto Islands, South Pacific, of a missionary mother and the high chief of the Island of Ana, he was often mistaken for a Sioux. In 1903 the State ordered the Soldiers' and Sailors' Home transferred from Cheyenne to Fort McKinney.

FORT SANDERS, established as **FORT JOHN BUFORD** for a Civil War general killed in 1863, was for the protection of the Overland Trail and workers on the Union Pacific Railroad. It was built near Laramie on Soldier Creek in 1866. Several months after it was garrisoned, the name was changed to Fort Sanders in honor of General William P. Sanders, a cavalry officer who died of wounds in 1863. Fort Sanders was the meeting place in the summer of 1868 of Generals U. S. Grant, Philip H. Sheridan, and William T. Sherman when they discussed gradients and curves on the railroad with rail officials. Calamity Jane, an Army scout, was stationed here in 1871–1872 after completing a campaign with troops in Arizona. The *Frontier Index,* a newspaper, was printed in a boxcar of the equipment train. The fort was abandoned in 1882. Little remains of the old fort. A golf course crosses the parade ground, and a transcontinental highway cuts through the site. An old guardhouse and magazine and stone buildings are on the site.

FORT FRED STEELE, on the North Platte River east of Rawlins, was established in 1868 to protect the Union Pacific Railroad as its tracks were laid farther westward. The fort was named in honor of a general who distinguished himself in the Civil War. Brevet

Colonel Richard I. Dodge, commanding four companies, was ordered to protect the railroad from Rock Creek to its crossing of the North Platte River, a distance of over sixty-five miles. To do this he stationed his companies at intervals along the line. It was from this fort that Major Thomas F. Thornburg, in the fall of 1879, led 150 soldiers to the aid of Nathan C. Meeker, agent to the White River Ute in northwestern Colorado. Thornburg was ambushed before he could reach Meeker, who was killed. In the fight Thornburg counted 12 dead and 47 wounded, and the Indians later admitted to 6 dead.

Jo Rankin, an Army scout, escaped and carried news to Rawlins. Troops were rushed from Fort Douglas, Utah, and Fort D. A. Russell, Wyoming, but in the meantime Chief Ouray of the Utes had ordered the revolt stopped. The fort was abandoned in 1886, and today transcontinental trains cut through the ruins.

FORT D. A. RUSSELL (FORT FRANCIS E. WARREN) was established in 1867 near Cheyenne to protect men working on the

Union Pacific Railroad. In time it became one of the most elaborate posts of the West. First known as the **POST ON CROW CREEK,** it later was officially designated **FORT DAVID A. RUSSELL** in honor of a brigadier general of that name killed in the Civil War. However, it was called Fort D. A. Russell. General John J. Pershing was stationed here, and married the daughter of Senator Francis E. Warren. The Pershing House still stands, and in 1930 the name of the post was changed to Fort Francis E. Warren. In 1948 it was transferred to the Department of the Air Force.

FORT FETTERMAN, established not far from the present-day town of Douglas, was used as a supply base in the later Sioux Wars. Built in 1867, it was named in honor of Brevet Lieutenant Colonel W. J. Fetterman, killed at Fort Phil Kearny. It was the last Army outpost along the Indian border after the Laramie Treaty of 1868. It was abandoned in 1882, and cattlemen took over and for a time made it a lively town.

FORT WASHAKIE, established in compliance with the terms of the treaty with the Shoshone and Bannock Indians in 1869, was first named **CAMP AUGUR** in honor of Brigadier General Christopher C. Augur, who negotiated the treaty. A year later it was renamed **CAMP BROWN** to commemorate Captain Frederick H. Brown, killed in the Fetterman Massacre. Originally a subpost of Fort Bridger, it was made an independent post in 1870 and was moved seventeen miles north to a location one and one-half miles from the Shoshone Agency on the right bank of the Little Wind River, opposite its confluence with the North Fork. When the fort first was established on the site of present-day Lander, Chief Washakie of the Shoshone met the soldiers and avowed his friendship, and from that time on served as scout in campaigns against the Sioux, Arapaho, Ute, and other hostile tribes. In 1878 the name of the post became Fort Washakie, in honor of the friendly chief. Washakie died in 1900 and was buried with military honors in the fort's cemetery. In 1909 the fort was abandoned as a military post, and the reservation was turned over to the Department of the Interior.

FORT YELLOWSTONE, a little-known and unique post, was

established in 1886 in Yellowstone National Park when the Department of the Interior asked for troops to protect the area. Captain Moses Harris and Company M, 1st United States Cavalry, first established **CAMP SHERIDAN** at Mammoth Hot Springs, but the name was changed to Fort Yellowstone in 1891. It was abandoned in 1916.

CAMP STAMBAUGH, near present-day Atlantic City, was established in 1870 in Smith Gulch on the Oregon Trail when the miners demanded protection as boundaries of the Shoshone Reservation were drawn almost adjoining the mining district. It was named for Lieutenant George B. Stambaugh of Camp Brown (Fort Washakie) who had been killed by Indians. The fort was abandoned in 1878.

FORT MACKENZIE, near Sheridan, was established as a military outpost in 1899 and named for General Ranald S. Mackenzie, famous Indian fighter. Abandoned in 1918, today it belongs to Veterans Administration Facility No. 86, and some of the seventy-five buildings are those of the old fort.

The Southwest States

UTAH

COLORADO

NEW MEXICO

NEVADA

ARIZONA

CALIFORNIA

FT. HUMBOLDT

FT. BIDWELL •

• FT. McDERMIT
• FT. McGARRY
• CAMP WINFIELD SCOTT

FT. DEFIANCE •

FT. BRAGG

FT. HALLECK •
• FT. RUBY

SIERRA

Sacramento R.

RANGE

• FT. CHURCHILL

FT. SHELLBOURNE •

FT. BAKER
FT. BARRY
FT. MILEY
FT. POINT
PRESIDIO

• FT. ROSS
FT. FUNSTON
FT. McDOWELL
FT. WINFIELD SCOTT
FT. MASON
CAMP AT ALCATRAZ

• SUTTER'S FT.
STOCKADE AT GENOA

FT. DESE

NEVADA

FT. CAMERON •

• FT. HA

THE PRESIDIO OF MONTEREY

NEVADAS

COAST

LAS VEGAS FT. •

• FT. TEJON

CALIFORNIA

FT. MOJAVE

PRESCOTT BARRACKS •

• FT. MacARTHUR

FT. GUIJARROS
EL PRESIDIO REAL
FT. STOCKTON

Colorado R.

FT. ROSECRANS

FT. YUMA

Gila R.

FT. I

SCALE OF MILES

0   50   100   150   200

FT. BUENAVENTURA

Great
Salt
Lake

UINTAH RANGE

FT. DAVY CROCKETT

FT. UTAH

FT. DUCHESNE

WASATCH RANGE

Green R.

Colorado R.

UTAH

FT. NAMAQUA

FT. COLLINS

South Platte R.

FT. SEDGWICK

FT. WICKED

FT. ST.VRAIN

FT. MORGAN

FT. VASQUEZ

FT. JACKSON

FT. LUPTON

FT. LOGAN

ROCKY MOUNTAINS

COLORADO

FT. CRAWFORD

FT. REYNOLDS

FT. LYON

FT. BENT

BENT'S NEW FT.

Colorado R.

San Juan R.

Arkansas R.

FT. MASSACHUSETTS

FT. LEWIS

FT. GARLAND

EL PUEBLO

CANTONMENT BURGWIN

FT. DEFIANCE

FT. MARCY

FT. UNION

FT. WINGATE

POST OF ALBUQUERQUE

FT. BASCOM

VERDE

Pecos R.

ARIZONA

Rio Grande

FT. SUMNER

FT. APACHE

NEW MEXICO

NT

FT. CONRAD

FT. CRAIG

FT. STANTON

AYPA

CAMP GRANT

FT. BAYARD

FT. BOWIE

FT. CUMMINGS

FT. SELDON

FT. CRITTENDEN

FT. BUCHANAN

FT. FILLMORE

FT. HUACHUCA

301

UTAH

Admitted to the Union in 1896 as the forty-fifth state.

Something unusual was going on at Fort Douglas. Brigham Young himself put his eye to the telescope mounted atop Beehive House and looked toward the fort. Although nearly midnight, it was ablaze with lights. There was a lot of activity.

As he watched, there came a sudden roar of a cannon. "Call out the Militia at once!" ordered Brigham Young.

The cannon at the fort boomed again. President Young of the Church of Jesus Christ of Latter-day Saints, commonly known as Mormons, urged more speed in assembling the Militia around Beehive House, his official residence. This house, built much like a New England colonial house, had a "widow's walk" around its square cupola—a kind of walk from which the surrounding country could be viewed. Since the establishment of Fort Douglas in 1862 near Salt Lake City, and the passage of the Federal antipolygamy laws, there had been rumors that Brigham Young would be arrested. The garrison was supposed to protect the Overland Mail route, but everyone knew it was there to control the Mormons. Therefore a continual vigilance was kept, and when any unusual maneuver was noticed at the fort the Mormon Militia rushed to guard Brigham Young.

On this night, however, although the cannon was fired eleven times, no threatening move was made against the Mormon leader. Later it was learned that a celebration had been going on at the fort in honor of Colonel Patrick E. Connor, who had just been notified that he had been brevetted a brigadier general.

FORT DOUGLAS was established first as **CAMP DOUGLAS** by six companies of the 3rd California Volunteer Infantry and four companies of the 2nd California Volunteer Cavalry which had marched overland from Benicia Barracks, California. In 1878 the name of the post had been changed to Fort Douglas.

A few months after the establishment of the post, Colonel Connor and his men fought the last major Indian battle in the vicinity of northern Utah on Bear River north of Lewistown. In subzero weather, with the trail covered by snow, Connor and his men engaged the Indians in a gorge 20 feet deep and 40 feet wide. The troops lost 14 killed and 49 wounded, while 70 soldiers were disabled by frozen feet. The Indians lost 224 killed, and Connor is said to have ordered: "Take no prisoners, fight to the death; nits breed lice."

In 1901 Fort Douglas was recommended as a permanent military post. It was used as a training camp in World War I, and many German prisoners, alien enemies, and draft evaders were interned there. Today the fort resembles a small town with its 170 buildings on the 9,000-acre reservation northeast of Salt Lake City.

FORT DUCHESNE was built some years after Fort Davy Crockett, Colorado, a few miles from this fort up the Uintah River. The fort became the agency for the 84,000-acre Uintah and Ouray Indian Reservation. One notable thing happened here in 1885. Samuel H. Gilson, prospector, scout, and Pony Express rider, was informed by an Indian chief of a black, lustrous, brittle asphalt to be found in the hills near the fort. Gilson investigated. He discovered the substance would not burn. He called it Gilsonite, and today it is used in varnishes, paints, in rotogravure ink, electrical insulation, waterproofing compounds, telephone receivers, and many other things.

FORT BUENAVENTURA was the first fort erected west of the Wasatch Range, and was built by Miles Goodyear on the site of Ogden in 1844–1845. He was an Indian trader and the earliest white settler in Utah. With him was Jim Baker, a noted mountain man. The Mormons bought Goodyear's cabin and stockade in 1847 for $2,000. Today the Goodyear cabin of cottonwood logs stands in Tabernacle Park, Ogden, as the oldest manmade structure in the state.

FORT UTAH was built near the site of the town of Provo in 1849 when the Mormon empire began to spread in the mountain valleys south from Great Salt Lake City. This fort was typical under rules of colonization laid down by Brigham Young. He had ordered, following troubles with the Ute Indians, that first a fort should be built not only for protection but also to allow for social life and religious activities. Irrigation ditches followed, then fenced farmlands and log or adobe houses. John S. Highbee, with thirty families, established the colony on the Provo River and built Fort Utah. It was here that Chief Sowiette, of the friendly Ute, moved into the fort with his warriors and prepared to help defend it against Chief Wakara (Walker) of the unfriendly Ute. Walker and his men whooped and danced around the fort all night, but withdrew next day without actually making an attack. On the site of Fort Utah in Sowiette Park in Provo is a pioneer museum. The park was named for the friendly Ute chief.

FORT HARMONY, built on the site of present-day New Harmony at the base of the Pine Mountains, was the first settlement in that section in 1852. The fort was built by John D. Lee, but was abandoned by Lee and his followers because of the so-called Walker War led by Chief Wakara (Walker). The chief was angered at prohibition by the Mormons of the slave trade and also because of continual white encroachment. Lee returned two years later to the spot and erected a second **FORT HARMONY,** but a rainstorm that lasted twenty-eight days demolished it. The colonists then established the town of New Harmony.

FORT DESERET, near Delta, was erected on order of Brigham Young in 1866 as a protection against Indians during the Ute Black Hawk War. The fort was built of adobe, and part of the walls are still standing. The name Deseret came from a word in the Book of Mormon which meant "honey bee." Brigham first had called his territory the "State of Deseret," but Congress would not accept the name and termed the territory Utah. The Mormons were unhappy with this word, for they claimed it was descriptive of a "dirty, insect-infested, grasshopper-eating tribe of Indians."

COVE FORT, a unique structure, embraced by canyon walls lined with volcanic rock, was built in 1867 by the Mormons during the Ute Black Hawk War. The fourth wall of the structure is the stockade itself. Inside the 100-foot square area, the original rooms backed against the enclosing wall. A well was in the center of the square, and hanging in the front arch of the entrance was a huge bell to be rung as warning of an Indian attack. The fort, located some twenty miles north of Beaver, served for many years as a communications center for the Church, a supply station, and cattle ranch. One of the twelve rooms in the place was fitted up as a telegraph station of the Church's newly completed Deseret Telegraph Line. Later the fort was sold and used as a private tourist camp, but today it is a state monument.

Ruins of Cove Fort

FORT CAMERON, first known as the **POST AT BEAVER** on Beaver Canyon, was established in 1872 by the Government for a better maintenance of the laws of the general government in southern Utah against the aggression of the Mormons. The name was changed in 1874 to Fort Cameron in honor of Colonel James Cameron, who was killed at the Battle of Bull Run. The reservation was abandoned in 1885.

COLORADO

Admitted to the Union in 1876 as the thirty-eighth state.

First through the door of the lodge tumbled the great Kit Carson. As he sought to regain his feet he was knocked down again by a bundle of blankets and furs. Then his trusty rifle clattered beside him. His Spanish saddle, horse gear, moccasins, buckskin coats, and all sorts of clothing followed. Soon everything Kit Carson possessed was scattered on the ground outside the lodge, and in the doorway, hands on hips and a frown on her face, appeared Kit's Cheyenne Indian squaw, Making-Out-the-Road.

A crowd had gathered to watch the fun.

Making-Out-the-Road shouted to them in her anger: "He say I spend too much! He say I want too many things! One thing I don't want—that's him!"

Kit got up, brushed himself off and looked about at his belongings. "Honey, one thing you didn't throw out was my bag of gold dust!"

"I've thrown you away!" screamed Making-Out-the-Road. "You shall never sleep in my lodge again!"

She turned back into the lodge. Kit gathered up his belongings and rode over to Fort Bent. He might have hoped things would be straightened out, but they never were; and Making-Out-the-Road ran off with a cousin, and Kit eventually married a beautiful Spanish girl at Taos.

Making-Out-the-Road was Kit's second wife. His Arapaho wife had died some time before. He had met the vivacious Cheyenne girl while patroling the Indian camps under orders of William Bent after the latter had called a council of Cheyenne, Arapaho, Kiowa, and Comanche, and talked them into making peace in 1840. Bent wanted this peace to last, and Kit was to see that no liquor was sold in the camps. Kit had been impressed by Making-Out-the-Road's beauty—and cleanliness—and had thrown a blanket about her and thus married her. Her unusual name was said to have come from

an ancestor who was good at reading sign and had once set his people on the right path by determining the proper road.

There was never a dull moment in and around **FORT BENT.** It was trading post, social center, Indian gathering place, and stronghold of the Bent brothers—Charles and William and their partner Céran St. Vrain, reputedly a French nobleman. This imposing fort of adobe, 180 feet by 135 feet with walls 15 feet high and 4 feet thick topped with growing cacti, was begun in 1828 on the banks of the Arkansas River near the present site of La Junta and completed four years later. It was called **FORT WILLIAM,** for William Bent, and later Fort Bent or **BENT'S FORT.**

Indians and fur trappers and mountain men came here from far and wide. Jim Bridger, among the greatest of the mountain men, frequented this post. So did Jim Baker, Tom (Broken Hand) Fitzpatrick, and "Uncle Dick" Wootton, known as a "swapper," as he was always ready to swap. Jim Beckwourth, a mulatto who became a war chief of the Crow, was a visitor here. The Crow thought so much of Beckwourth that to keep him from leaving them they tried to poison him, so he said. Kit Carson, of course, was here. He was

Conestoga wagons approaching Fort Bent

employed as a hunter from 1831 to 1842, when he joined John C. Frémont's first expedition into the Rocky Mountains. Frémont used the fort as a base for supplies.

General Stephen Watts Kearny and his Army of the West paused at the fort in 1846, and in the following year General Sterling Price, en route to Mexico, stopped at the fort and enlisted William Bent as guide to Taos. As a result Bent became an honorary colonel in the Army. In 1852 Bent sought to sell his fort to the Army; finally, becoming disgusted with the delay in negotiations, he loaded all his goods on twenty large oxen-drawn wagons, touched off the powder magazine, and blew up the fort.

Today, with its walls outlined by adobe brick laid by the State Historical Society of Colorado, the National Park System has designated this as Bent's Old Fort National Historic Site.

Bent moved five miles down the Arkansas River to Short Timber Creek, but by the next year he was forty miles down the river and had built **BENT'S NEW FORT.** This was about eight miles west of Lamar. This also was an imposing fort, built of stone on a high bluff overlooking the Arkansas River.

In 1859 Bent leased his fort to the Government and went to live with his daughter near the Purgatoire River. The Army promptly named this fort **FORT FAUNTLEROY** for a Colonel T. T. Fauntleroy of the Old 1st Dragoons. Then, when he defected to the Confederates, they changed it to **FORT WISE** in honor of Henry Alexander Wise, governor of Virginia, but the name of Wise, who ordered the execution of John Brown for his raid on Harpers Ferry and who became a Confederate brigadier general, also proved embarrassing, so once more the fort's name was changed—this time to **FORT LYON,** in honor of Nathaniel Lyon, first Union general to fall in the Civil War.

In 1864 the name of Fort Lyon became associated with one of the most disgraceful and tragic acts in the annals of western Indian warfare. Black Kettle and his band of Cheyenne were encamped at Sand Creek, not far from the fort, in compliance with the call of the agent that all friendly Indians should come there for roll call and protection. Colonel C. M. Chivington of the 1st Colorado Cavalry led his troops by forced march to Fort Lyon, induced some of the United States troops there to join him, and at daybreak of November 27 fell on the friendly Indians, slaughtering men, women, and children. This treacherous act was variously known as Chivington's Massacre and the Sand Creek Massacre, and brought on an uprising of the Plains Indians that cost the Government $30,000,000 to put down.

Two years later the river began cutting away the bank at Fort Lyon, and a new fort was built twenty miles upstream. This fort is not far from present-day Las Animas. It was at this fort that Kit Carson, then fifty-nine, died on May 23, 1868. He was buried there with military honors, but later his body was removed to Taos. Today Veterans Administration Facility No. 80 is located on the reservation of 1,140 acres. There also is the Kit Carson Museum.

William and Charles Bent had entered upon the fur trade in 1824, and with Céran St. Vrain built a stockade on the banks of the Arkansas on the site of the city of Pueblo. This was abandoned when they built Bent's Fort.

The site of Pueblo at the confluence of the Arkansas River and Fountain Creek appeared to have been a favorite spot, for Lieutenant Zebulon Montgomery Pike camped here in 1806 after throwing up a breastwork of logs. His party remained five days while he himself went north to try, unsuccessfully, to climb the peak that bears his name. Later, in February, 1807, he built winter quarters on the Conejos five miles upstream from the Rio Grande. This stockade, near Alamosa, has been faithfully reconstructed.

But it remained for James P. Beckwourth, the mulatto mountain man and onetime chief of the Crow Indians, to build the first permanent structure here in 1842. It was a fort, **EL PUEBLO,** sixty yards square and made of adobe. It had round blockhouses at two opposite corners. Five years later the place was reported as a hangout for loafers and smugglers of liquor from New Mexico. The Ute Indians wiped out the settlement on Christmas, 1854.

FORT JACKSON, first of the so-called Platte Valley fur posts, four of which were all built on a fifteen-mile stretch of the South Platte River some forty miles from Denver, was established in 1833 near present-day Ione. Peter Sarpy and Henry Fraeb built the fort for the Pratte, Chouteau Company of St. Louis, and are said to have shipped $10,000 worth of furs in one season. The fort was bought by Céran St. Vrain in 1838 and later abandoned.

The second of these posts was **FORT VÁSQUEZ,** built in 1836 by Louis Vásquez and Andrew Sublette for the Rocky Mountain Fur Company, the most active competitors of the Bents. While this post did a thriving business, it was not as well liked as Bent's Fort, and in 1840 it was sold and two years later captured and looted by Arapaho raiders. Reconstruction on the site at Platteville shows an imposing structure with a large court of 125 by 100 feet surrounded by heavy adobe walls pierced with rifle loopholes. At each corner are towers for riflemen and footpaths on top of the walls. While the fort was once on the South Platte, the stream now runs five miles farther west.

FORT LUPTON was the third of these forts, built in 1836 on the site of present-day Fort Lupton by Lancaster P. Lupton, former Army lieutenant. It was first called **FORT LANCASTER.** At times

Indians gathered here for council. The fort was abandoned in 1844, and a rich farming community sprang up here and soon the town of Fort Lupton was established. The ruins of the fort are on a dairy farm whose barn is built around some of the original adobe walls of the fort.

FORT ST. VRAIN, south of Greeley at St. Vrain, was the largest of the South Platte trading posts, and third largest in the Rocky Mountain West. Only Fort Laramie on the North Platte and Fort Bent on the Arkansas exceeded it in size. It was established in 1838 by William Bent and Céran St. Vrain, to compete with Fort Lupton and Fort Vásquez, and first called **FORT GEORGE.** Built of adobe, the fort was 125 by 100 feet, with walls 2 feet thick and 14 feet high. Being halfway between Fort Bent and Fort Laramie it was a popular rendezvous of traders, emigrants, and adventurers. This fort was abandoned in 1844 when the American Fur Company and Lancaster P. Lupton agreed to give up their competing South Platte Valley fur trading posts. The site of Fort St. Vrain is identified by a marker, erected in 1911.

FORT DAVY CROCKETT, on the left bank of the Green River in Moffat County near the Colorado-Utah line, was not an imposing affair. It was built in 1837 by Philip Thompson and William Craig as a one-story trading post of cottonwood logs with three wings and no stockade. The post, though visited by trappers, never prospered and was nicknamed by them "Fort Misery." Dr. F. A. Wislizenus of Germany, author of *A Journey to the Rocky Mountains,* visited the post in 1839 and found the inhabitants eating dog meat. He tried some and said it was "not bad." Mountain men and their squaws deserted the place in 1840. This spot is in Dinosaur National Park at a place known as Brown's Hole, which had been a rendezvous of mountain men since 1830.

FORT MASSACHUSETTS was built in 1852 in the San Luis Valley and is believed to have been the first United States military post in Colorado, as well as the first settlement in the valley. The fort lay in a swampy hollow surrounded by foothills, and soldiers not slain by Indians were mortally sickened by the stagnant waters. It was abandoned in 1858 for Fort Garland, established six miles to the south.

FORT GARLAND, which replaced Fort Massachusetts, was built in 1858 and named for Brigadier General John Garland, Commander of the Department of New Mexico. It was primarily established to check the Ute Indians, but also was a refuge for settlers and a social center. In 1866–1867 Kit Carson commanded the post, and did very well because of his familiarity with the Ute language. Prior to the arrival of Kit Carson, the most exciting event at Fort Garland was the affair of the Espinoza gang. The leader, Felipe Nerio Espinoza, had sworn to kill one hundred Americans for each of his six relatives slain in the Mexican War. Operating in and around Fort Garland, he had wiped out forty persons when Tom Tobin, veteran Indian scout and colorful character, took up the trail. Tobin met and killed Espinoza as well as one of his gang. To collect a reward offered by the legislature, he placed the heads in a jar of alcohol. A doctor at Fort Garland is supposed to have tried to make off with the heads, and in fleeing broke the jar. Tobin had to use "Taos Lightning," a fiery alcoholic drink from Taos, to preserve his trophies. He eventually obtained a $2,500 bounty, a handsome rifle, and fancy buckskin suit.

The old fort, with most buildings well preserved, is today a state historic monument and stands on the southern edge of the town of Fort Garland. A highway cuts across the parade ground.

FORT LEWIS, eight miles from present-day Durango in the San Juan Basin, was established in 1880 and garrisoned with troops from Fort Garland. By 1883 all troops at the latter fort had been moved to Fort Lewis. This was the second fort of this name, both being built to guard the Ute Indian Reservation. The first was at Pagosa Mineral Springs, a group of hot mineral springs, established in 1878 and named for Lieutenant Colonel William N. Lewis, who died of wounds inflicted by Cheyenne in a fight on Famished Woman's Creek that same year. First called **CAMP LEWIS** it became Fort Lewis the same year. In 1880 it was removed to near present-day Durango. The old fort now became a subpost to the new under the name of **CANTONMENT PAGOSA SPRINGS,** and was partially dismantled to build the new one. The second Fort Lewis was abandoned in 1891.

FORT COLLINS, in Larimer County fifty-eight miles north of

Denver and on the site of present-day Fort Collins, was established as a small military post in 1864. It was first called **CAMP COLLINS** and later Fort Collins for Lieutenant William O. Collins, commanding officer at Fort Laramie, Wyoming, and was garrisoned mainly for the protection of a few scattered ranchers and farmers in the Cache la Poudre Valley, as well as to guard the Overland Trail. The post was abandoned in 1871. The Auntie Stone Cabin, built as the first dwelling at Fort Collins and used later as a mess hall for officers, today is the meeting place of the Larimer County Pioneers Association.

FORT SEDGWICK, west of Julesburg, was established as a military post in 1864 to protect travelers. It was named for General John Sedgwick of the Union Army. A granite marker identifies the site of this fort, which was garrisoned until 1871 when the Indians were subjugated.

FORT MORGAN, on the site of the present-day Fort Morgan, seat of Morgan County, was built during the gold-rush days and first known as **CAMP TYLER** and later as **CAMP WARDELL.** It was named Fort Morgan in 1866 in honor of its first commander, Colonel C. A. Morgan. The site of the old fort is marked by a monument.

FORT CRAWFORD was established in 1880 in the Uncompahgre Valley south of present-day Montrose, to restrain the Ute Indians. It was first called **CANTONMENT ON THE UNCOMPAHGRE** but later named Fort Crawford in honor of Captain Emmet Crawford, 3rd Cavalry. The entire Valley was a part of the Ute reservation until 1881, when it was opened for settlement. The garrison was withdrawn in 1884. Chief Ouray, famous leader of the Uncompahgre Ute, and his wife, Chipeta, are buried in Ouray-Chipeta Park not far away.

FORT LOGAN, three miles from Denver, was established in 1887 about the time the Government abandoned all other military posts in the state. The grounds embrace some 1,000 acres with 136 buildings, barracks, warehouses, officers' quarters, and so on. This is the only garrisoned post in Colorado today.

FORT WICKED, a fortified ranch and station on the Overland

Trail near Merino, gained its name when Indians rode off in disgust without being able to take it during the uprising in 1865. They called the stationmaster, H. Godfrey, "Old Wicked," and his nickname was given the fort.

FORT REYNOLDS, near Manzanola, was an Army post during the Civil War. **FORT NAMAQUA,** in what is today Loveland, was the first settlement in that community, when Mariano Modeno in 1858 built his fortified ranch house, which later was to become a stage station for the Overland Stage Line.

NEW MEXICO

Admitted to the Union in 1912 as the forty-seventh state.

Captain Paddy Graydon ordered two mules brought up. He then personally supervised the strapping on their backs of several hundred pounds of explosives. To the explosives he attached short fuses.

"Them pore old mules," groaned one trooper.

"Shut up!" cried another. "This is war, man! War!"

It was war and it had come to New Mexico. The first clash between Union and Confederate forces in the Southwest occurred at Fort Craig, on February 16, 1862. General Henry H. Sibley and his Texans had appeared before the fort and were at once engaged by Union cavalry from the garrison. Sibley retired across the Rio Grande, but the Union men followed up their advantage. They began to harass the Texans. One of Kit Carson's troopers lassoed a Confederate cannon and "snaked" it back to the Union camp amidst loud cheers.

But on the night of February 20th Captain Graydon believed he had the ideal plan to wipe out the enemy. He would rig up two mules with sufficient explosives to blow up the Confederate camp. All he had to do was to light the fuses, prod the mules, and send them on their way into the midst of the rebels.

Captain Graydon was a smart man and knew how to keep his company at full strength by impressing peons and giving them the names of his missing soldiers, so his roster was always full—but he

did not know about mules. It is traditional that not even the most hard-bitten old Army sergeant could ever understand an Army mule.

When the fuses were lighted and began to sputter, Captain Graydon said hopefully and encouragingly to his walking bombs: "Get along, mules—trot right into that Confed camp."

With that, he and the rest of his company turned and ran as fast as they could toward Fort Craig. They began to run even faster when they saw that the mules, instead of going toward the Confederate camp, were running right along after them. Their feed bags were back there at Fort Craig. And the two mules now considered Graydon and the others their bosom friends. But the short fuses burned down, and there was a terrific explosion. The Confederate camp came awake with a start, and surprise was impossible. The next day there was the Battle of Valverde, seven miles north of the fort, at which the Union forces were disgracefully trounced. General Sibley went on to capture Albuquerque and Santa Fe.

FORT CRAIG was established in 1854 on the west bank of the Rio Grande, at the northern entrance of the Jornada del Muerto. (Journey of Death—*jornada* meaning colloquially "a day's journey without water," and the Jornada del Muerto in the dry season was without a drop of water for eighty miles!) The purpose of the fort was to protect westbound miners from Navajo and Apache Indians and to patrol the road between Santa Fe and El Paso. The fort figured in the Navajo and Apache conflicts of the 1850's and, following the Civil War, in the Apache wars of the 1860's and 1870's. It was abandoned in 1885, and its eighteen adobe buildings began to crumble until today only parts of them remain. A New Mexico historical marker on U.S. 85, some five miles to the west of the fort site, identifies it.

FORT CONRAD, on the west bank of the Rio Grande, was established in 1851 but did not last long. In 1853 Colonel Joseph King Fenno Mansfield, in making an inspection of military posts of the West, informed the War Department that "a better site, I have no doubt, can be found some 10 miles further south between this post and Fra Cristobalm, that will more effectively intercept the trails of the Indians, and I would accordingly recommend breaking up this post and building an entire new one." His recommendations were followed out, and next year Fort Craig was built and all troops at Fort Conrad moved there. Fort Conrad was named for the then Secretary of War Charles M. Conrad.

FORT MARCY, established in 1846 on a hill overlooking Santa Fe, was the first American fort built in New Mexico. It was erected by General Stephen Watts Kearny, commanding the Army of the West, when he took over New Mexico as a territory of the United States during the War with Mexico, and declared himself governor. This fort, which never fired a shot in anger, was named for the Secretary of War William L. Marcy. It was an "irregular hexagonal pentagon," with adobe walls 9 feet high and 5 feet thick, the whole surrounded by a wide ditch or moat; 13 cannon were mounted on its walls.

Santa Fe was a gay town at this time. When Brevet Colonel Edwin Vose Sumner took over command of the Department of New Mexico in 1851, he was appalled at conditions at Fort Marcy. He reported: "I reached Santa Fé on the 19th of July and assumed command of the Department. My first step was to break up the post at Santa Fé, that sink of vice and extravagance, and to remove the troops and public property to . . . Fort Union. I left one company of artillery there."

The post was abandoned when the Confederates invaded Mexico in March, 1862, but was reoccupied by New Mexico Volunteers shortly thereafter. Complete abandonment was ordered in 1867. Then an odd situation developed. In 1875 the District of New Mexico ordered the relief of "certain detachments assigned to the District Headquarters located at Fort Marcy," and shortly thereafter the Assistant Adjutant General at Washington requested post returns from the fort. The commander of the company ordered to relieve the garrison reported "there was no post at Fort Marcy." The Assistant Adjutant General then wrote to the Commanding Officer, District of New Mexico, and that officer forwarded the returns, thereby re-establishing Fort Marcy. The fort was finally abandoned in 1894. A group of mounds on the hilltop overlooking Santa Fe marks the site.

FORT UNION, one of the most important military posts established after the United States acquired the Spanish Southwest in the War with Mexico, was built in 1851 at what today is Watrous in Mora County. The ruins of this fort, erected on a reservation of eight square miles in a broad valley at the base of the Turkey Mountains, are now preserved as the Fort Union National Monument. It was strategically placed to protect traffic on the Santa Fe Trail and was a supply center for smaller forts of the area and a base for troop movements. During the Civil War it became the principal objective of Confederate forces under General Henry R. Sibley following his capture of Albuquerque and Santa Fe. But on the way to Fort Union the Confederates were surprised in Apache Canyon and defeated at the Battle of Pigeon's Ranch in Glorieta. The failure of the Confederates to capture Fort Union completely ruined their plans for occupying New Mexico and within a few months the Civil War in that Territory was over. There actually were two Fort Unions. The first had been built at the foot of a mesa, and Colonel Mansfield's report of 1853 stated: "It is too close under the mesa for a tenable position against an enterprising enemy, unless the immediate heights can be occupied by a blockhouse which can readily be done." In 1861 the old fort was abandoned and a second one built a mile from the side of the mesa. It was constructed in the shape of a large star. Kit Carson, as a lieutenant colonel, served here with the New Mexican Volunteers during the troubles with the Apache Indians. Geronimo, the great Apache chief, was confined in a cell here at one time, as was Billy the Kid, notorious killer in the Lincoln County (Cattle) War. Fort Union's latter years "were full of army red tape, brass, social life, and pretty women—it was gay," as one writer put it. After the Apaches were subjugated and the railroad came, there was little use for the fort. It was abandoned in 1891. Not until then did the Government learn that its fort was on private property—a part of the Spanish Mora Grant. The heirs of General Benjamin Butler, who acquired large holdings of the grant, have graciously donated to the Government 720 acres and the right of way to the site of this National Monument.

FORT SUMNER was established on the east bank of the Pecos

River at Bosque Redondo (Circle of Trees) in 1862 to guard the reservation of the Navajo and Mescalero Apache conquered by Kit Carson. This had been the site of a trading post licensed in 1851, and when a fort was built here in accordance with the plan of General James H. Carleton it was reported as "beyond comparison the handsomest and most picturesque in the Union." In 1863 Carson had to pursue the discontented Navajo, and after rounding up some 8,000 he marched them hundreds of miles back to Bosque Redondo. The Navajo called this the "long walk." They were held here until 1868, when on promise of good behavior they were allowed to return to their homeland along the Arizona–New Mexico border. After this the fort was demilitarized and put up for auction. Lucien B. Maxwell bought it and remodeled the officers' quarters into a house of twenty large rooms. He lived here until 1875 when his son, Peter, inherited the property. It was in Peter Maxwell's room in 1881 that Billy the Kid was killed by Sheriff Pat Garrett. He was buried in the fort cemetery. Three years later a group of cattlemen bought the property but abandoned it in 1894. The ruins of this fort were washed away by a flood in 1941.

FORT WINGATE, as it later became known, was established as **FORT FAUNTLEROY** in 1860 at Ojo del Oso near present-day Gallup on the site of the town of Fort Wingate. A year after it was built the name was changed to **FORT LYON** after Nathaniel Lyon, first Union general to fall in the Civil War. Colonel Thomas Turner (Little Lord) Fauntleroy, of the old 1st Dragoons, for whom the fort first was named, had joined the Confederate Army and his name became anathema. In 1862 the fort was re-established sixty miles to the west and renamed Fort Wingate in honor of Captain Benjamin Wingate who had been killed a short time before at the Battle of Valverde. The fort served actively in Colonel Kit Carson's campaign against the Navajo in 1863–1864, but when the Indians were allowed to return home in 1868 Fort Wingate was moved back to the original location of Fort Fauntleroy-Lyons. From 1882 on, the fort was often used as headquarters and outfitting post for ethnological and archeological expeditions. It was retained as a Government post until 1910. In 1914 the old buildings were used to house 4,000 Mexican troops and families who fled Mexico during the Pancho Villa War. In 1925 Congress appropriated a half million dollars for a Navajo School on the Fort Wingate Military Reservation. The Wingate Ordnance Department, designated in 1918 and still in use, was moved to a new site nearer the Santa Fe Railroad.

FORT SELDEN was established in 1865 north of Las Cruces on the Rio Grande as a protection against raids of the Gila Apache. It was at the southern end of the Jornado del Muerto (Journey of Death), the eighty-mile stretch of arid road at whose northern end was Fort Craig. South of Fort Selden, named for Colonel Henry R. Selden, 1st New Mexico Volunteer Infantry, was Mount Robledo,

which was used by the Army as a heliograph station during the Apache uprising. Messages by heliograph, a device for signaling by flashing the sun's rays from a mirror, were received here from Fort Bliss, Texas, some fifty miles away. The fort was permanently abandoned in 1891. Crumbling walls of some twenty-five buildings are to be seen on the site. A New Mexico historical marker on U.S. Highway 85 gives a brief history of the fort.

FORT FILLMORE was established on the east bank of the Rio Grande, south of present-day Las Cruces, in 1851, to operate against the Apaches of the White Mountains and the Gila River. It was named for President Millard Fillmore. In July, 1861, Lieutenant

Colonel John R. Baylor of the Confederate Army captured the fort as well as the entire command of Major Isaac Lynde. Baylor made his headquarters at Mesilla across the river and named himself military governor, with Mesilla as the capital of the Territory of Arizona, which included all of New Mexico south of the 34th parallel, a part of Texas, and all of Arizona, Nevada, and California. But a year later General James H. Carleton at the head of the California column ran the Confederates out and set up his own military headquarters. Fort Fillmore had the distinction in 1860 to be commanded for a short time by a woman, Mrs. Lydia Spencer Lane. In her book *I Married a Soldier* she explained that when the entire garrison was ordered out on patrol with the exception of a sergeant and ten men, "I was left in command of Fort Fillmore." All public funds were turned over to her and the sergeant made his daily report to her. Only traces of the old adobe fort are to be seen today in the shifting sands.

FORT STANTON, established in 1855 in Lincoln County five miles west of present-day Capitan, was garrisoned to protect white settlers from the Mescalero Apache. It was first called **CAMP STANTON** in honor of Captain Henry W. Stanton, 1st U.S. Dragoons, who was killed nearby by Mescalero Apache Indians about four months before the camp was established. The fort at first consisted of a blockhouse surrounded by an adobe wall on a level hilltop. When the Confederates invaded New Mexico during the Civil War, the Union forces abandoned the fort. But after the war it was reestablished when Colonel Kit Carson was sent to subdue the Apache, who had gone on the warpath again. In 1868 many of the old adobe buildings were replaced by stone structures that still stand today. The fort was abandoned in 1896 and became a U.S. Public Health Service Hospital for the Merchant Marine three years later. Today it is a tuberculosis sanitarium operated by the New Mexico Department of Public Welfare.

FORT CUMMINGS in Dona Ana County near Florida was established in the fall of 1862 by General James Henry Carleton for the purpose of keeping New Mexico from joining the Confederacy, as well as to control the depredations of the Apache led by Cochise,

Geronimo, Victoria, and other warlike chiefs. Another duty was to protect the Butterfield Trail and the road from Fort Selden to California. The establishment of the Ojo Caliente Reservation in 1868 and the submission of a substantial portion of the Apache brought a more peaceful state of affairs to the Territory of New Mexico,

Apache

and in 1870 the fort was abandoned except for a caretaker. However, in 1881 when Chief Victoria went on the warpath the post was reoccupied for four more years. Ruins of adobe walls mark the site today, while a tablet commemorating the Butterfield Overland Mail identifies the site as a stage station from 1858 to 1861.

POST OF ALBUQUERQUE, at present-day Albuquerque, was occupied in 1847 by Captain J. H. Burgwin of the First U.S. Dragoons and continued as a military installation until 1867. Captain Burgwin had **CANTONMENT BURGWIN** near Taos named for him in 1851. It was located so as to reinforce the garrisons at Fort Union, Fort Marcy and others in the area, as well as to command the wagon road between Santa Fe and Taos. Today the Fort Burgwin Research Center, founded by Ralph M. Rounds, occupies the site, and the fort site is being restored.

FORT BASCOM was a military post on the south bank of the Canadian River in San Miguel County in 1863. It was named in honor of Captain George N. Bascom, killed at the Battle of Valverde. In 1870 the garrison and stores were transferred to Fort Union.

FORT BAYARD was established two miles from the present town of Bayard in 1866 to afford protection to the miners of that section against the Warm Springs Apache under Chief Victoria. It was named in honor of Captain George D. Bayard, cavalry officer and brigadier general of volunteers, who died of wounds received at Fredericksburg. In 1900 the reservation and all buildings were turned over to the Surgeon General of the Army for use as a sanitarium for the treatment of officers and enlisted men suffering from pulmonary tuberculosis. It is now a United States Veterans Hospital.

NEVADA

Admitted to the Union in 1864 as the thirty-sixth state.

"I wouldn't mind being shot by one of them Indians—just so the bullet lodged in a fleshy part—" began one soldier.

"And didn't kill you and you could get the bullet after the doctor dug it out," said a second soldier, finishing out the sentence of the first.

"That's right!" exclaimed the first.

"Well, I'd be willing to have two or three bullets hit me as long as they didn't do too much damage," went on the second.

"You're right! Them kind of bullets, especially!"

It would not be hard to imagine two soldiers at Fort Schellbourne having a discussion such as this in the 1860's. For it was reported that the Paiute Indians—at least some of them—were using bullets cast out of pure gold! The Pony Express riders thundering through this isolated and rugged section had often heard this story. Plenty of bullets had come their way—but they had stopped none of the golden ones, apparently.

Yet the story that went about this mining section evidently had some foundation, as later discoveries seemed to confirm it. The Indians apparently used whatever metal they could get to make their bullets, and silver and some gold were in those hills around Schell Creek and in Schellbourne Canyon and Egan Canyon in White Pine County.

Schell Creek was the site of a relay station on the Pony Express and Overland Stage Route from 1859 to 1869. After the Indians destroyed the first building in 1860, troops were moved in to protect the mail and travelers. The military post was called **CAMP SCHELL-BOURNE** and later **FORT SCHELLBOURNE.** It was abandoned in 1869 when transcontinental stagecoaching ended in those parts with completion of the Union Pacific Railroad. Today the site of Fort Schellbourne is part of a ranch, and remains of the stage station and military post are to be seen at Schell Creek.

FORT BAKER, more generally known as **LAS VEGAS FORT** or **STOCKADE AT LAS VEGAS,** was originally established by thirty Mormons under William Bringhurst in 1855. Brigham Young at the City of the Great Salt Lake sent Bringhurst and his men to build a fort, the usual precaution of the Mormons, to protect immigrants and the United States mail from the Indians and to teach the latter how to raise corn, wheat, potatoes, squash, and melons. These settlers cleared away the mesquite in the basin known as Las Vegas by the Spanish because of its fertile and marshy plains, and built an adobe stockade 14 feet high and 150 feet long, then cabins, and finally planted crops. They called their stockade **THE FORT.** The Mormons were "released" from the mission in 1857 when Brigham Young had trouble with the Federal Government and called for a concentration at Great Salt Lake City. During the Civil War Union troops were stationed there briefly and called the place Fort Baker. The Las Vegas Fort today has been partially restored and is on property owned by a Las Vegas fraternal club.

The Mormons also are credited with establishing the oldest settlement in Nevada at what is today Genoa in Douglas County when that section was a part of western Utah. This was the stockade at Mormon Station, built in 1849 by H. S. Beattie, who had come to trade with travelers on the road to California. In 1855 Judge Orson Hyde, one of the Twelve Apostles of the church, renamed the place

Genoa, and the fortification became known variously as the **STOCK-ADE AT GENOA** or the **FORT GENOA STOCKADE**. By then it enclosed an acre of ground. Genoa began to prosper when the Comstock Lode was uncovered a few miles to the northeast and Virginia City roared into existence. Today the stockade has been restored as a museum.

FORT CHURCHILL, the pride of Nevada as far as military posts went, was established in 1860 just after the rush to the Comstock Lode, although it was not the discovery of this richest silver vein in the county that caused its erection. The fort was built in the Carson River Valley just southeast of present-day Reno as the direct result of the killing of seven white men at the James Williams Station (east of Carson City) on the Overland Trail. It is believed that the kidnaping of two Bannock Indian women by white men had caused the Indians to seek revenge. Nevertheless troops were sent in from California to aid Nevada volunteers, and finally the Indians were subdued. Fort Churchill, named in honor of Captain Charles C. Churchill, 3rd U.S. Artillery, then was ordered built. The reservation was a rhomboid containing 1,400 acres, within which was a small parade ground with officers' quarters, barracks, mess hall, guardhouse, commandant's office, and other necessary buildings. During the Civil War this post became a recruiting station.

Fort Churchill was a relay station during the brief Pony Express Service, and such famous riders as William F. ("Buffalo Bill") Cody, Robert H. ("Pony Bob") Haslam, and Johnny Fry rode this section. Haslam made a sensational ride of 380 miles in 36 hours during the Paiute uprising. The post was abandoned in 1871, and the Government realized but $750 at the public auction sale of the post buildings. Much of the timber used in the big white Towle house at Carson River Crossing on the Fernley-Yerington Highway came from the fort buildings. In 1935 CCC workers began to clear the old reservation under sponsorship of the State Park Service for the Sagebrush Chapter of the Daughters of the American Revolution. One of the buildings was reconstructed as a future museum, but this has crumbled into ruins. The remainder is merely sections of adobe walls. The site is a state park.

FORT RUBY, also known as **CAMP RUBY,** was established at the southern end of the Cave Creek Road (near Cave Creek, White Pine County) in the Ruby Valley in 1862, at a time when Indians throughout the nation were giving the Civil War as an excuse to make war themselves upon the whites. During the first year of Fort Ruby's existence the Goshute and Paiute Indians directed their attacks mainly on Overland Mail relay stations. The Fort Ruby garrison fought several skirmishes before the troubles ended. In 1864 the Nevada Volunteers were relieved by Californians, who held the post until its abandonment three years later. The site is on the Fort Ruby Ranch, where two one-story log structures, the old post office and a residence, are to be seen adjacent to modern ranch buildings.

FORT HALLECK was established in 1867 near the route of the proposed Central Pacific Railroad in Elko County at the western base of the Ruby Mountains near Secret Canyon. It was built after Fort Ruby was abandoned and the garrison of the latter fort moved there. The fort was named in honor of General Henry Wager Halleck, then commander of the Military Division of the Pacific. While the troops engaged in no Indian fighting, their presence encouraged settlement in the surrounding valleys. This was one of the coldest posts in winter in the United States, the thermometer sometimes going down to 50 below zero. The fort was abandoned in 1886. The buildings have disappeared and the site is identified by a historical marker.

FORT McDERMIT, near the present town of McDermitt, at the present McDermitt Indian Reservation, was erected in 1865 on the site of the Quinn River station, a stagecoach stop. The fort was named in honor of Colonel Charles McDermit, the name of the town being misspelled as McDermitt through a mapmaker's error. Colonel McDermit, commander of the Nevada Military District, had led a troop of cavalry to Paradise Valley where Indians had attacked the settlement. He was shot and killed from ambush and his body taken to Fort Churchill for burial. Immediately thereafter Fort McDermit was established on a reserve of 2,000 acres. In 1886 it was turned over to the Department of the Interior for an Indian Reservation.

FORT (CAMP) McGARRY was established on the shores of Summit Lake in the present Paiute and Shoshone Indian Reservation, in 1867. It was located on the Applegate Cutoff, an early road to Oregon. The soldiers first lived in tents, and finally stone buildings were erected and the fort placed on a permanent basis. It was named for Colonel Edward McGarry, of the 2nd California Volunteer Cavalry. The fort was abandoned in 1871.

CAMP WINFIELD SCOTT was established just south of Fort McDermit in 1866. It was named for General Winfield Scott. The fort was abandoned in 1871.

ARIZONA

Admitted to the Union in 1912 as the forty-eighth state.

It was a strange sight. The soldiers at Fort Defiance stood about and gaped. Some made critical remarks. But the forty-seven heavily laden camels seemed at peace with the world. They chewed their cuds, swished their short tails to dislodge flies, and now and then grunted in their odd fashion.

"Wonder what's holding up things?" asked one soldier.

Apparently there was an animated discussion going on among some Arabs and the American in charge of this attraction—Edward Fitzgerald Beale. The Arabs one by one threw down their camel whips and turned away. Only one man stood beside Beale.

"Well, Hi Jolly, it looks like we'll have to go it without the Arabs," said Beale.

Hi Jolly, whose real Syrian name was Hadji Ali, understood and nodded his head. He was the only camel driver left. The Arabs during the previous evening and that morning had been hearing frightening stories about the forests, plains, deserts, and especially the fierce Indians along the proposed route through Arizona, so they refused to go.

Beale gave orders for the caravan to move out. The camels carried not only about 600 pounds each in baggage, but water and feed for the mules that were to be taken along. Beale proceeded south from Fort Defiance to approximately the 35th parallel and then

westward along this imaginary line across the entire state to the Colorado River. He had been authorized by the Government in this year of 1857 to open up a wagon road from Texas to California, which he successfully did.

The use of camels in the western desert country had been Beale's idea. He had been a Navy man and had fought with Commodore Stockton when the latter seized California in the War with Mexico. Beale and Kit Carson were sent to Washington with dispatches. Later Beale interested Jefferson Davis, Secretary of War, in the idea of using camels. The storeship *Supply* made two trips to the Orient to obtain the animals.

The Civil War put a stop to this experiment. The camels that formed the United States Army Camel Corps based at Fort Tejon, California, were sold to a circus and private owners in 1864. Some were turned loose and became something of a terror in the desert. They frightened other pack animals as they suddenly loomed up in their path. Mule drivers and others gradually exterminated them.

The camel driver, Hadji Ali, later bought himself a mule and began prospecting for precious metal in the mountains. Following his death he was buried at Quartzsite.

FORT DEFIANCE, the starting point in Arizona of this survey, was the first military post established in the Territory. It was built in 1852 under the direction of Colonel E. V. Sumner as a base for his campaigns against the Navajo. After years of almost continual skirmishing, the Navajo in the spring of 1860 attacked the fort. But they were beaten off. The next year the fort was abandoned and later Fort Defiance served as the Navajo agency. The site is now occupied by a Navajo tribal school and hospital. The town of Fort Defiance has grown up around it. All that remains of the old fort is a three-story stone building.

FORT BUCHANAN, established as the first of two military posts in what was known as the Gadsden Purchase, was built in 1857 in Santa Cruz County three miles west of present-day Sonoita. It was named for President James Buchanan. By the Gadsden Purchase the United States in 1853 had acquired from Mexico 45,535 square miles of territory which represents the extreme south of New Mexico and Arizona below the Gila River. Fort Buchanan guarded the Butterfield Overland Mail, and its garrison operated against the hostile Apaches. Shortly after the start of the Civil War, the fort was evacuated and destroyed. After the war **FORT CRITTENDEN,** named for General Thomas L. Crittenden of the Union Army in the Civil War, was built on a hill just east of the ruins of Fort Buchanan. This post was abandoned in 1873. Ruins of both forts are to be seen today.

FORT GRANT, which had a succession of names and several previous sites, finally was located on a reservation of 42,341 acres in Graham County, at the town of Fort Grant, twenty-five miles north of Wilcox. This post originally was established as the second military installation in the Gadsden Purchase in 1860 when it was provided that the location of Fort Buchanan be changed to the junction of the Arivaypa and San Pedro rivers. In the meantime a post was built by the garrison of Fort Buchanan at the mouth of the San Pedro River and named **FORT ARIVAYPA.** A few months later the name was changed to **FORT BRECKENRIDGE,** for John J. Breckenridge, Vice President under Buchanan. At the start of the Civil War this post was destroyed by fire and abandoned, as was Fort Buchanan. In 1862 California troops rebuilt and occupied the post and named it **FORT STANFORD,** for Leland Stanford, then governor of California. The post was abandoned before the year was out and destroyed by a flood. In 1865 California troops established a new site at the junction of the Arivaypa and San Pedro rivers and called it **CAMP GRANT,** but this spot proved so malarial and unhealthful that the post was removed seventy miles southeast to a point at the foot of Mount Graham in the latter part of 1872. Seven years later the name Fort Grant was given the post. The garrison saw much service here in endeavoring to intercept Apache renegades who fled the San Carlos Reservation, and pursuing Apache raiding parties into Mexico. With the surrender of Geronimo in 1886, the fort lost its importance. It was ordered discontinued in 1905 and abandoned in 1907. In 1911 it was given to the State of Arizona, and the reform school was moved there from Benson. It is still the State Industrial School, and several of the old buildings of the fort are in use.

FORT LOWELL, established as **CAMP TUCSON** in 1860, close to the present site of a Tucson hotel, was one of the key outposts in the long and deadly war carried on against the Apache Indians. It was captured by Texas Mounted Volunteers in the early part of 1862, but a few months later the California Column of Union troops retook it and named it the **TUCSON POST SUPPLY DEPOT.** After the war the post was maintained as a supply depot for military posts in southern Arizona. In 1866 the name was changed to **CAMP LOWELL** in honor of Brigadier General Charles R. Lowell, who was killed at the Battle of Cedar Creek, Virginia. This was a very popular post at the time, and was the scene of much of Tucson's social life. Presumably because of the town's unhealthy condition, the post was moved in 1873 some seven miles southeast. Here large adobe bricks were used in the construction of a permanent post, and in 1879 it was renamed Fort Lowell. It was abandoned in 1891, soon after the end of the Apache War. The City of Tucson acquired part of the former military reservation and planned to create a park and restore at least one adobe structure.

FORT BOWIE had its origin in the desire of California troops during the Civil War to protect a spring at the eastern entrance of Apache Pass at what is today Bowie or Bowie Junction. General James H. Carleton, commander of the California Column of Volunteers, on his way to New Mexico detached a company to guard the spring known as Puerto del Dado in the Chicahua Mountains. Shortly afterward occurred the Battle of Apache Pass in which warriors led by Mangas Coloradas and Cochise attacked the troops. Field artillery was used here for the first time against the Apache. After the defeat of the Indians temporary huts were erected and the post was called Fort Bowie, in honor of George W. Bowie, colonel of the regiment, who then was commanding the District of Southern California. Occupation of the post was continuous until 1894, when the troops were withdrawn and the post was abandoned. The names "Camp" and "Fort" appear to have both been used officially in referring to this post. After being named Fort Bowie, five years later it was called **CAMP BOWIE** until 1879, when once more it became Fort Bowie. The reservation was sold at auction to local farmers in 1911.

FORT WHIPPLE (WHIPPLE BARRACKS) was established in 1863 by California Volunteers in the Chino Valley, some twenty miles north of the present site of Prescott, to protect miners in the gold fields near the San Francisco Mountains from Indian raiders as well as to preserve peace and order among the miners. It was named Fort Whipple in honor of Brigadier General Amiel W. Whipple, who was killed in the Battle of Chancellorsville, and who as a first lieutenant of Topographical Engineers in 1853 explored the road leading from Albuquerque, New Mexico, to the regions around the San Francisco Mountains. This had been known as the "Whipple Route." In 1864 the location of the fort was changed to a point on Granite Creek, two miles from Prescott. That same year it became the territorial capital when Governor John N. Goodwin arrived there. The governor later moved into a mansion across Granite Creek. In the meantime the military post in Prescott known as **PRESCOTT BARRACKS** and Fort Whipple were designated in 1879 as one establishment to be known as Whipple Barracks. In 1898 Whipple Barracks was discontinued by official order. Today on the 1,700-acre reservation is a Veterans Administration Hospital, and within the military compound is the 75-acre Yavapai Indian Reservation.

"FORT MISERY" was a name given a two-story log structure in

Fort Misery

the heart of Prescott in Pioneer Square. This house, which has been reproduced, was the first built in Prescott (named for William Hickling Prescott, the historian) in the winter of 1863–1864 by Manuel Yesesea, who arrived with the escort of the territorial governor, John N. Goodwin. It was used as a residence for the judge, and the first court of the Territory convened there. One night there was an alarm of an Indian attack. All prisoners were freed to fight, and after the battle all were given their liberty. Later the house was turned into a boardinghouse, and settlers named it "Fort Misery."

FORT VERDE, established in 1866 as **CAMP LINCOLN** on the Verde River in the Verde Valley of central Arizona, was the headquarters of General George Crook's campaign against the Yavapai, or Apache-Mojave Indians, in 1872–1873. In the latter year the Indians surrendered unconditionally. By that time the post had become known as **CAMP VERDE;** then, in 1879, it was designated as Fort Verde. The name Camp Verde clung to it, and a town on the site is known as Camp Verde. The fort was abandoned in 1890. Three sets of officers' quarters still are standing and today are private residences. The Camp Verde Improvement Association maintains a small museum in the old administration building.

FORT APACHE, established in 1870 on the north side of the White River on the site of the present-day town of Fort Apache, was important in the Apache Wars of 1872–1873 and 1881–1886. It was located on the northern edge of the San Carlos Reservation, which was an extension of the White Mountain Reservation. Several times after the Apache were settled on the reservation, renegade bands under such chiefs as Geronimo, Natchez, Chato, and Chihuahua escaped and were pursued by the fort's garrison but without success. Fort Apache first was named **CAMP ORD,** but the same year the name was changed to **CAMP MOGOLLON** and then **CAMP THOMAS.** In 1871 it became known as **CAMP APACHE,** and in 1879 was officially termed Fort Apache. It is not certain whether the Camp Apache established in 1871 later became Fort Apache, as there is some evidence that it was a temporary post located nearby and discontinued about 1873. Most available sources, however, indicate that Camp Apache and Fort Apache were the same post under different designations. The Fort Apache Military Reservation was transferred to the Secretary of the Interior in 1922. The fort is now used by the Bureau of Indian Affairs as headquarters of the Fort Apache Indian Reservation. Officers' row, the barracks, adjutant's office, commissary, guardhouse, quartermaster warehouse, and cavalry stables still are standing. One of the old log buildings at the end of officers' row is said to have been occupied by General George Crook during his campaign.

FORT HUACHUCA, established in 1877 as **CAMP HUACHUCA** to protect settlers and travelers from the fierce Apache Indians, played an important part in the campaigns against Geronimo between the time it was built until 1886 when the Apache chief surrendered. In 1882 the camp was made permanent and called Fort Huachuca but saw little activity until the Madero Revolt in Mexico in 1911. It then became the base for border patrols. It was declared surplus by the War Department in 1947 and is now the United States Army Electronics Proving Ground. The large adobe houses built in 1880 have been remodeled and are in present-day use, while other buildings dating from the time this was a fort still are in good condition. One interesting group of adobe huts located one-half mile north of the parade ground was built around 1900 to house Apache scouts, who had previous to this lived in wickiups, or temporary Indian shelters.

FORT MOJAVE was established in 1859 under the name of **CAMP COLORADO** by an expedition up the Colorado River as directed by the Department of California. The site of the fort at the head of the Mojave Valley on the east bank of the river had been suggested two years earlier by Edward Fitzgerald Beale, as a shelter for emigrants to California and a base of operations against the Mojave Indians. The post was named Fort Mojave by the post commander, but lasted only three years. It was re-established by California Volunteers in 1863, but finally, in 1890, was turned over to the Indian Service. The Indian Service gave it up in 1935, and the buildings were destroyed in 1942.

Of the numerous camps established in Arizona during the Indian troubles and Civil War, the majority lasted but a short time.

CALIFORNIA

Admitted to the Union in 1850 as the thirty-first state.

In December, 1841, Commandant Aleksander Rotchev of **FORT ROSSIYA** (Russia), which would be shortened to **FORT ROSS** by the Californians, was in something of a quandary. He had received orders from Czar Paul I to withdraw from California soil. The sea otter, which had provided a brisk business in furs, was almost extinct; the experiment in shipbuilding had proved unsuccessful, and farming had been a failure. Commandant Rotchev could not just pull out and leave everything. It would be too costly to transport all the goods and chattels that had been accumulated since the building of the fort in 1812.

But the problem was solved when Captain John Augustus Sutter, a Swiss aristocrat and former army officer in his native land, and founder of New Helvetia (Sacramento), appeared on the scene. Nearly everything the Russians had would be useful to Captain Sutter, who had built Sutter's Fort two years earlier and started farming on a large scale. He offered $30,000 to the Russian to be paid in $2,000 cash and the remainder in yearly installments of produce, mainly wheat. Commandant Rotchev accepted, and the deal was closed.

Captain Sutter literally bought everything. He got the buildings, which he dismantled, the farm implements, 1,700 head of cattle, 940 horses and mules, 9,000 sheep, the fort's arsenal, including brass pieces, cannon, and muskets—all former French weapons picked up in 1813 in the path of Napoleon's retreat from Moscow—and even Madame Rotchev's prized conservatory. Not only all this, but Captain Sutter acquired the Russian twenty-ton schooner *Constantine*, which he promptly loaded with his goods and sailed off down the coast and up the Sacramento River to his own fort at New Helvetia.

Fort Ross, the chief outpost of Russian civilization in California, stood on a high shelf of land sloping from wooded hills to the edge of a cove on the Pacific Ocean seventy-five miles above San Francisco. The fort was laid out in a rectangle that was enclosed by a

14-foot stockade of hewn timber and guarded by two blockhouses at the north and south corners, with portholes for cannon. In all, there were 59 buildings. The few buildings left after Captain Sutter's purchase were neglected until, in 1906, after damage by an earthquake, the State began restoration. The stockade, the Russian Orthodox chapel, the blockhouses, and the commandant's house all have been restored. Fort Ross today is a State Historical Monument.

SUTTER'S FORT (New Helvetia), which has been completely restored on its original site at Twenty-sixth and L streets in Sacramento, was built in 1839. Captain Sutter, by swearing allegiance to the Mexican flag, had received a grant of 50,000 acres of land. He soon had a thriving colony at New Helvetia, became a rival of the Hudson's Bay Company as a trader of furs with the Indians, and laid the foundation for his reputation as the "founder of American agriculture in California." John C. Frémont visited the fort in 1844 and again in 1846. In the latter year Frémont raised the American flag at Monterey but three days later was forced to retreat to Sutter's Fort. On May 13 war was declared with Mexico, and on July 11 Sutter hoisted the American flag over his fort. Sutter was then the leading man of wealth and influence in California, and the United States was indebted to him to a great extent for the conquest of California. But Sutter's troubles began when gold was discovered in January, 1848, at his sawmill on the south fork of the America River, near Coloma, some forty miles from the fort. In the stampede that followed, gold seekers overran his property, stole his livestock, and drove off his Indians. Sutter soon found himself impoverished. He died in Pennsylvania in 1880, a poor man. In the Fort Sutter Historical Museum in the restored fort, which is now a state historical monument, are to be found many interesting things. Inside the gate is the bell of Young America Engine Co. No. 6 which rang for Lincoln's election and tolled for his assassination. Near the bell are the cannon that guarded the fort. The original pine door frames are from Fort Ross. Here are relics of early California days, including Pony Express saddles (Sacramento was the western terminus of the Pony Express), Indian artifacts and agricultural implements.

The **PRESIDIO** of San Francisco is a post of considerable antiquity, and while still an active installation rivals in age some of the forts on the Atlantic seaboard. It was originally built in 1776 by Don Bautista de Anza to guard the Franciscan mission of San Francisco de Asis (later known as *Misión Dolores*). It was the custom to build presidios, or forts, to guard the missions from hostile natives and possible invaders, and between 1769 and 1823 the Franciscan friars founded twenty-one missions along the coastwise Camino Real (Royal Road), with the first at San Diego and the last at Sonoma. The missions with their presidios were spaced just a day's journey apart. The Presidio at San Francisco, with its mission restored, is now on a military reservation of 1,542 acres, the largest in the United States within a city—the entrance to which is at Lincoln Boulevard and Lombard Street. It extends from Lyon Street west to the ocean and from West Pacific Avenue and Lobos Creek north to the rim of the Golden Gate. The establishment of a United States fort at the Presidio may be said to date from April, 1847, when a detachment of troops was left there. The post was abandoned briefly from February to June, 1851, but since that year has been continually occupied.

FORT WINFIELD SCOTT, forming one of the defenses of San Francisco Harbor, is located near the northern limits of the Presidio. It is headquarters of both the Ninth Coast Artillery District and the harbor defenses distributed among Forts Barry, Baker, Miley, and Funston. In 1921 this fort was designated as a saluting station to return salutes of foreign vessels of war visiting the Port of San Francisco.

FORT POINT, on the promontory beyond Fort Winfield Scott and on the northernmost point of the San Francisco Peninsula beside the southern anchorage of the Golden Gate Bridge, was established in 1861. It stands on the shoreline and marks the site of **CASTILLO DE SAN JOAQUIN,** built by the Spanish in 1794 as a subpost of the Presidio. In 1881 Fort Point was renamed Fort Winfield Scott, for General Winfield Scott, but today the old name Fort Point is being used. This old fort, the largest of its kind on the Pacific Coast, was designed after Fort Sumter, South Carolina, with walls 36 feet thick and mounting 146 guns. Plans are under way to preserve it as a historical monument, with the old artillery pieces remounted and their muzzles pointing out over the Golden Gate. The Officers' Club, once the Spanish commandant's headquarters, is a low adobe structure and the oldest building standing in San Francisco. Nearby is the Presidio marker, which records its history, and in front are two old Spanish guns named "Poder" and "San Pedro," bearing the Spanish coat-of-arms and inscribed "Lima, Peru—1673."

FORT BAKER, part of the defenses of San Francisco, near Sausalito, was established in 1897. It was named for Colonel Edward Dickinson Baker, California Volunteers. In 1904 the military reservation of Fort Baker was divided into two forts, with the eastern portion retaining the name of Fort Baker and the western portion being named **FORT BARRY** for General William F. Barry, of Civil War fame. **FORT MILEY,** another of the defenses of the city, was established in 1900 just south of Lincoln Park, overlooking the Golden Gate. It was named in honor of Lieutenant Colonel John D. Miley, who died the year before at Manila. **FORT FUNSTON,** also one of the defenses, on the rim of the Golden Gate bordered by the Skyline Boulevard, was established in 1898 during the Spanish-American War and was known as the Laguna Merced Military Reservation. In 1917 it was named for Major General Frederick Funston, who policed San Francisco after the 1906 earthquake disaster.

FORT MASON, established as **FORT POINT SAN JOSE** in 1863, is built on the site of old Spanish fortifications erected in 1797 as **BATTERY SAN JOSE.** It is at Van Ness Avenue and Bay and Laguna streets on what is called today Black Point, and as an Army supply depot contains residences of the commanding general and ranking staff officers of the 9th Corps Area. This 67-acre reservation was once the home of General and Mrs. John C. Frémont, who built a house here in 1853. As others took up residence on the point, in 1882 Colonel Richard Barnes Mason was ordered to clear it of all who claimed squatters' rights, including General Frémont. Frémont issued a challenge to Mason to fight a duel, but this never came about. Following this, the fort was given the name Fort Mason.

FORT McDOWELL, established on Angel Island, the largest island in San Francisco Bay, in 1863, was first named **CAMP REYNOLDS** in honor of Major General John F. Reynolds, who was killed at Gettysburg. Abandoned in 1866 and reoccupied the same year, the name of the installation was changed to **POST OF ANGEL ISLAND.** Some time later it became a prison camp for hostile Arizona Indians. In 1900 its name was changed to Fort McDowell in honor of General Irvin S. McDowell, of Civil War fame. The War Department declared the post surplus in 1946, and it is now San Francisco's quarantine and immigration station.

CAMP AT ALCATRAZ was established on the island of that name in San Francisco Harbor in 1854. Between that time and 1882 the Government appropriated $1,697,500 for fortifications, and powder magazines were blasted from the rock and a citadel built on its crest. In 1868 the post was designated as a disciplinary barracks for prisoners serving long sentences. In the 1870's troublesome Indians were sent there. In 1907 it was designated the Pacific Branch of the United States Military Prison, but in 1934 it became a Federal Prison for civilian incorrigibles, and some of the nation's toughest gangsters served time on "The Rock." Among these were Al Capone, "Machine Gun" Kelly, and the mail robbers Albert Bates, Gene Colson, and Charles ("Limpy") Cleaver. For years San Francisco civic bodies demanded the abandonment of the grim prison, but it was not until recently that this finally was done.

FORT HUMBOLDT, located on a high plateau in Eureka, overlooking Humboldt Bay, was built in 1853 to protect settlers from hostile Indians. It was here that Captain Ulysses S. Grant, bored with garrison life after fighting in every battle of the Mexican War from Vera Cruz to Mexico City, resigned his commission. He proved a failure in civilian life and was one of the first volunteers for the Army when the Civil War started. The garrison was withdrawn from the fort in 1865. The restored headquarters building of the commissary department stands today, and the site has been set aside as the Fort Humboldt State Historical Monument.

FORT BIDWELL, in the present town of Fort Bidwell in Modoc County, was established in 1865 to protect settlers of Surprise Valley from Indian raids. Named for the Honorable John Bidwell, leading citizen of California and at that time a member of Congress, the fort served as a base for troops operating against the Bannock, Paiute, Snake, and Modoc Indians. The Army abandoned the fort in 1892; it was taken over by the Bureau of Indian Affairs, and still functions as headquarters of an Indian reservation. All that survive from the military era are the stable, a school, and the parade ground. The site is marked by a bronze plaque as California Registered Historical Landmark No. 430. It is interesting to note that in 1865 the name was changed to **CAMP BIDWELL** and restored to Fort Bidwell again in 1879. Bidwell had been a member of the first overland party in the 1840's to cross the Sierra Nevada. He had later planted vineyards, and after two years plowed them under and ran for President on the Prohibition Ticket.

THE PRESIDIO OF MONTEREY became a United States military post in 1847 upon arrival of a company of the 3rd Artillery under command of Lieutenant E. O. O. Ord. The Navy had captured it in 1846 during the War with Mexico. This venerable Presidio had been built in 1770 by Governor Gaspar de Portola when he formally took possession of the country in the name of Carlos III of Spain. When the Navy raised the Stars and Stripes over the post they called it **FORT MERVINE.** The Army upon garrisoning it called it **MONTEREY REDOUBT** and **POST OF MONTEREY.** It was abandoned in 1852, but re-established in 1865 as **MONTEREY BARRACKS.** Developed as a cantonment in 1902 for troops returned from the Spanish-American War, the name was changed to **POST ORD BARRACKS** in honor of its first commander. But finally, two years later and after sixty-eight years, the original name of The Presidio of Monterey was given the post, a name it bears today. It still is an active post. The entrance is on Pacific Street north of Decatur Street in Monterey, and covers 360 acres.

EL PRESIDIO REAL (The Royal Garrison) was built in 1769 in what is today Presidio Hill Park in San Diego's Old Town. It was the first outpost of Spain's effort to protect California from encroachments of foreign powers, and was garrisoned until 1835.

Today, within a hollow square that has been surrounded by a modern adobe wall, are a few mounds and ruins of the old walls, outlining the ground plans of the original presidio. The San Diego Historical Society has plans to reconstruct some of the original presidio buildings, such as the adobe barracks and the red-tile-roofed mission. The restored landmark will be presented to the community on San Diego's bi-centennial, celebrated July 16, 1969, two hundred years after Father Junipero Serra dedicated the first California presidio.

FORT STOCKTON, formerly a small fort built in San Diego in 1838 by Mexicans as a protection against Indians, was renamed for Commodore Robert F. Stockton after its occupation by American troops during the Mexican War in 1846. It first was held by Commodore Samuel Dupont and named Fort Dupont. But shortly thereafter Commodore Stockton took over the command of the fort. Its site is a short distance from the entrance of Presidio Hill Park, and a trench, roughly outlining a quadrangle, still is visible. Inside this area is an old Spanish cannon cast in Manila in 1783 and engraved with the name *El Jupiter*. This ancient cannon, with *El Capitán*, another which stands in Old Town Plaza, are from the original ten that formed the armament of old Fort Guijarros.

FORT GUIJARROS, on the neck of Ballast Point, called by the Spanish *La Punta de los Guijarros* (Cobblestone Point), was built around 1800. After a rather uneventful existence, broken only when it fired on an American merchant ship that entered the harbor illegally, the fort was abandoned in 1835. Nothing remains today of this historic fortification.

FORT ROSECRANS, first known as the **POST AT SAN DIEGO,** was established in 1849 following the American occupation of California. It was abandoned and reoccupied several times and had such names as **MISSION OF SAN DIEGO** and **SAN DIEGO BARRACKS** until 1903 when by official order it received the permanent name of Fort Rosecrans in honor of Major General William S. Rosecrans of Civil War fame. The installation was within the military reservation that took in the entire southern end of Point Loma and also included a naval wireless area and the old quarantine and coaling station. Fort Rosecrans, to which fortifications had been added from time to time until it was considered impregnable, saw service during both world wars, but was declared surplus on December 31, 1949.

FORT TEJON, in Grapevine Canyon near Tejon Pass, was established in 1854 by Lieutenant Colonel Edward F. Beale as a protection for travelers over the mountain trail and administrative post for Indian affairs, of which he had been appointed administrator for California and Nevada. Three years later, when Beale was director of the wagon-road survey from Texas to California, he brought his camel train into Fort Tejon after a successful trip. It then became the home of the United States Army Camel Corps, which had been formed by Secretary of War Jefferson Davis, at Beale's suggestion, to utilize the Asian animals in the desert regions of the West. Here the camels were based for seven of Fort Tejon's years as a military post. When the fort was abandoned during the Civil War, some of the camels were auctioned off to a circus and others as pack animals, while still others were turned loose. In 1858, a year after the camels came to Fort Tejon, the first stagecoach of the Butterfield Overland Mail arrived. Upon the abandonment of the fort, its reservation became a part of Beale's Rancho Tejon, and the buildings were used as stables and residences. Three adobe buildings have been restored, and today this fort is a California State Historical Monument.

FORT YUMA, directly across the Colorado River from Yuma, Arizona, was established in 1850 to protect the Yuma Crossing from raids of the Yuma and Mojave Indians. The fort was erected on the site of the Misión de la Puríssima Concepción, which had been built in 1779, and where two years later Indians killed the Franciscan priests as well as soldiers and colonists. Fort Yuma was associated with the Yuma Quartermaster Depot across the river, and not only was a stopping place for California immigrants but also a processing point for supplies and personnel for Arizona forts. The fort is now headquarters for the Yuma Indian Reservation, and a dozen buildings date from the military period.

FORT BRAGG was made a military post within the boundaries of the Mendocino Indian Reservation in 1857. It was named for General Braxton Bragg, of Mexican War fame. The reservation, which covered ten acres, was thrown open for purchase in 1867, and the lumber town of Fort Bragg developed. The town was badly damaged by the earthquake of 1906 but was rebuilt.

FORT DEFIANCE, at Susanville on the Susan River and commanding a view of the Honey Lake Valley, was nothing more than a cabin owned by Isaac N. Roop, who built it in 1853. Ten years later one hundred men held the cabin during the so-called Sagebrush War, fought to establish the California-Nevada line. Susanville was placed in California, and the cabin became famous as "Fort Defiance." Today it is the oldest building in Susanville.

FORT MacARTHUR was established in 1914 not far from Hermosa Beach on Paseo de Mar to guard the approach to Los Angeles Harbor from the edge of the ocean bluffs. It was named for Lieutenant General Arthur MacArthur, father of General Douglas MacArthur but often spelled "McArthur." The post was declared inactive in 1947.

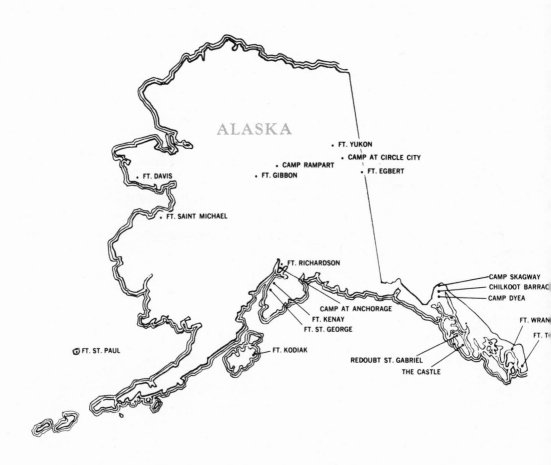

ALASKA

• FT. YUKON

• CAMP AT CIRCLE CITY

• CAMP RAMPART
• FT. GIBBON
• FT. EGBERT

• FT. DAVIS

• FT. SAINT MICHAEL

FT. RICHARDSON

CAMP SKAGWAY
CHILKOOT BARRAC
CAMP DYEA

CAMP AT ANCHORAGE
FT. KENAY
FT. ST. GEORGE

FT. WRAN
FT. T

ⓞ FT. ST. PAUL

• FT. KODIAK

REDOUBT ST. GABRIEL
THE CASTLE

SCALE OF MILES

0   50   100   150   200

ALASKA

Admitted to the Union in 1959 as the forty-ninth state.

At 3:30 P.M., Friday, October 18, 1867, after alternate salutes from the artillery of the United States and Russia, with the United States taking the lead as instructed by the Department of State, the flag of Imperial Russia was lowered on the staff at **THE CASTLE** (Sitka). Then fifteen-year-old George Rousseau, son of the United States commissioner, with the help of a midshipman, ran up the Stars and Stripes. Captain Alexei Pestchouroff, of the Russian Imperial Navy, as commissioner of the czar, spoke a few words, after which Brigadier General Lovell H. Rousseau, the United States commissioner, signified his acceptance of the Territory in the name of the United States Government. The Americans cheered, and the Russians "all seemed as if they had attended the funeral of the Czar." Alaska now belonged to the United States. It was termed variously "Seward's Icebox" and "Seward's Folly," for which Secretary of State William H. Seward had paid, in behalf of the nation, $7,200,000.

The **POST OF SITKA**, never officially designated Fort Sitka, but often termed thus, was the first military post in Alaska, garrisoned just eleven days after the flag went up, and commanded by Brevet Major General Jefferson Columbus Davis (not to be confused with Jeff Davis of the Confederacy).

Alexander Baranof, a Siberian, had arrived in Sitka in 1799 from Kodiak. He was accompanied by thirty Russians and several hundred Aleut Indians. As head of the Russian American Company, he bartered with the Tlingit Indians, who had a fortified town there, for a site six miles north. Here he built **REDOUBT ST. GABRIEL** (Old Sitka). Two years later there was an uprising of the Tlingit, and they captured and burned the redoubt, killed twenty Russians, and took women and children prisoners. Baranof, who escaped, was back in 1804 with a force. He captured the new fort of the Tlingit near the mouth of the river, rebuilt the village on the hill, and

Post of Sitka

named it Novo Arhhangelsk (New Archangel). However, the old Indian word "Sitka," meaning "By the Sea," persisted, and the place continued to be called by that name. Baranof built a rough-hewn fortress and lived in style in what he termed The Castle. He had many luxuries, including a library of 1,200 volumes. In 1818 he was displaced by officers of the Imperial Russian Navy, including Baron Ferdinand Petrovich von Wrangel, who occupied the site until the American purchase. The American Army abandoned the Post at Sitka, as well as other posts, in 1877, following scandals involving soldiers, and two years later the American Navy was placed in charge of Alaska. Today at the Naval Air Station at Sitka is to be found Baranof's old log fort.

FORT KODIAK was established in 1868 on the site of the first Russian settlement in Alaska. In 1792 Gregor Shelikof anchored in Paul's Harbor in Three Saints Bay (named for his ship) and landed on Kodiak Island. Here he erected headquarters for the Russian American Fur Company. After the purchase of Alaska by the United States Major General Henry W. Halleck, commanding the Military

Division of the Pacific, sent an artillery unit to establish the fort. The post was abandoned in 1870.

FORT KENAY (KENAI) was built on the site of **FORT ST. NICHOLAS,** a Russian post established in 1791 by Grigor Konovalof, in command of the ship *St. George.* Five years earlier the Russians had settled here on the Kenai Peninsula, near Kasilof, building two log houses, surrounded by a stockade, which they called **FORT ST. GEORGE,** probably from the ship *St. George.* However, this became a "lost village," and apparently had been burned. After the purchase of Alaska a company of artillery was sent to build an Army post on the site of Fort St. Nicholas. The company was shipwrecked on a rock near Port Graham, and after being rescued they spent the winter at Fort Kodiak, which had just been established. They built Fort Kenay, named for the Kenai Indians of that region, the following year. This post was mainly to aid in establishing friendly relations with the Aleut and Kenai. It was abandoned when the Army pulled out of Alaska.

FORT WRANGELL (WRANGEL) was established in 1868 on the north end of Wrangell Island in the crescent along Etolin Bay (now Wrangell Harbor) on the site of an earlier Russian fort. This

Fort Wrangell

latter was **REDOUBT ST. DIONYSIUS,** built by the Russians in 1834 to resist encroachments of Hudson's Bay Company traders. After acquiring Alaska the Army built Fort Wrangel (*sic*) in 1868, naming it for Baron Ferdinand Petrovich von Wrangel, Russian naval officer and former governor of Alaska. A detachment from Fort Tongass erected the fort, which was discontinued in 1877. However, it was again occupied in 1898 by the Army during the gold rush, but finally abandoned in 1900.

The town of Wrangell grew up around the fort, and the name of the fort itself was spelled Wrangell.

FORT TONGASS was established just a month before Fort Wrangell on a small island near the southern boundary of the Alexander Archipelago south of Ketchikan. It was named for the Tongass Indians, and, like other military posts, was abandoned in the 1870's.

FORT ST. PAUL, one of the most remote posts, was established on St. Paul Island, forty-four miles north of St. George Island. Erected in 1869, it was garrisoned by a detachment of an artillery company, and abandoned in 1870.

FORT SAINT MICHAEL, at St. Michael near the mouth of the Yukon River, was established in the fall of 1897 following the Klondike gold strike and because of the increased traffic on the Yukon River. The purpose of the fort was for protection of life and property of Americans. In 1874 Private Lucien M. Turner had been ordered by the Chief Signal Officer of the Army to open a meteorological station at the fort. Fort Saint Michael was not abandoned until 1922.

FORT YUKON, just in the Arctic Circle on the northern point of the Yukon River where it begins its southerly course, was established in 1897 as a military post a month before Fort Saint Michael had come into service. Major General Nelson A. Miles had recommended to the Secretary of War that a military expedition be sent to the Klondike Region to take supplies and prevent starvation among the miners there, many of whom were American citizens. They had swarmed into the Klondike since the sensational gold strike. However, this expedition did not materialize until the following year. In the meantime thousands had become caught by the winter ice below Fort Yukon and had to be rescued. Fort Yukon was the site of the oldest English-speaking settlement in Alaska. It had been established in 1847 by the Hudson's Bay Company, and for more than twenty years was the chief trading post of that section. The Russians had by agreement allowed the British to remain here, but in 1869, two years after the purchase of Alaska by the United States, the British were ordered to leave. The town of Fort Yukon, a trapping center, is on the site of the old fort.

FORT EGBERT, originally known as the **CAMP AT EAGLE CITY,** was established as a result of General Nelson A. Miles's recommendation that a military expedition be sent into the Klondike to take supplies and prevent starvation to American citizens drawn there by the lure of gold. In 1898 the expedition got under way and established a camp at Circle City. The following year the War Department decided to retain the **CAMP AT CIRCLE CITY** and instructed that a new post also be established at Eagle. Fort Egbert was built and garrisoned, and the Camp at Circle City became a subpost of it. The latter post was abandoned in 1900, and Fort Egbert in 1911. Deserted buildings may still be seen near the town of Eagle.

CHILKOOT BARRACKS (FORT WILLIAM H. SEWARD) originated from a post at Haines's Mission now known simply as Haines, which was established in 1898. The War Department decided to make a permanent post here, and in 1904, before it was garrisoned, it was named Fort William H. Seward in honor of the purchaser of Alaska. In 1922 the name was changed to Chilkoot Barracks, from the Chilkoot Indians of that section. This post was on the Lynn Canal, which extends eighty miles northeast from Chatham Strait and was fifteen miles from Skagway. There was a **CAMP SKAGWAY,** established in 1898 at Skagway, but the post was abandoned in 1904 and the garrison moved to Fort William H. Seward. Chilkoot Barracks was abandoned in 1943.

At the turn of the century, when Alaska was in a ferment because of the gold fever, many camps, posts, and forts were established. There was **CAMP DYEA,** established in 1898 to relieve destitution among miners and natives. It was destroyed by fire the following year. **FORT GIBBON** was a garrisoned post of three companies on the north bank of the Yukon River at its junction with the Tanana River. Built in 1899, it was not abandoned until 1923. **CAMP RAMPART,** established in 1899 to guard property at Rampart City, lasted until 1901. **FORT DAVIS,** a garrisoned post of two companies three miles east of Nome, was established in 1900 and named in honor of General Jefferson Columbus Davis. It was discontinued in 1919. The **CAMP AT ANCHORAGE** was established in 1919 to protect Government property during construction of the United States Railroad. It was abandoned in 1926. The big military installation at Anchorage is **FORT RICHARDSON,** headquarters of the Army's Alaska Department. With many forts in the forty-ninth state, it can safely be said that not one ever "fired a shot in anger."

HAWAII

Admitted to the Union in 1959 as the fiftieth state.

John Young watched anxiously as the Russians erected a block-house near the waterfront in Honolulu, hoisted the Russian flag, and then began to lay out plans for a large fort. He had seen enough. He dispatched a messenger by canoe to King Kamehameha, who was then on the island of Hawaii engaged in suppressing a minor revolt. The king ordered the Russians expelled from the island of Oahu, and told the Corps of Okaka, a body of picked warriors, to do the job. The Russians, some eighty or ninety of them from the ships *Kadiak* and *Ilmen,* headed by Dr. George Anton Scheffer, a German adventurer sent by the Russians to establish trade in the Sandwich Islands, fled the island, leaving behind a brass cannon marked "1807–Kadiak."

John Young, one-time boatsman of the ship *Eleanora* who had been sent on shore by his British captain to inquire about the fate of the captain's son, had been held in 1790 by King Kamehameha and, with another British seaman, Isaac Davis, proved of great value to the king. They were made chiefs, and Young especially had the confidence of the great Hawaiian ruler. When the Russians quitted the island, Young told the king he thought the idea of a fort to protect the harbor of Honolulu was a good one. The king agreed, and instructed Young to build a "papu," or fort, and name it *Kekuanohu.* Young started in January, 1816, and completed it in February, 1817. The new Hawaiian flag, a flattering combination of both British and American ensigns, with eight stripes representing the eight islands, was flown over the fort.

This historic structure, which stood on the waterfront at the foot of what is today Fort Street, was rectangular, 340 feet long and 300 feet wide. It was built of adobe, faced inside and out with coral rock. The walls, 20 feet thick at the base and 12 feet high, were lapped by the tide. The main entrance was at Fort Street. The 40 guns (some say 60) of various calibers, which had been acquired at

353

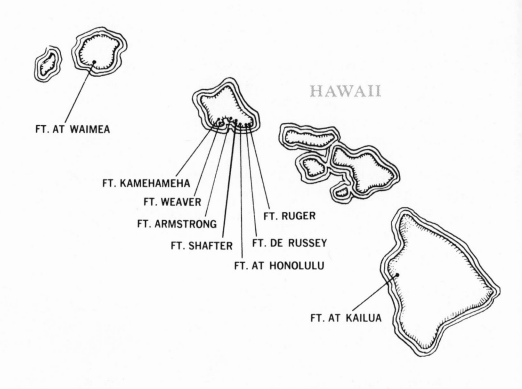

FT. AT WAIMEA

FT. KAMEHAMEHA

FT. WEAVER

FT. ARMSTRONG

FT. SHAFTER

FT. AT HONOLULU

FT. RUGER

FT. DE RUSSEY

FT. AT KAILUA

HAWAII

SCALE OF MILES

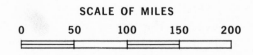

0   50   100   150   200

times from various ships, were *en barbette* on old-fashioned carriages on a sort of parapet—their muzzles high enough to fire over the walls. While three walls were straight, the fourth, on the harbor side, was curved outward to give it a battle frontage of 336 feet. As none understood the workings of the great guns, George Beckley, a British sea captain who had remained in Honolulu, was the fort's first commandant. Inside the fort were houses and barracks for officers and soldiers. Guards pacing the tops of the thick walls sang out every ten minutes in English "All is well!"

FORT KEKUANOHU, or, as it was more commonly called, **FORT AT HONOLULU,** played an important role in Hawaii's history for half a century. In 1830–1831 it was the scene of a contemplated revolt by Liliha, governess of Oahu, in the absence of King Kaahumanu. Liliha's father finally persuaded her to give up plans for the revolt. In 1840 the fort was the scene of the island's first infliction of capital punishment when Kamanawa, relative of the king, was hanged for poisoning his wife. Three years later the Hawaiian flag was lowered and the English flag raised over the fort when Hawaii was ceded to Great Britain. A twenty-one-gun salute was fired and a British band played "God Save the Queen." The British flag floated over the fort from February 25 until July 31, when Hawaii's independence was once more restored.

In 1849 two French warships arrived in the harbor of Honolulu and Rear Admiral Legoarant de Tromelin sent ten demands to King Kamehameha III. These included equality of worship, reduction of duty on French brandy, and punishment of certain young Hawaiians "who had impiously put their hands in holy water." To back up his demands he landed a force that took over the customhouse and other Government buildings, spiked the guns of the fort, poured all its gunpowder into the waters of the harbor, and smashed public buildings. The king's yacht was destroyed, and a few foreign vessels were seized. The French consul was removed for ten days until the matter was settled.

This practically spelled the end of Fort Kekuanohu. In 1857, after it had served as police headquarters and prison, it was demolished. The white coral stones helped build 2,000 feet of waterfront. Fort Street was widened and continued to the waterfront, running through the fort site. Salutes, which had been fired from the fort, were now given from the battery on Punchbowl Hill overlooking the city and harbor.

The **FORT AT WAIMEA** on the island of Kauai was built by Dr. George Anton Scheffer, the German adventurer who was trying to gain control of the islands for Russia. He went to Kauai after he was expelled from Oahu by King Kamehameha for trying to build a fort on the waterfront at Honolulu. In May, 1816, after signing a secret document with King Kaumaulii of Kauai, putting the island under the protection of Russia, Scheffer erected his fort at the mouth of the Waimea River. It was an irregular 8-sided, or octagonal, affair with walls from 10 to 20 feet high and 30 feet thick, built of native rock. Forty guns were mounted on the fort's walls. Scheffer had hardly completed his fort before he was forced to abandon it. King Kamehameha learned of the secret agreement as well as the fort over which floated the flag of Russia. He had been promised the island of Kauai as a part of his empire, and was determined to have it. Scheffer had been forced to use former American sailors then living on Kauai as interpreters, and these Americans gave away the plot to American traders, who complained to King Kamehameha. With some bloodshed Kamehameha took possession of the island, and Scheffer and the other Russians were forced to leave. This ended the Russian threat to take over the Hawaiian Islands.

The fort was a formidable structure embracing 2½ to 3 acres of land. Inside was a huge room in the ground, roofed over with enormous Lehua trees, covered with earth, which formed a powder magazine. The fort was garrisoned until 1853 but saw no action. From 1854 to 1860 a captain and a few soldiers lived there and each year fired a salute on the king's birthday. When the men died they were not replaced. In 1864, by order of the Government, the fort was dismantled and thirty-eight guns shipped to California and sold there. Two others still are at the bottom of the bay where they sank when a boat capsized.

The **FORT AT KAILUA** on the island of Hawaii had been a

heiau, or temple of worship, on the western shore of Kailua Bay
before it was fortified in the early part of the nineteenth century.
It was believed that John Adams Kuakini, governor of the island
of Hawaii, had converted this place into a fort following the death
of King Kamehameha I, in 1819. At that time King Kamehameha II,
commonly known as Liholiho, son of Kamehameha I, broke the
kapu system, or taboo, of the ancient Hawaiian religion in the
belief that this would encourage more trade with Americans and
Europeans. Idolatry was abolished. So all the idols but three in
the *heiau* at Kailua were destroyed by the governor, who had in-
cidentally adopted the name of President John Adams of the United
States. He then mounted eighteen cannon on the stone walls,
spacing them between the three remaining idols which stood
as sentinels. He also placed two 8-pound brass mortars at the entrance to the fort. These pieces were said to have been given to
King Kamehameha I by Dr. George Anton Scheffer. There is no
record of any action by this fort, whose armament overlooked the
bay. In 1845 a visitor there reported he had found workmen breaking up several cannon and using the metal to make agricultural
implements; one, he said, was fashioning an *oo,* or native spade.
By 1855 the annual report made to the Government listed "one
powder keg" at the fort. But in 1861 there is a record that a number of old cannon from the Fort at Kailua had been brought by
steamer to Honolulu and sold for export. All that remains of this
old fort today is a mass of rocks on the western shore of the bay.

These forts, the details of which have been gleaned from reports
and papers of the Hawaiian Historical Society, comprise all of the
earlier defenses of the eight islands of the group. President McKinley, by proclamation in 1898 and 1899, established several land
areas for the naval and military establishments. Over the years
before World War I, fortifications were built on the island of Oahu
for protection of Pearl Harbor and the city of Honolulu. These
included **FORT ARMSTRONG** at the entrance of Honolulu Harbor to the east; **FORT DE RUSSEY** at Waikiki; **FORT RUGER**
behind Diamond Head; **FORT KAMEHAMEHA** ("The King's
Post"), and **FORT WEAVER** to guard Pearl Harbor.

FORT SHAFTER, on the outskirts of Honolulu toward Pearl Harbor, was the first permanent Army post in Oahu. Some of its buildings were finished and occupied as early as 1907, and it was to become the headquarters for the Army in the Territory. The Government's plan from the beginning was to concentrate all important naval and military installations on the island of Oahu.

Glossary

ABATIS. A barricade of felled trees with the branches toward the enemy. (In the modern sense this term can be applied to a barbed-wire entanglement.) See *Fort Tyler*, Georgia; *Fort Watson*, South Carolina.

BARRACKS. A permanent building for the housing of soldiers. Frequently interchangeable with the United States Army's conception of "fort" or "military post." See *Jefferson Barracks*, Missouri; *Whipple Barracks*, Arizona.

BASTION. A projecting outwork of a fortification, placed to give a wider firing range. See *Fort Marion*, Florida; *Fort Ticonderoga*, New York; *Fort McHenry*, Maryland.

BATTLEMENT. A low wall or parapet with open places or indentations for shooting; mainly for cannon placed on top of a fort, tower, or some types of blockhouses.

BLOCKHOUSE. A fort of logs or heavy timbers, with an overhanging second story, with loopholes for rifles and sometimes gunports for cannon. Generally placed on diagonal corners of stockades similar to bastions on larger forts. A blockhouse might stand alone, as the one at Pittsburgh, Pennsylvania.

BREASTWORK. See PARAPET.

CAMP. A temporary post for soldiers. When camps become permanent military posts the United States Army designates them as "forts." See *Camp Supply*, Oklahoma.

CANNON. A large mounted piece of artillery for discharging heavy shot. Usually designated as "piece" or "gun" or "great gun."

CASEMATE. A vaulted, shellproof chamber in a fortification, with openings for guns. See *Fort Pulaski*, Georgia.

CAUSEWAY. A raised road or way leading to a fort's entrance—usually over a moat or ditch. See *Fort Caroline*, Florida.

CHURCH FORT. A fortified structure serving as a fort as well as a place of worship. See *Fort Herkimer*, New York.

COVERED WAY. A depression in the outer edge of a fort's moat or ditch where soldiers could stand behind a dirt breastwork. See *Fort Marion*, Florida.

CROWN WORKS. A fortification consisting of two or more fronts for protecting an advantageous position. Usually a defense with a jagged outline. Sometimes termed HORN WORKS.

CURTAIN. A wall of a fort between bastions. See *Fort Ticonderoga*, New York.

DEMILUNE. See LUNETTE.

DITCH. See MOAT.

DRAWBRIDGE. A bridge at a fort's entrance across a moat; it can be let down or raised. See *Fort Niagara*, New York.

EMBRASURE. An opening in a wall or parapet with the sides slanting outward so that the angle of fire of a cannon may be increased.

EN BARBETTE. Arrangement of guns on a platform high enough to permit firing over the fort's wall. See *Fort at Honolulu*, Hawaii.

FASCINES. Bundles of sticks tied together, mainly used by attacking troops to make a pile high enough to enable them to scale the fort's walls. Used double at *Fort Caroline*, Florida, and packed with dirt in between to make the fort's walls.

FLANKERS (LOG). Ordinarily described as a fortified position at either flank of a fort for protection or attack. See *Old Fort*, New Hampshire.

FORT. An enclosed place with walls or stockades, and bastions or blockhouses, and containing soldiers or fighters and armed with various defense mechanisms. Also the name for a permanent Army post as distinguished from a "camp" or temporary one. In France, Marshal Sebastian le Prestre de Vauban (1638–1707), and in Holland, Baron Menno van Coehoorn (1641–1704), established the basic principles of forts. However, in the rapidly expanding West of America, an Army fort might not even be fortified.

FORTALICE. A small fort or defensive outwork, illustrated by such defense works at Vicksburg, Mississippi.

FORTIFICATION. A fortified place or position or the act or science of fortifying.

FORTRESS. A popular term, but not an official one, for some forts in the United States. See *Fortress Monroe*, Virginia.

FORTRESS ARTILLERY. See CANNON.

FOSSE or FOSS. See MOAT.

FRAISE. A defense of pointed stakes driven into the ramparts of a fort in an inclined or horizontal position.

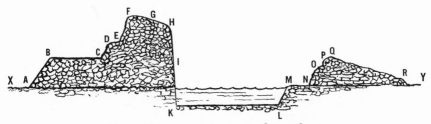

Vertical section of a typical fortification

X-Y: Ground line. X-A: Place to be defended. A-B-C-D-F-G-H: Rampart with its parapet. A-B: Interior slope of rampart. B-C: Terreplain. D-E: Banquette. E-F-G: Parapet. H-I: Revetment. H-K: Escarp. K-L: Ditch. L-M: Counterscarp. N-O-P: Banquette. Q-R: Glacis.

GABION. A round bottomless wicker basket filled with earth, sand, or stones and used for revetments (supporting walls) in field works or forts. See *Fort Hoke*, Virginia.

GATE. The entrance to a fort, designated as a portal in large forts, but in pioneer forts of America usually a log gate, swinging on iron hinges.

GLACIS. A defensive slope, as of earth, in front of a fort.

HORN WORKS. See CROWN WORKS.

HOT SHOT. Cannon balls made red-hot in a hot-shot oven and used for setting fire to enemy ships. See *Fort Marion*, Florida.

LOOPHOLES. Slots or openings in forts or blockhouses through which a rifle or cannon may be fired.

LUNETTE. A projecting fieldwork having the shape of a half moon, usually a defensive fortification erected by troops in the field. An example of a lunette, or demilune, is to be seen in the Vicksburg National Military Park, Mississippi.

MAHAN TOWER. A structure used to elevate riflemen above the walls of a fort so they can fire down within the fort. Named for its inventor, Colonel Hezekiah Mahan. See *Fort Ninety-six*, South Carolina.

MARTELLO TOWER. An isolated tower of masonry, formerly erected on coasts for defense against invasion. Named for Mortello Point, in Corsica, where such a tower was attacked by the British fleet in 1794. See *Fort Constitution*, New Hampshire.

MOAT. A defensive ditch or fosse on the outside of a fort's walls. See *Fort Macon*, Georgia.

OUTWORKS. Outer defenses beyond the ditches or moats of a fort, much the same as demilune (lunette), ravelin, salient, or fortalice. See *Fort Ticonderoga,* New York.

PALISADE. A fence or fortification made of strong timbers, stakes, or pickets, set endwise in the ground. See *Fort Nashborough,* Tennessee.

PARADE. An open space in the center of a fort where military reviews are held or where troops assemble for parade. See *Fort McHenry,* Maryland.

PARAPET. A low wall to protect defenders, usually on the top of a fort's rampart. A breastwork.

PICKET. See PALISADE.

PORTCULLIS. A grating that can be lowered quickly to close the portal of a fortified place. See *Fort Pulaski,* Georgia.

POWDER MAGAZINE. A compartment usually lined with lead and placed underground for storing gunpowder. See *Fort Waimea,* Hawaii.

PRESIDIO. A military garrison; a fortified place or post. See *The Presidio of San Francisco.*

RAMPART. The embankment surrounding a fort on which the parapet is raised. A bulwark or defense. See *Fort McHenry,* Maryland.

RAVELIN. A fort's outwork with two faces forming a salient angle at the front end. See *Fort Ticonderoga,* New York; *Fort Marion,* Florida, and *Fort Pulaski,* Georgia.

REDAN. A jagged or notched front to a fort. A triangular fortification of two walls or parapets, with its apex extended toward the enemy. The "Big Redan" and "Little Redan" at Sevastopol became famous during the Crimean War. A good example has been preserved in the Vicksburg National Military Park, Mississippi.

REDOUBT (REDOUT). An enclosed fortification of various forms, of which the square redoubt was the most common. Usually an outlying fortification or breastwork. *Fort Pitt,* Pennsylvania, was a typical American redoubt.

REVETMENT. A sloping wall of brickwork or other material supporting the outer face of the rampart, and lining the side of the ditch or moat.

SALIENT. A part of a fort projecting farthest toward an enemy. The points of a redan meet at a *salient* angle.

STOCKADE. A line of stout posts or stakes set upright in the earth to form a barrier. An enclosure is often said to be surrounded by a stockade. Many pioneer forts were termed stockades.

TERREPLEIN. The upper surface of a rampart behind the parapet on which guns were mounted. See *Fort Marion,* Florida.

TRENCH. A long, irregular ditch with the earth thrown up in front as a parapet. The Vicksburg National Military Park, Mississippi, shows two types: the *parallel,* which ran parallel with the enemy's line, and the *approach,* or *sap,* which ran at right angles. At the end of the *approach* mines were usually set and exploded.

WATCHTOWER. A fort's tower on which a sentinel was posted. At *Castillo de San Marcos (Fort Marion),* Florida, small watchtowers were built on the point of each bastion. See also *Fort Snelling,* Minnesota, which had one watchtower.

Selected Bibliography

Adams, Henry. *History of the United States.* 9 vols. New York: Charles Scribner's Sons, 1889–1891.

"American Guide Series." Compiled by the workers of the Writers' Program of the Work Projects Administration of the fifty states and major cities.

Bancroft, George. *History of the United States.* 10 vols. New York: D. Appleton & Co., 1834–74.

Billings, John S. *A Report on Barracks and Hospitals, with Descriptions of Military Posts.* (No. 4.) Washington, D.C.: Surgeon General's Office, 1875.

Brandes, Ray. *Frontier Military Posts of Arizona.* Tucson: Dale Stuart King, 1960.

Building Alaska With the United States Army. (No. 355-5.) Alaska: United States Army Headquarters, 1962.

Cullum, George W. *Campaigns of the War of 1812–15 . . . with Brief Biographies of American Engineers.* 1879.

Grant, Bruce. *Northwest Campaign: The George Rogers Clark Expedition.* New York: G. P. Putnam's Sons, 1963.

Hammond, John M. *Quaint and Historic Forts of North America.* Philadelphia: J. B. Lippincott Co., 1915.

Hart, Herbert M. *Old Forts of the Northwest.* Seattle: Superior Publishing Co., 1963.

———. *Old Forts of the Southwest.* Seattle: Superior Publishing Co., 1964.

Larpenteur, Charles. *Forty Years a Fur Trader on the Upper Missouri.* Minneapolis: Ross & Haines, 1933.

Linford, Velma. *Wyoming, Frontier State.* Denver: Old West Publishing Co., 1947.

Lossing, Benson J. *The Pictorial Field-Book of the Civil War in the United States.* 3 vols. Philadelphia: David McKay, 1866–68.

———. *The Pictorial Field-Book of the Revolution.* 2 vols. New York: Harper & Brothers, 1859–60.

———. *The Pictorial Field-Book of the War of 1812.* 1868.

———. *Popular Cyclopedia of United States History from the Aboriginal Period to 1876.* New York: Harper & Brothers, 1881.

McMaster, John B. *History of the People of the United States During Lincoln's Administration*. New York: D. Appleton & Co., 1927.

————. *History of the People of the United States from the Revolution to the Civil War*. 8 vols. New York: D. Appleton & Co., 1883–1913.

Mansfield, Joseph K. F. *Mansfield on the Condition of Western Forts, 1853–54*, ed. Robert W. Frazer. Norman, Okla.: University of Oklahoma Press, 1963.

Niles Weekly Register (Baltimore Weekly) from 1811 to 1836. *Niles National Register* from 1836 to 1849.

Nye, Wilbur S. *Carbine and Lance: The Story of Old Fort Sill*. Norman, Okla.: University of Oklahoma Press, 1957.

Permanent Fortifications and Sea-Coast Defenses. ("E. P. Blair, from the Committee on Military Affairs, made the following report . . . for the purpose of ascertaining what modifications . . . are required to repel improved methods of attack." House Report 86.) Washington, D.C.: Government Printing Office, 1862.

Peterson, Harold L. *Forts in America*. New York: Charles Scribner's Sons, 1964.

Prucha, Francis Paul. *A Guide to the Military Posts of the United States, 1789–1895*. Madison, Wis.: The State Historical Society of Wisconsin, 1964.

Rhodes, James F. *History of the Civil War, 1861–1865*. New York: Frederick Ungar Publishing Co., 1961.

————. *History of the United States from the Compromise of 1850 to the McKinley-Bryan Campaign of 1896*. 8 vols. New York: The Macmillan Co., 1912.

Roosevelt, Theodore. *The Winning of the West*. 6 vols. New York: G. P. Putnam's Sons, 1920.

Ruth, Kent. *Great Day in the West: Forts, Posts, and Rendezvous Beyond the Mississippi*. Norman, Okla.: University of Oklahoma Press, 1963.

Sarles, Frank B., Jr., and Shedd, Charles E. *Colonials and Patriots: Historic Places Commemorating Our Forebears 1700–1783*. Washington, D.C.: National Park Service, 1964.

Sites for Military Posts and Camp Grounds. (House Document 618, Fifty-seventh Congress.) Washington, D.C.: Government Printing Office, 1902.

Soldier and Brave, Military and Indian Affairs in the Trans-Mississippi West, Including a Guide to Historic Sites and Landmarks. (Vol. XII.) Washington, D.C.: National Park Service, 1963.

Webb, Walter Prescott. *The Texas Rangers: A Century of Frontier Defense*. Boston: Houghton Mifflin Co., 1935.

Index to Forts and States

Each fort is indexed by each of its names, but the most prominent name has been used to locate it on a sectional map, as indicated by the italic page numbers below.

372   INDEX